I0810100

IMAGES
of America

FORESTVILLE

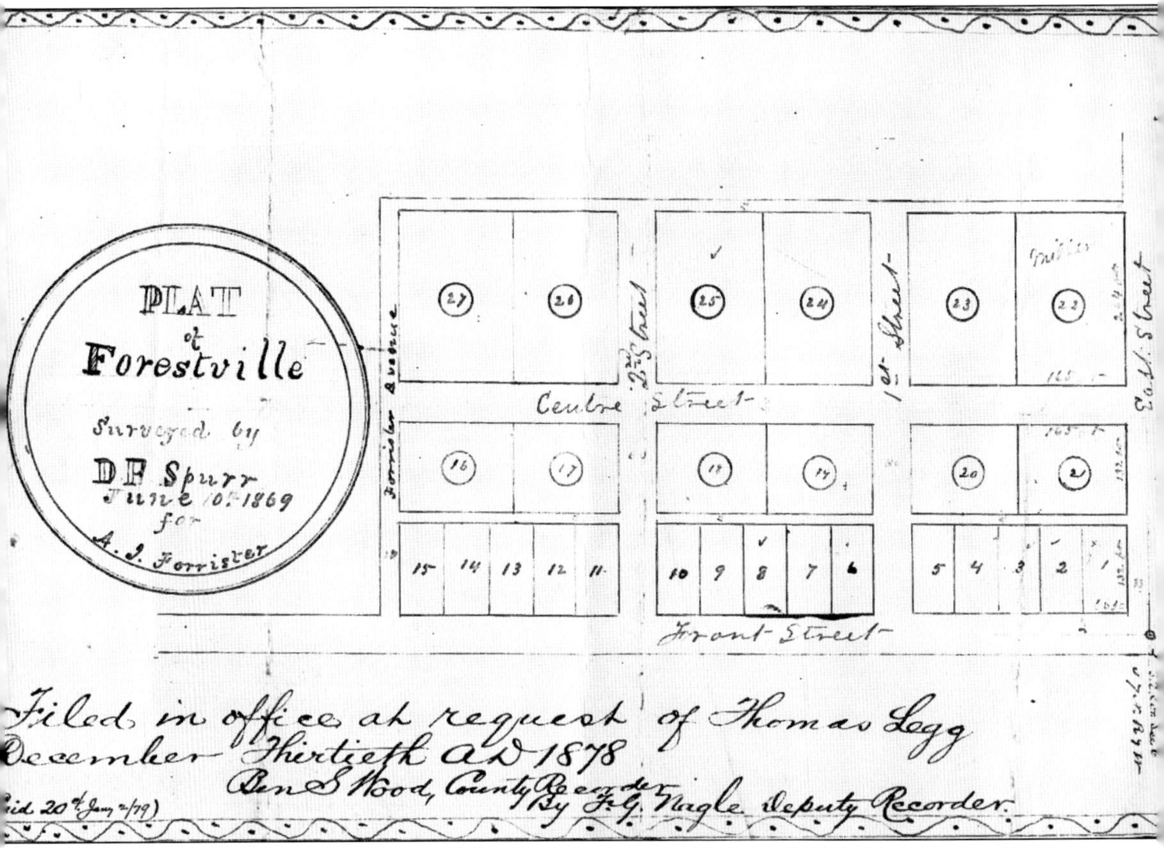

In 1878, this plat map was drawn of the downtown area of Forestville. Notice there is a Forrister Avenue next to where Fred's Liquor is today. Plat No. 1 on this map is where Andrew Jackson Forrister's saloon was located. It was surveyed in 1869 and filed in 1878. The recorder for this plat map was Thomas Legg, who lived in Forestville during that time. (Courtesy of the Dave Henry collection.)

ON THE COVER: Tom Silk, known as the unofficial first mayor of Forestville, is standing while Clyde Fouts and Margaret Silk sit in a 1914 Ford. Fouts often drove for Tom Silk, because as his daughter said, "He wasn't a very good driver." Tom Silk was the manager of the Analy Savings Bank and postmaster from 1900 to 1915. His wife, Ida, became postmistress from 1915 until 1945. Tom Silk managed the local baseball team, among other civic activities. In 1928, the bank building burned and was replaced by the stucco building seen later in pictures. (Courtesy of Lavon Speer Covington.)

IMAGES
of America

FORESTVILLE

Penny Hutten and
the Forestville Historical Society

ARCADIA
PUBLISHING

ISBN 978-0-7385-5805-9

Published by Arcadia Publishing
Charleston SC, Chicago IL, Portsmouth NH, San Francisco CA

Printed in the United States of America

Library of Congress Catalog Card Number: 2007939179

For all general information contact Arcadia Publishing at:
Telephone 843-853-2070
Fax 843-853-0044
E-mail sales@arcadiapublishing.com
For customer service and orders:
Toll-Free 1-888-313-2665

Visit us on the Internet at www.arcadiapublishing.com

To my grandchildren, Hunter, Brandon, and Katelyn,
may they develop a love of history,
viewing it as a puzzle that becomes
an adventure as the pieces come together.

CONTENTS

ACKNOWLEDGMENTS

My greatest debt is to Dave Henry and his wife, Kay, for giving so generously of their pictures, time, and knowledge. Secondly, thanks to Ross and Bernice Yeager for their perfect detailed memories of Forestville's past. This book would also not have been written with out the help of the Forestville Historical Society members Ron Davis, Lavon Speer Covington, Phil and Cheri Marcucci, Virginia Van Keppel Hughes, the late Verna Blanc, Warren and Florence Templeman, John Anderson, Darleen Speer, and Don Fulkerson, all of whom contributed writing and fascinating stories.

I wish also to thank Jeff Tobes for giving me all the research he completed with his class on Forestville History. At the same time, Hal Wood also collected a lot of information that I used in the book.

These sources were a bedrock of information during the writing of this book: first, Burton Travis's *History of El Molino Rancho and Forestville Town* (finished by his son Russell Travis); second, the Pacific Union College library, which allowed me to read the William Tommy Ross journals; third, the early histories of Sonoma County at the Sonoma County Library Annex; fourth, the San Luis Obispo Historical Society; and finally, Susan Synder of the Bancroft Library.

Special thanks goes to Sherri Martinelli for her hospitality and willingness to share the history of her family and Linda Burke for all her time and love of Forestville history. Thanks also to the following people for information to complete the book: the late Marvin Walters; Dave Bramham; Daniel Rohlfing; Barbara Uebel; Bob Burke; Jeani Martini; Lorna Drake; Deane McGowen for his interview of Margaret Silk; Ken Silk; Claudia McDermott for her slogan "Forestville the Good Life;" Gary Harris; the late Mondo Dagnello; Eric Haeberli; Martha Garfield; Harry Lapham; Barry Aldridge; Janet Sitton; Archie Hicks Jr.; Louis Lacabanne; Evelyn McClure; Pete Pearson; Frank Close; Gary Duignan (fire chief); Fred Bertheaud; Joe Martinelli; the late Eva Martinelli; Margie Healy of Korbel Winery; my editor at Arcadia Publishing, Kelly Reed; and finally Gaye Lebaron, who sparked my interest in local history many years ago.

INTRODUCTION

"Forestville the Good Life" is a motto that many of the town's people use to describe the sentiment of living in Forestville. The community working to nurture an atmosphere for their families to thrive started long ago. The roots of this evolved from the early years.

Twelve years before the Bear Flag Revolt of 1846, Gen. Mariano Vallejo divided up land north of San Francisco into land grants sanctioned by the Mexican government. The start of the town now called Forestville derived from the land grant Gen. Mariano Vallejo traded with his brother-in-law, Juan Bautista Rogers Cooper (better known as Capt. John Cooper) for the Rio Ojotska land. Cooper had started the first powered, commercial sawmill in California at this site. The land grant was called El Molino from the Spanish word for "the mill." Soon many people came from different areas of the United States to experience their own manifest destiny.

Andrew Jackson Forrister saw an opportunity to start the first hotel and saloon in this area. He had traveled from Missouri in 1846, marrying his wife, Cynthia Hooper, in 1851. Some of the first stories are of travelers being swindled going through town. The name of the town caught on as "Swindle Rig" or "Swindle Ridge," giving a very picturesque detail of the goings on at the saloon owned by a previous saloon keeper. Later the town was named after the saloon keeper A. J. Forrister. There has been much debate as to the spelling of Forestville; some people believe it should have two *R*s like some of the early land documents; this issue will not be resolved any time soon.

Forestville had the first manufacturing plant in Sonoma County. Maj. Isaac Sullivan started making rawhide and oak chairs. The Faudré family moved to Forestville from Kentucky with their four boys. Steve W. Faudré was a Methodist minister. Soon they began making the Faudré chair, which is being collected around the United States to this very day.

With a manufacturing base, hotel, and saloon, two railroads were now coming into town. The Petaluma and Santa Rosa Electric Railway (P&SR) brought freight to San Francisco and vacationers from the city, where they caught the Russell Stage to the Russian River from 1903 till 1919. Up until 1914, the second train, the Northwestern Pacific Railroad (NWP) from Santa Rosa, stopped near Forestville while going to Guerneville, crossing over the Russian River at the Hacienda Bridge. The NWP train depot was located close to the Johnson house, which is now the Farm House Inn.

One of the first farming families was the William Thomas Ross family in 1857. William married Sarepta Ann Turner in 1864, becoming one of the founding families. The crops they grew were fruit and hops. Rumor has it that they were beloved by all for their kindness and with a generous heart helped those in need. Many of town's people are descendants from this wonderful family.

Some of the tourists that stopped in Forestville stayed at the electric hotel. To meet the needs of this new community, Silk, Son, and Company became a dry-goods store and a branch of the Analy Saving bank. This store later housed the post office. John Egbert Jewett started the first pharmacy close to the Analy Savings Bank. There were many other establishments, including a blacksmith shop.

In 1900, to take advantage of all the tourists, Mirabel Park built a dance hall; later, big-name bands like Benny Goodman, Harry James, and Glen Miller brought more people from San Francisco to relax and stay in the resort area.

In 1934, the Forestville School burned to the ground. The Methodist church allowed classes to be held in their church until a group of citizens got together to rebuild the school. Forestville has always had a friendly, small-town attitude that values its youth. In 1962, a group organized in order to acquire land so that the community could have its first park. Andy Anderson and Bob Aldridge, the local bank manager, headed the Forestville Youth Park organization. The Youth Park has an annual barbeque to raise money for its own maintenance. Bob Aldridge was the first person honored as citizen of the year due to his efforts for the town. Once again, this demonstrates the history of community action to make "Forestville the Good Life."

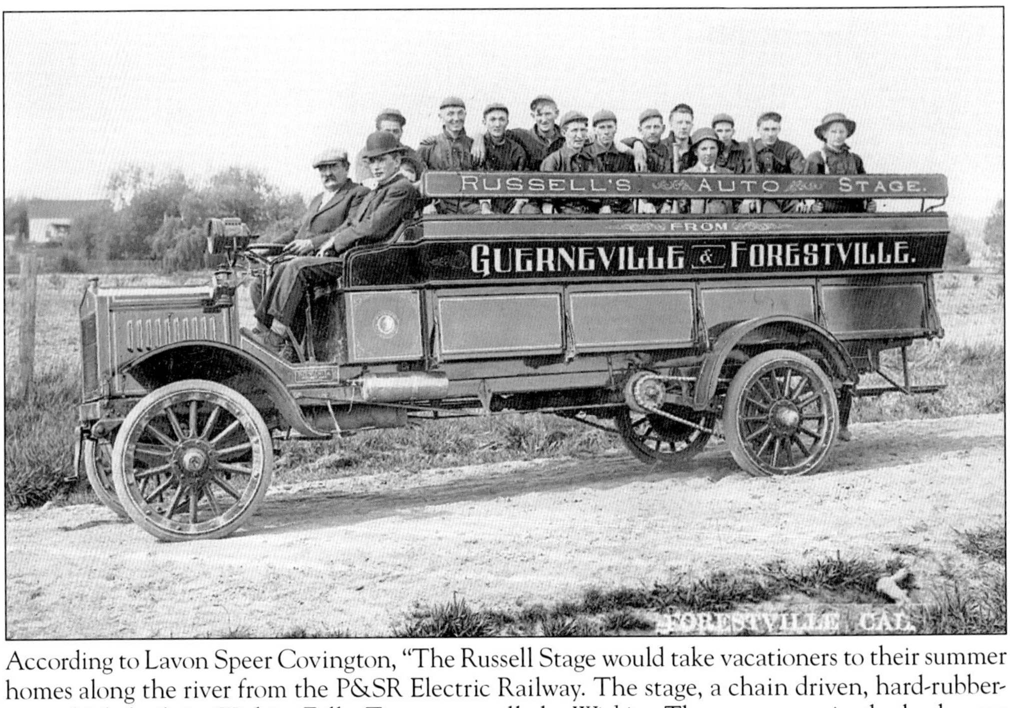

According to Lavon Speer Covington, "The Russell Stage would take vacationers to their summer homes along the river from the P&SR Electric Railway. The stage, a chain driven, hard-rubber-tire-vehicle built in Wichita Falls, Texas, was called a *Wichita*. The passengers in the back were Jack Williams, Everett Close, Archie Hull, Walter Kimes, Bert Marley, Howard Johnson, Clint Yeager, Jack Morris, Jack Morris's son (in front of them), Lewis Johnson, Ray Johnson, Fred Anderson (bat boy). George Russell is shown driving with James F. Speer Sr. in the front seat." (Courtesy of the Bob Aldridge collection.)

One

El Molino

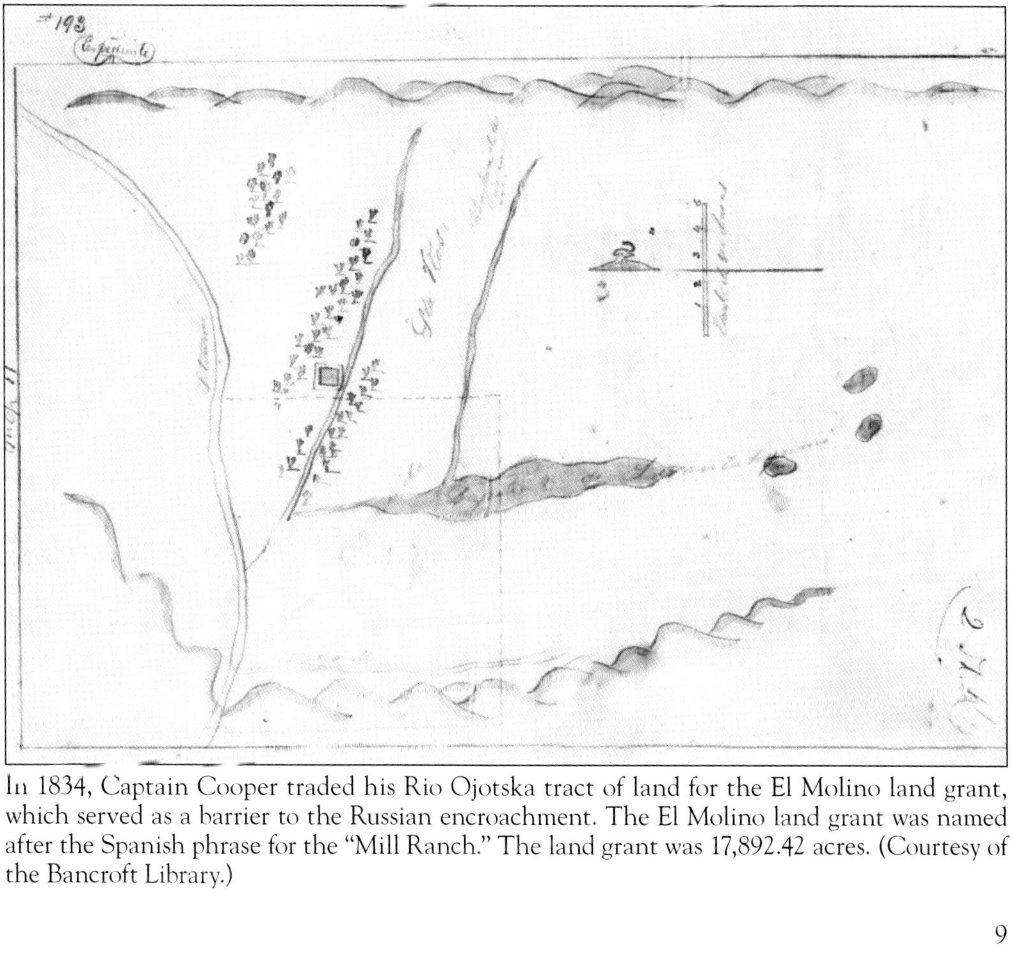

In 1834, Captain Cooper traded his Rio Ojotska tract of land for the El Molino land grant, which served as a barrier to the Russian encroachment. The El Molino land grant was named after the Spanish phrase for the "Mill Ranch." The land grant was 17,892.42 acres. (Courtesy of the Bancroft Library.)

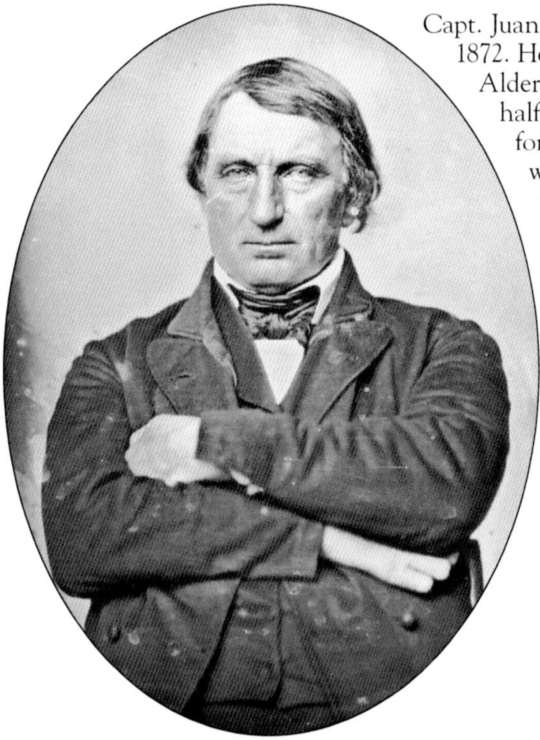

Capt. Juan Bautista Rogers Cooper lived from 1791 to 1872. He was born on the British Channel Island of Alderney and later moved to Massachusetts. His half-brother was Thomas Larkin, who was known for his part in early California history. They worked together in the lumber industry. Cooper married Gen. Mariano Guadalupe Vallejo's sister, Encarnacion Vallejo, on August 24, 1827, and they had four children. Captain Cooper built the first powered sawmill in California and owned several land grants: El Molino Rancho, El Sur, Rancho Punta de Quentin, and Nicasio Rancho, to name a few. His family lived on the El Sur Rancho in Monterey. (Courtesy of the Bancroft Library.)

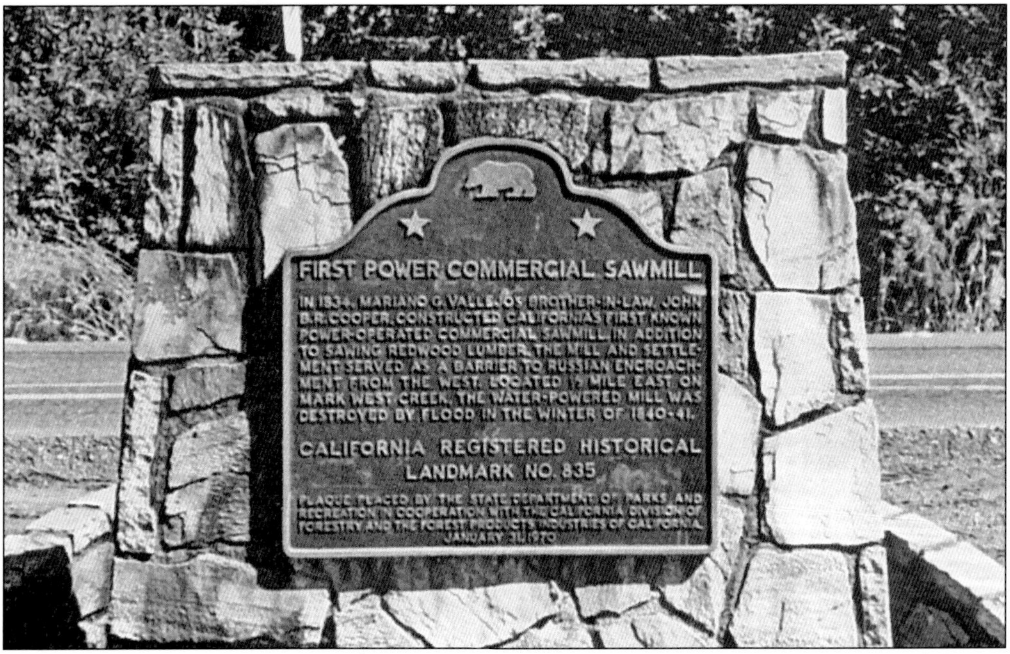

In 1834, Captain Cooper invested $10,000 to build the first power-operated sawmill in California. In 1841, when the Russian River had one of its floods, the mill floated down the river. On October 29, 1969, the mill was named California Historical Landmark No. 835. It was recognized as the birthplace of California's multi-billion-dollar timber-products industry by a committee of historians. (Courtesy of Jeff Tobes.)

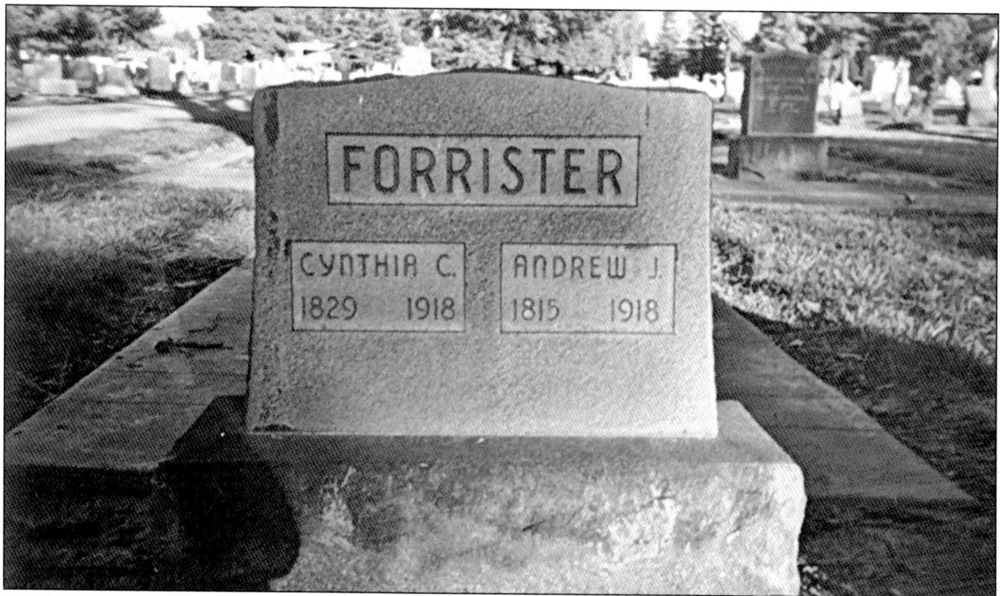

Andrew Jackson Forrister (June 28, 1815–April 13, 1918) died in Chico, California, after going blind. Forestville was named after him. No one knows why the spelling is different, but it adds to the charm of Forestville. Forrister was born in Missouri but moved to Forestville in 1853. In 1857, he married Cynthia C. Hooper, and they had four children. He was a saloon keeper in Forestville about the time the temperance league was gaining power. Within seven years, he moved to San Luis Obispo to take up farming. (Courtesy of Hannah Gross and Jeff Tobes.)

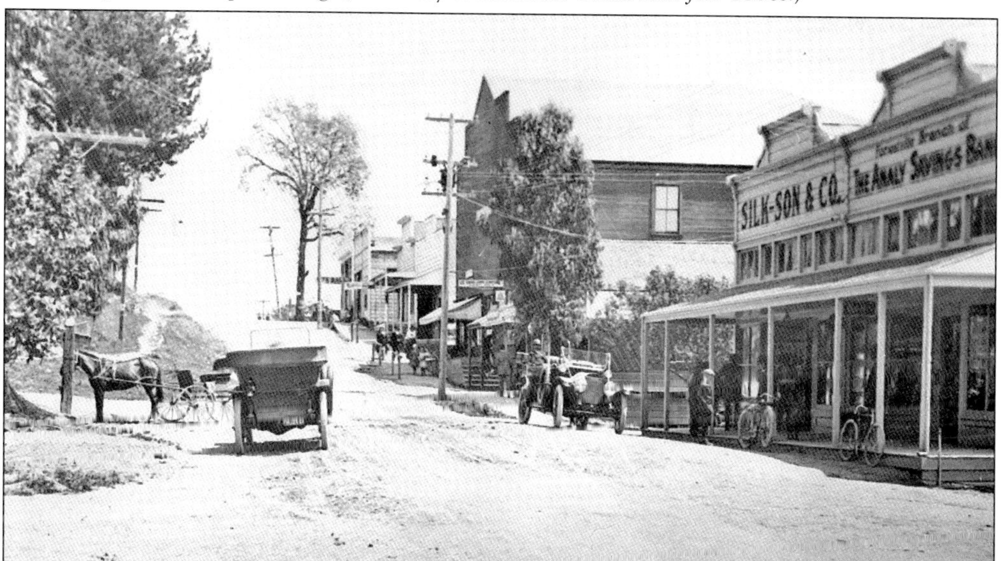

This 1912 picture of Forestville's downtown shows the Ross brothers' identical 1911 Cadillacs. Mondo Dagnello said, "The streets were not paved until 1918." Looking down the street, there is the corner of Silk, Son, and Company's variety store, Analy Savings Bank, and L.D. Yeager's barbershop. The tall building later became Dinucci Hall, which had a floating dance floor. Dinucci Hall was later turned into the I.O.O.F. Hall, which later moved to the current location. The top of the hill is where the Forestville Club is today, but it was Hick's Garage in years past, and before that it was the Rochedale store. (Courtesy of Lavon Speer Covington.)

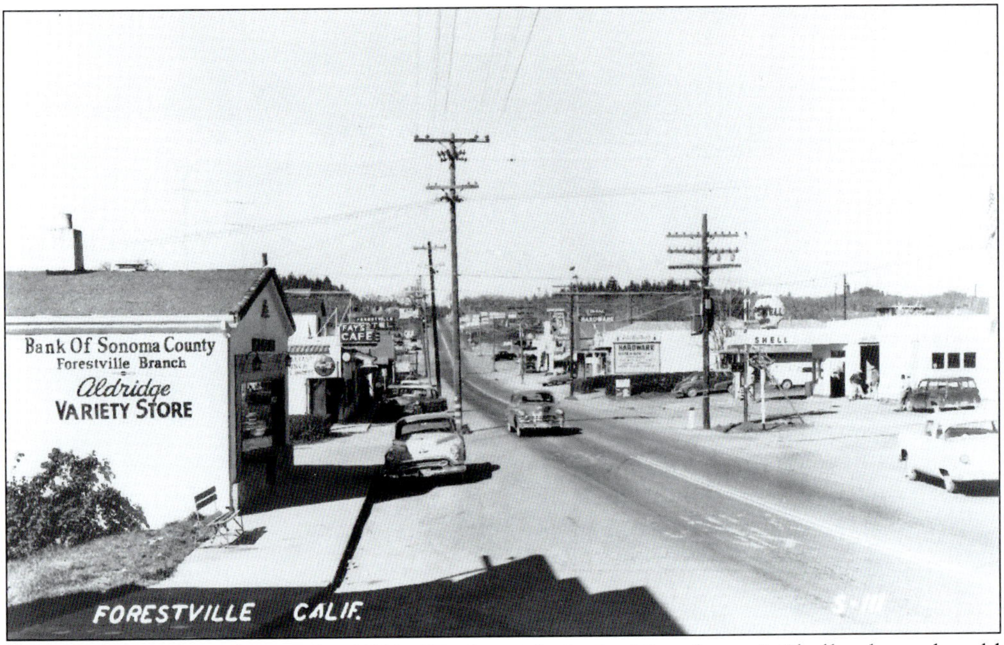

This is Main Street during the 1950s. To the right is the Templeman's Shell, where the old Templeman house was located. Next to the gas station is the Ideal hardware store, which is in the same location as it is today; it is now run by Bob Baba. On the left is the Bank of Sonoma County, run by Bob Aldridge, with his variety store next to it. Further down the street is Fay's Café, which moved across the street at a later time. The 1930s motel is where Gordon and Phyllis Grabe later ran the hippie-culture crafts shop, the Griffin Mind Shop, in the 1960s. In the 1970s, it became a popular Mexican restaurant. (Courtesy of Lavon Speer Covington.)

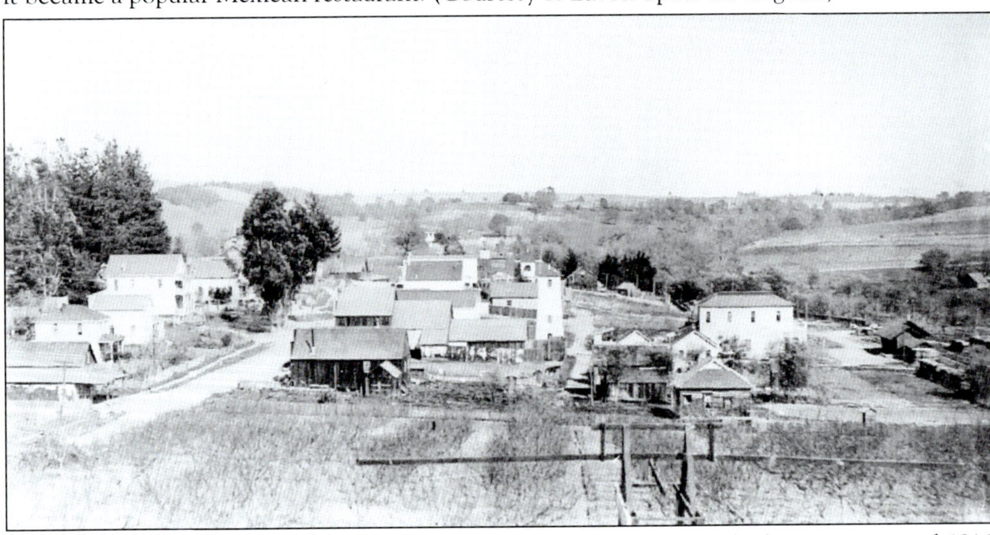

This view of Forestville must have been taken from the Evans house looking east around 1914. To the far right is the Electric Hotel; the train depot would have been a little further to the right but is not shown. On the right side of the street are the blacksmith shop and the livery stable, and the tallest building is the Dinucci–I.O.O.F. Hall with its floating dance floor. On the left side of the street is the Russell house, which was also a hotel; to the right are the Templeman and Clark family homes. (Courtesy of Ron Davis.)

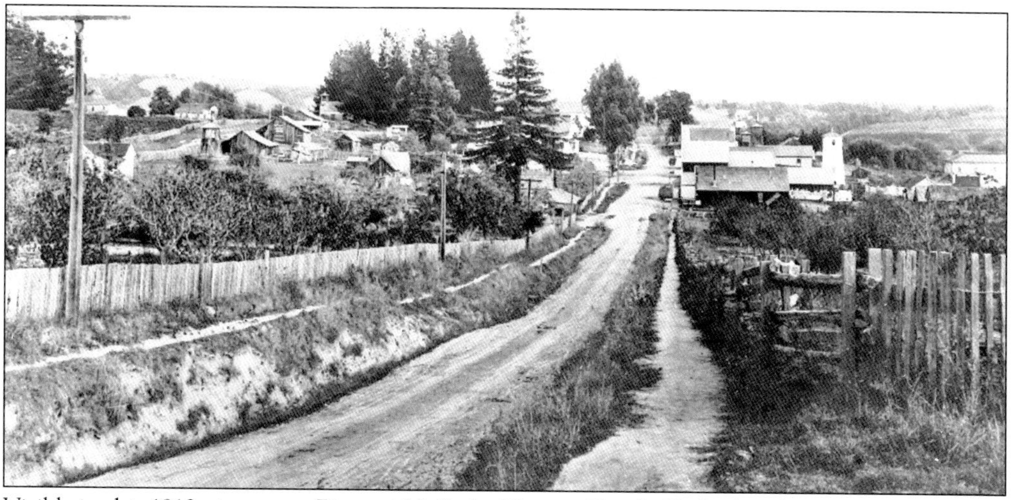

Visible in this 1912 picture are Dinucci Hall, the Electric Hotel, Clark's butcher shop, the school in the background, and, to the right, the Tilton House, considered to be the oldest house in town. The road must have been very muddy when it rained. (Courtesy of the Dave Henry collection.)

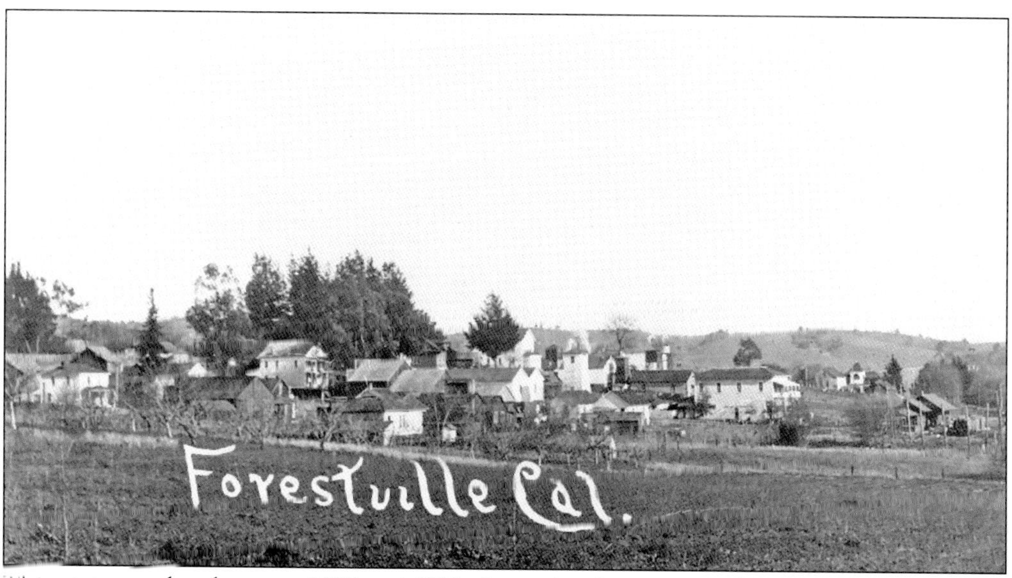

This picture, taken between 1906 and 1912, shows the electric train depot to the right and the Electric Hotel across the street from the train depot. The Forestville School is also visible in the background. Toward the center of the picture is an outhouse, very typical with homes of that day. (Courtesy of the Dave Henry collection.)

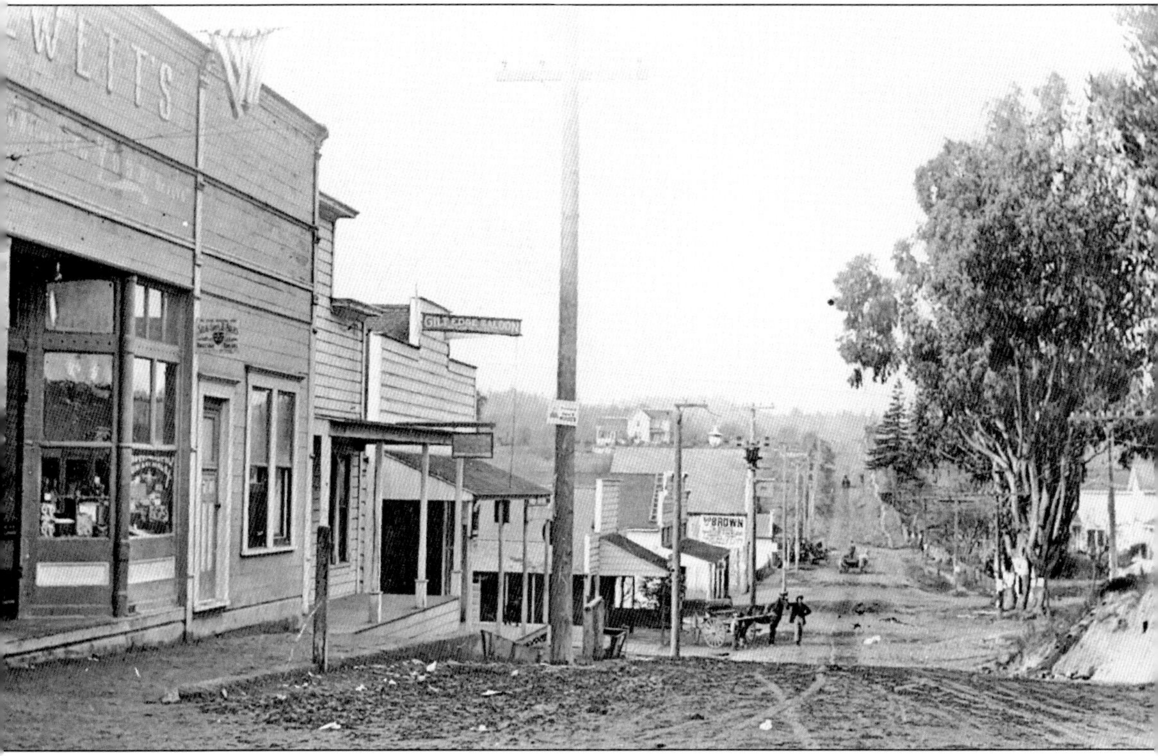

This town view is from the top of the hill looking toward Mirabel Road. The first store is John Egbert Jewett's drugstore, then Dr. Fred Newton Folsom's office, Jack Alten's Gilt Edge Saloon, Bill Clark's butcher shop, Tom Silk's grocery store, Charles C. Oliver's livery stable, L. D. Yeager's barbershop, and then the Evans house on the top of the hill. At various times there have also been a dance hall, bowling alley, restaurants, gas station, a library, an appliance store, antiques stores, a pool hall, and many other businesses. Virginia Van Keppel Hughes remembers her mother telling of going to town for an ice cream and having to duck into a building because a large herd of long-horned cattle were being driven down the middle of Main Street. (Courtesy of the Dave Henry collection.)

Two

CHANGING MONEY

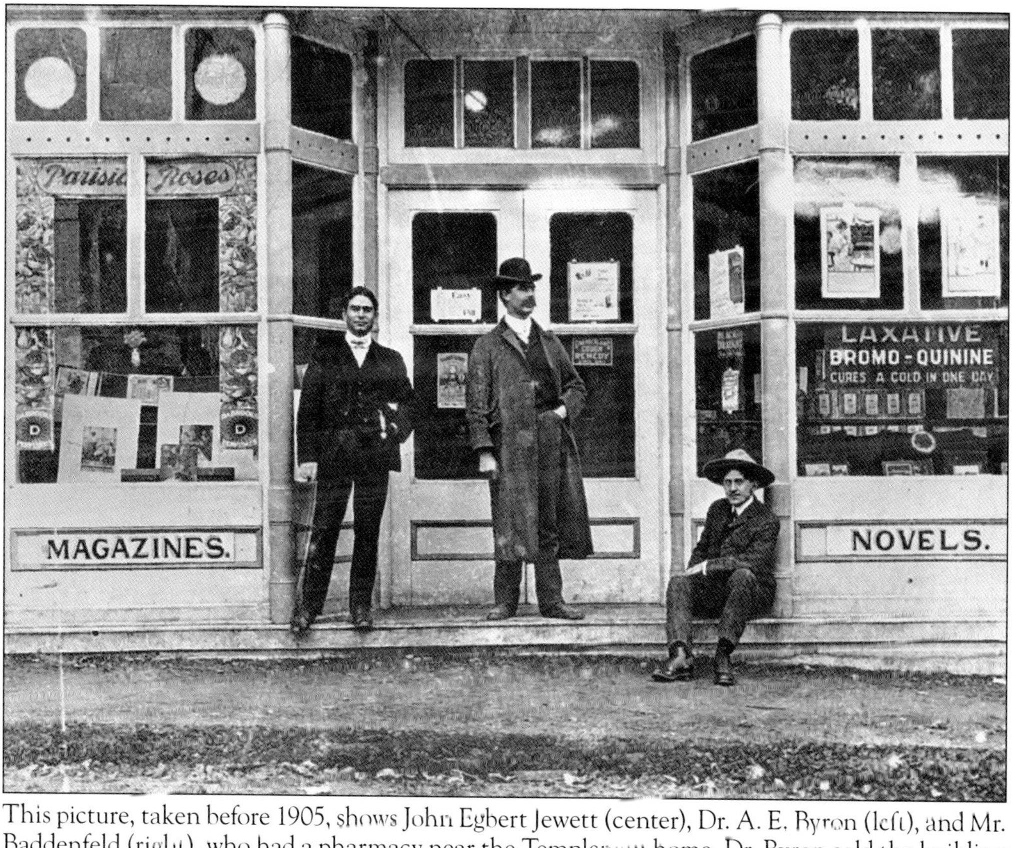

This picture, taken before 1905, shows John Egbert Jewett (center), Dr. A. E. Byron (left), and Mr. Baddenfeld (right), who had a pharmacy near the Templeman home. Dr. Byron sold the building to Jewett on February 25, 1905. Margaret Silk said, "Jewett's pharmacy and ice cream parlor had the best ice cream in the country." Her mother was Ida Jewett Silk, sister of Bert Jewett, so she probably enjoyed her uncle's ice cream a little more than others. "Notice the Bromo-Quinine that probably didn't cure a cold in one day and the cough remedy," said Dave Henry. (Courtesy of the Dave Henry collection.)

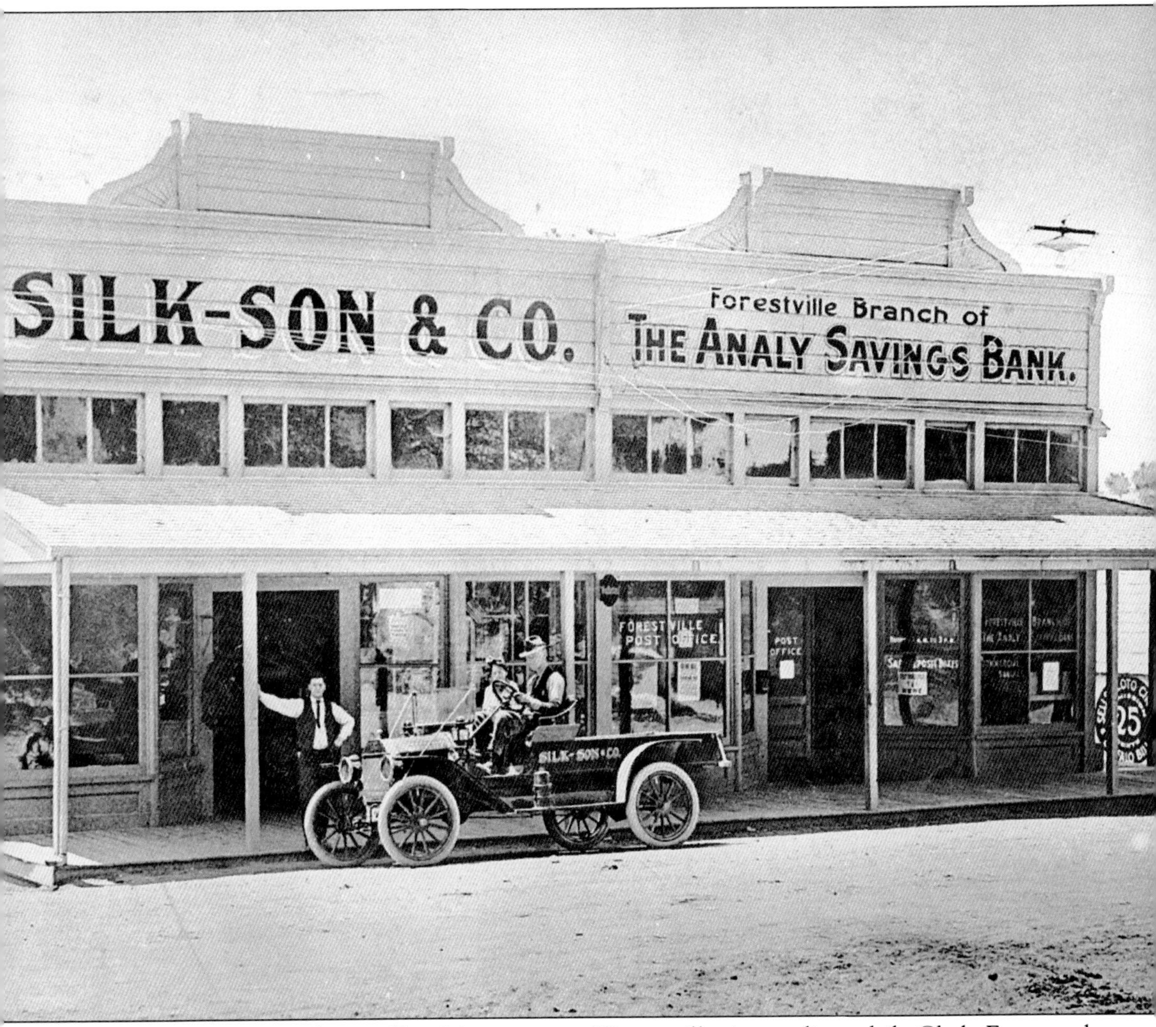

Tom Silk, known as the unofficial first mayor of Forestville, is standing while Clyde Fouts and Margaret Silk sit in the 1914 Ford. Fouts often drove for Tom Silk, because as his daughter said, "He wasn't a very good driver." Tom Silk was the manager of the Analy Savings Bank and postmaster from 1900 to 1915. His wife, Ida, became postmistress from 1915 until 1945. Tom Silk managed the local baseball team, among other civic activities. In 1928, the bank building burned and was replaced by the stucco building seen later in pictures. (Courtesy of Lavon Speer Covington.)

This shows the early days of commerce. Inside of Tom Silk's store are Howard Johnson and Naomi Gillespie. It looks like it was a real variety store, stocking daily items to run a home or ranch. Margaret Silk remembers riding out to the hop fields with Clyde Fouts and taking orders for groceries before delivering them. (Courtesy of Lavon Speer Covington.)

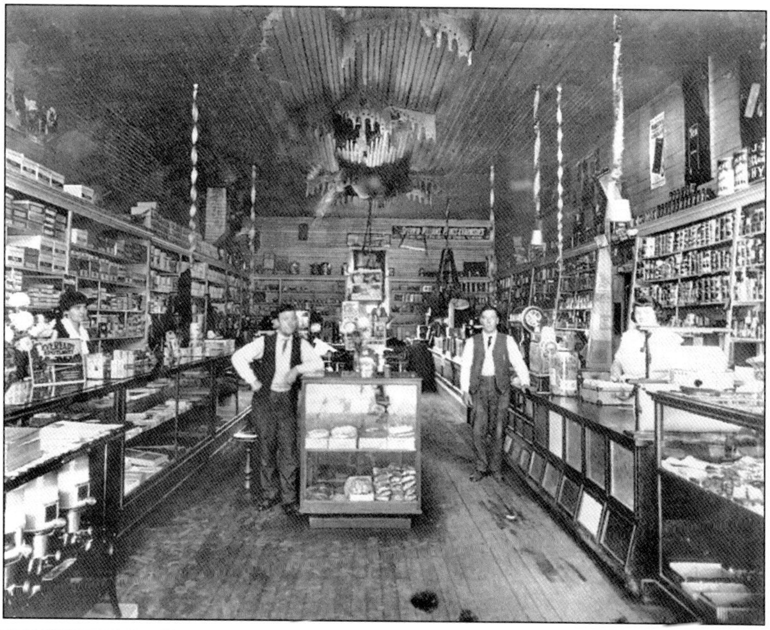

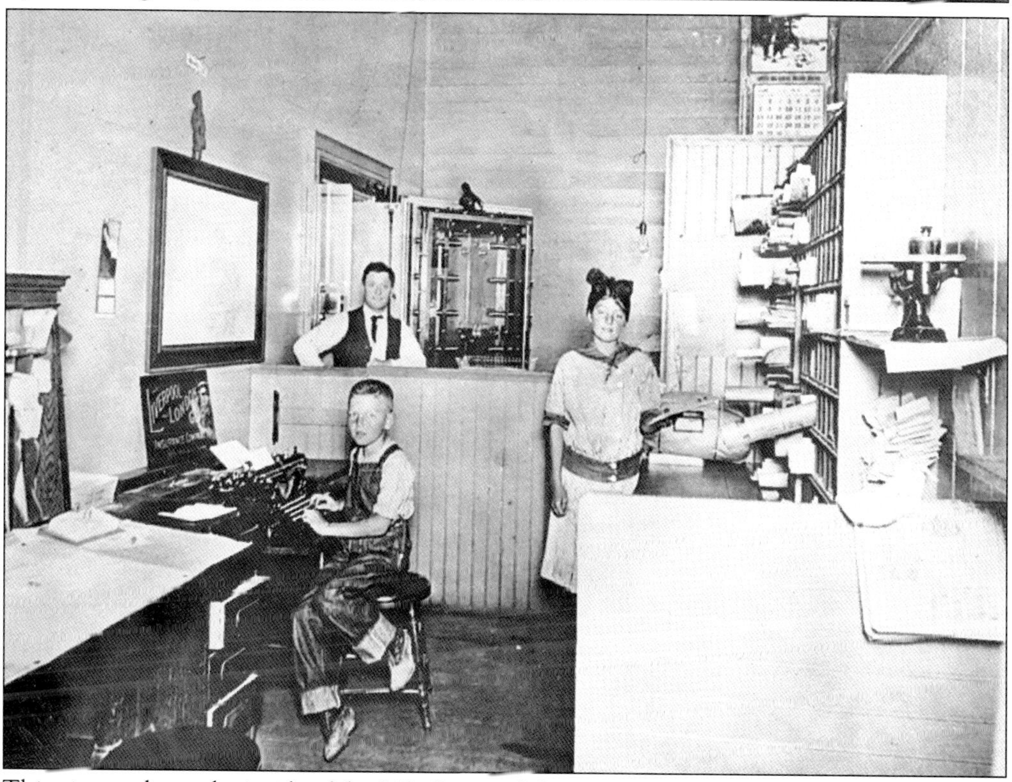

This picture shows the inside of the Silk, Son, and Company bank and post office. Margaret Silk is standing next to the post office, and her brother Thomas Silk Jr. is seated. Tom Silk had wanted his son, Tom Wesley Silk Jr., to take over the banking business when he retired, but young Tom went into teaching and became a professor at Cornell University. Tom Silk Sr. is standing by the bank vault, which was robbed in 1946. (Courtesy of Lavon Speer Covington.)

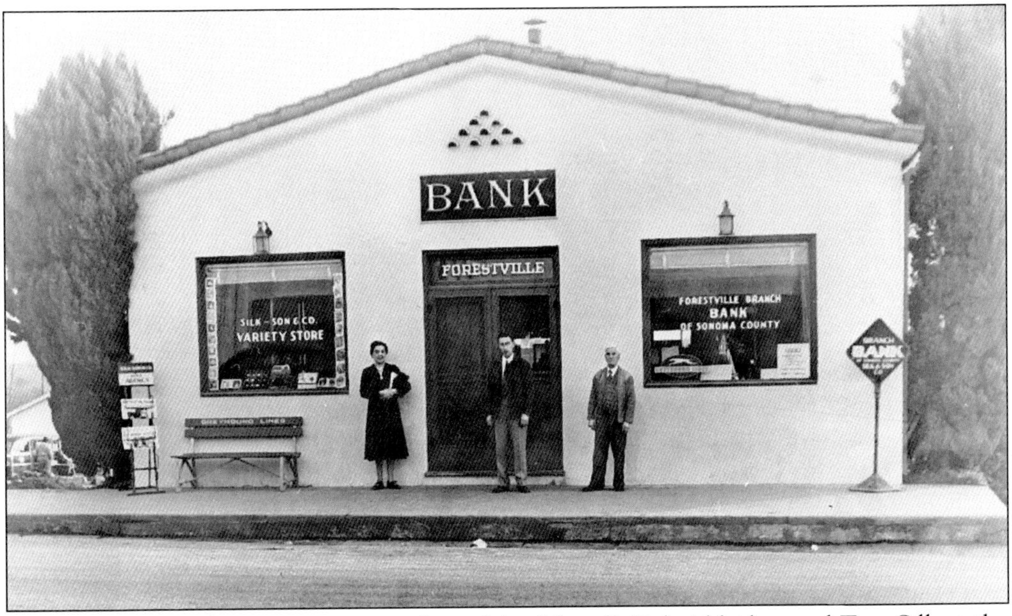

This Silk, Son, and Company picture shows Mrs. Morrell, Bob Aldridge, and Tom Silk at the variety store and bank. Bob Alridge worked for Tom Silk at the Bank of Sonoma County, the successor to the Analy Savings Bank. In 1948, he and his wife, Marda, bought the Silk, Son, and Company store and changed the name to Aldridge Variety Store. The bank and the variety store were in the same building until the 1960s, when the Alridges sold the variety store and concentrated on banking. (Courtesy of Janet Aldridge Sitton.)

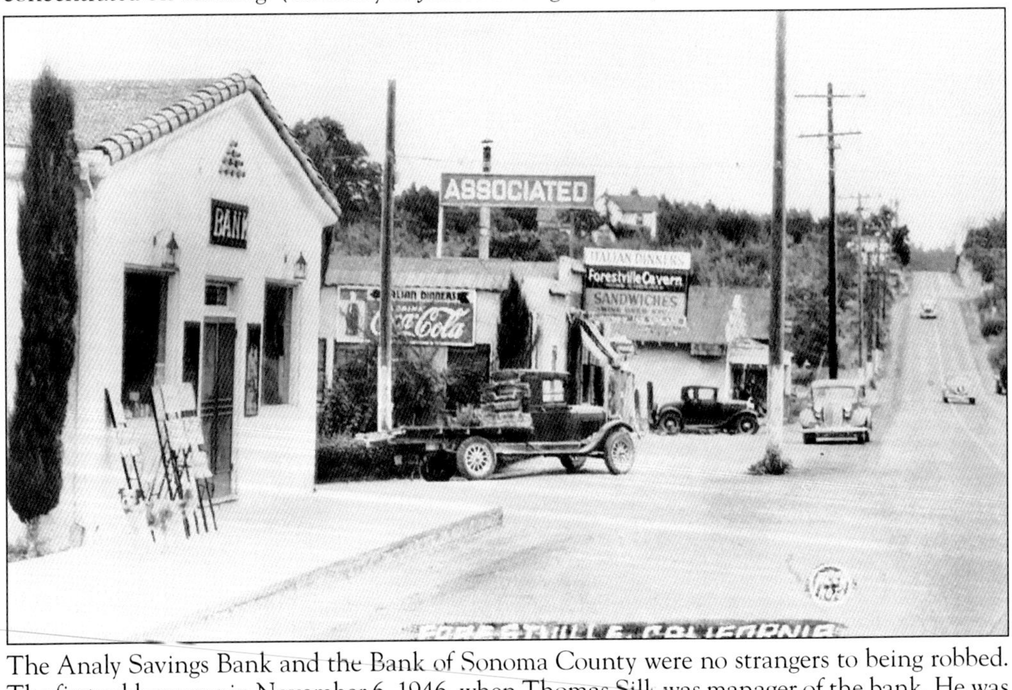

The Analy Savings Bank and the Bank of Sonoma County were no strangers to being robbed. The first robbery was in November 6, 1946, when Thomas Silk was manager of the bank. He was brutally beaten, and the robber escaped with $103 in small bills. Tom Silk continued to manage the bank until his death in October 1947. (Courtesy of the Dave Henry collection.)

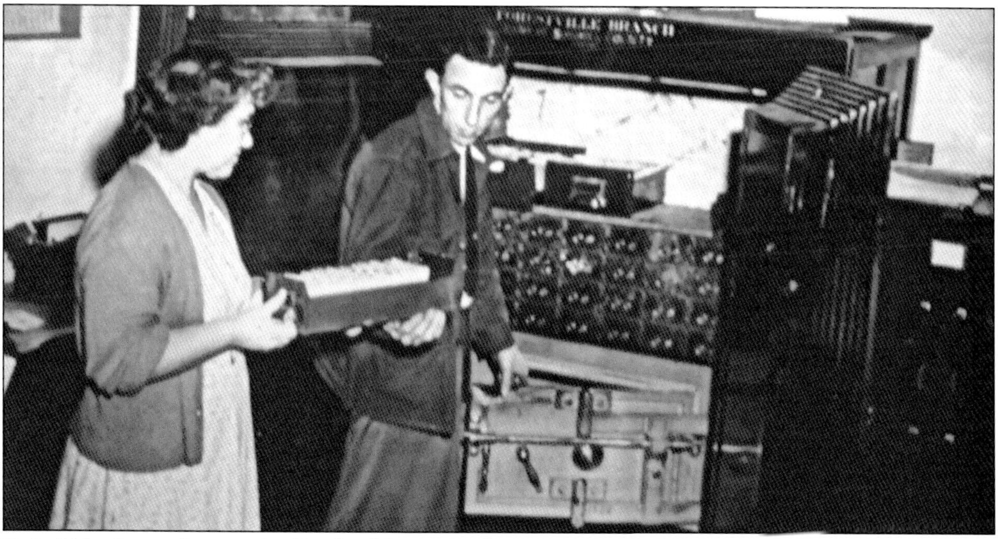

Bob Aldridge took over the Bank of Sonoma County in 1947 when Tom Silk passed away. Here Bob Aldridge and Iris Havenstrite Speer work in the vault. Bob Aldrige was bank manager when, in September 5, 1967, it was robbed again. Three gunmen held Bob Aldridge, his wife, Marda, and their son, David, hostage in their home until the bank vault time lock was released the next morning. The robbers were apprehended with $33,000. (Courtesy of the Dave Henry collection.)

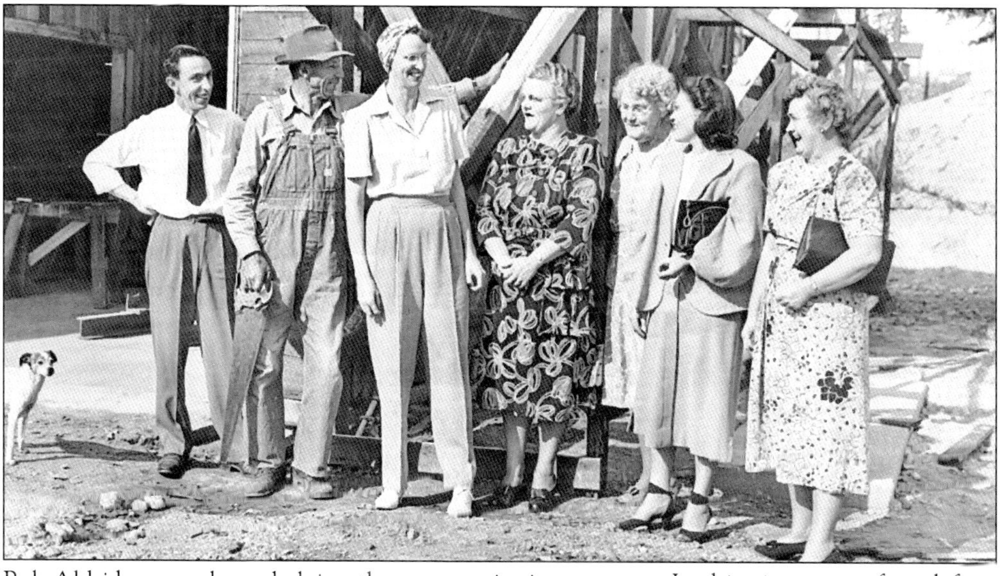

Bob Aldridge was always helping the community in some way. In this picture are, from left to right, Bob Aldridge, Ken Templeman, Marge Templeman, Edna Ludolff, Mrs. Gillespie, Myrna Athey, and Anne Orchard. Bob was helping with the creation of Templeman gas station. He was the first recipient of the Chamber of Commerce "Man of the Year" award in 1967. He was president of the Forestville School Board, director of Forestville Fire District, and contributed to the Forestville Lighting District and Forestville Sanitation District, the volunteer fire department, and the Forestville Water District. He also was instrumental in the formation of the Forestville Youth Park development. He spearheaded many drives to make the community a better place to live. "If it weren't for Bob Aldridge, many of the existing businesses wouldn't exist today," said Dave Henry. (Courtesy of Janet Aldridge Sitton.)

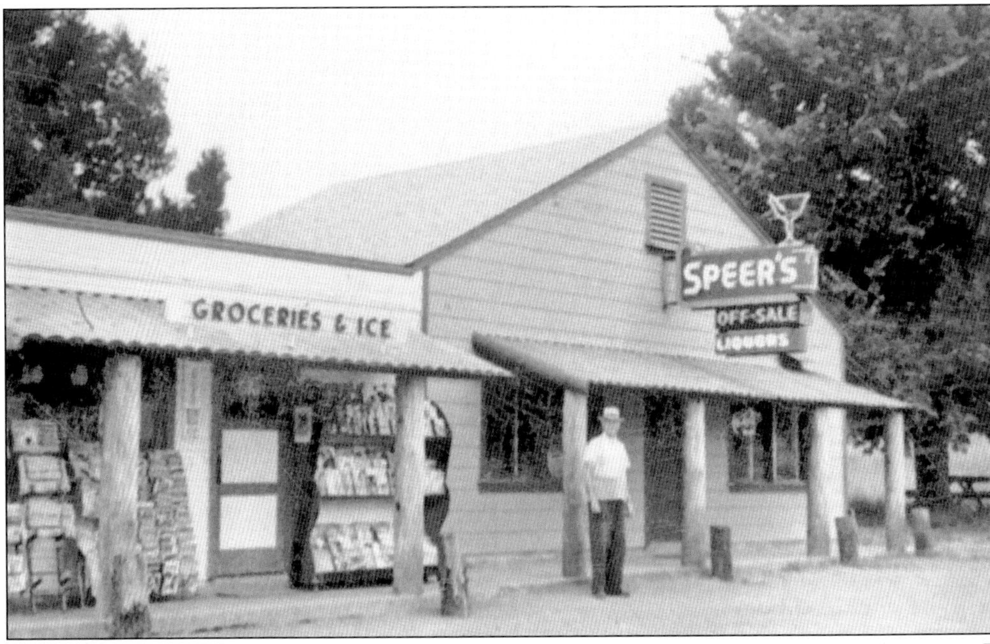

The property where Speers market now stands was originally 70 acres purchased by James F. Speer Sr. from Sarah A. Covey, and it included Mirabel Heights. James Speer Jr. ran it until 1937 when he managed an apple ranch on Vine Hill also owned by his father. After World War II, Howard Speer and his wife, Lillian, bought it and ran it as a gas station and store, later adding a bar and card room. This 1953 picture of Speers Market shows Lillian Speer's father, George Walsh, standing in front. (Courtesy of the Bob Aldridge collection.)

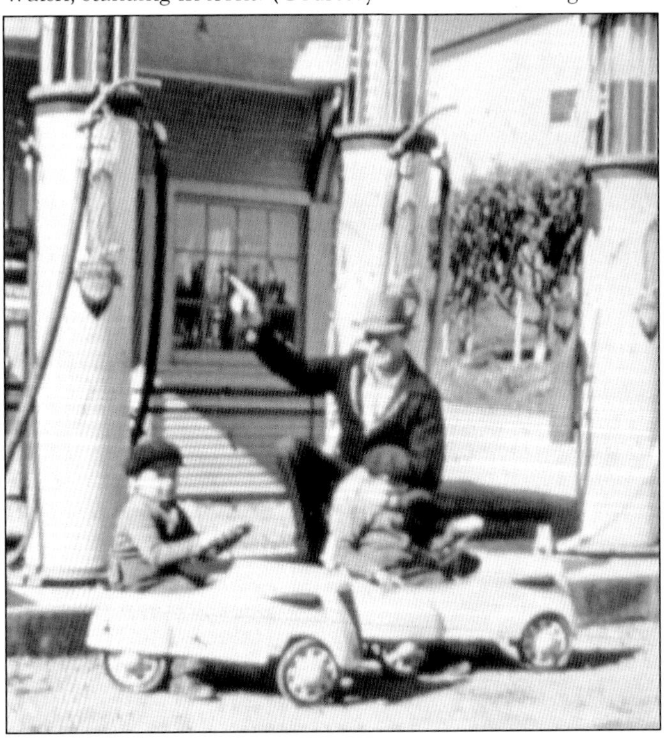

The Speers gas station was built in 1931, and this picture is of Howard Speer with his twin sons, Stanley (right) and Stanford. They are getting gas for their own cars at their dad's station. The gas station was torn down in the late 1940s, when the store and bar were rebuilt. It has been rebuilt several times into the store seen today. Their mother, Lillian Speer, was a memorable woman. In 1985, when a robber came to her home and wanted Howard Speer to open the store, Lillian, at the age of 74, said no. The robber shot her 79-year-old husband, so she shot the robber dead. She was a woman before her time. (Courtesy of Lavon Speer Covington.)

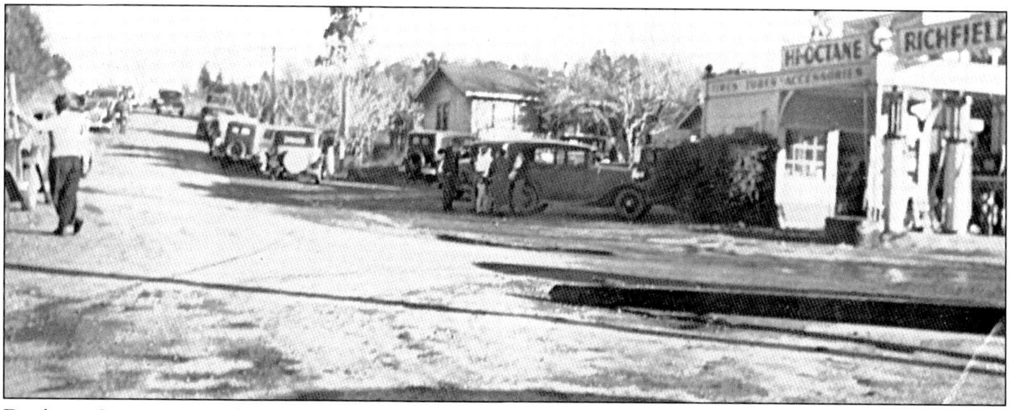

Darleen Speer remembers the story of when her grandfather first came to Forestville after the 1906 earthquake to help rebuild San Francisco. He later bought the property that Speers market is on today. This picture of the 1930s shows a time when Paul Speer worked the gas station and James Speer Jr. worked the market. Son Howard Speer later bought the gas station and started the changes continued by his son, Stanley ("Stan") Speer. Today the owner of the Speers market property is Howard Speer, Stan Speer's son. (Courtesy of Lavon Speer Covington.)

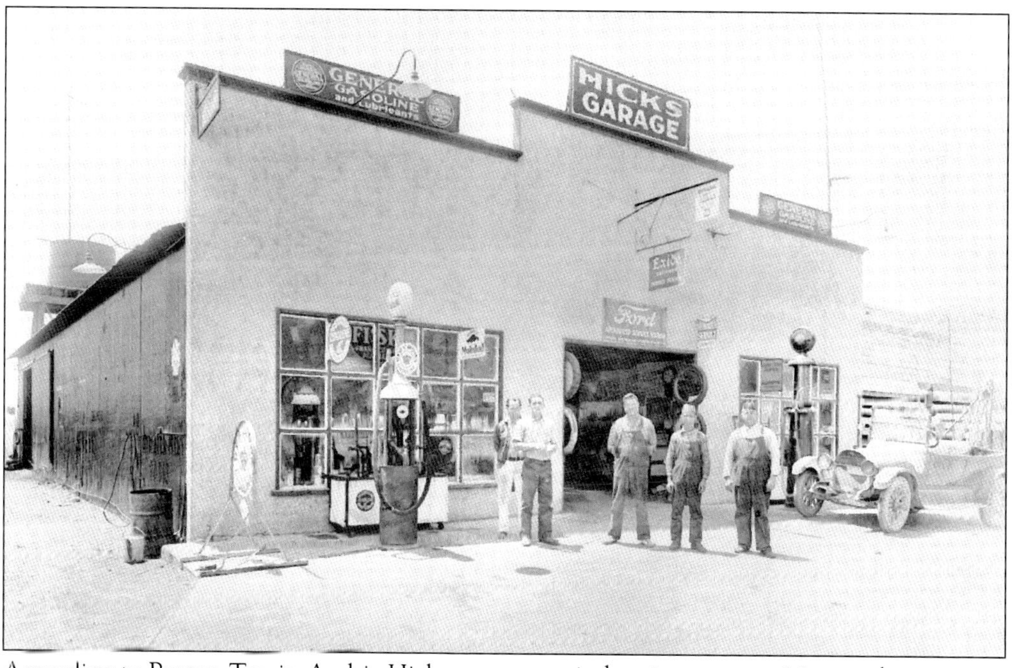

According to Burton Travis, Archie Hicks was a most industrious, enterprising, and progressive businessman. He set up this garage, which was an authorized Ford mechanic. This garage is located where the Forestville Club is today. It was destroyed by fire on August 20, 1922, and then rebuilt. On January 16, 1910, Hicks married Hazel Clark, daughter of the local butcher W. L. Clark. (Courtesy of Dave Henry collection.)

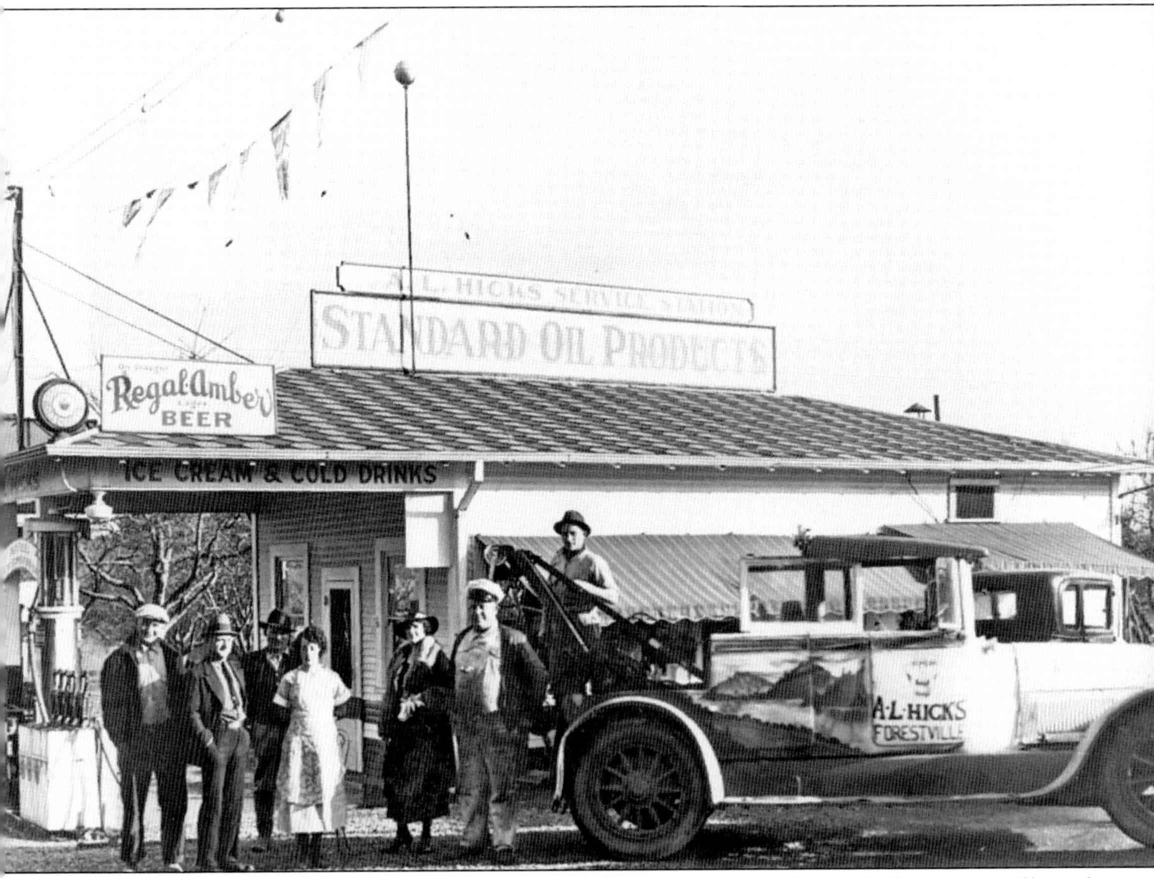

This picture of Archie Hicks's service station and ice cream store shows Archie in overalls and cap and his wife, Hazel, in a fur coat. Archie Hicks was an excellent businessman who liked to please his customers. His wife helped by serving ice cream. His station is located where the package store is today. He also owned the garage next door that later became the Forestville Club. Archie was involved in his community; he saw a need and tried to help with it. In 1938, after watching many fires, he made the first fire truck using an old Maxwell car. (Courtesy of the Dave Henry collection.)

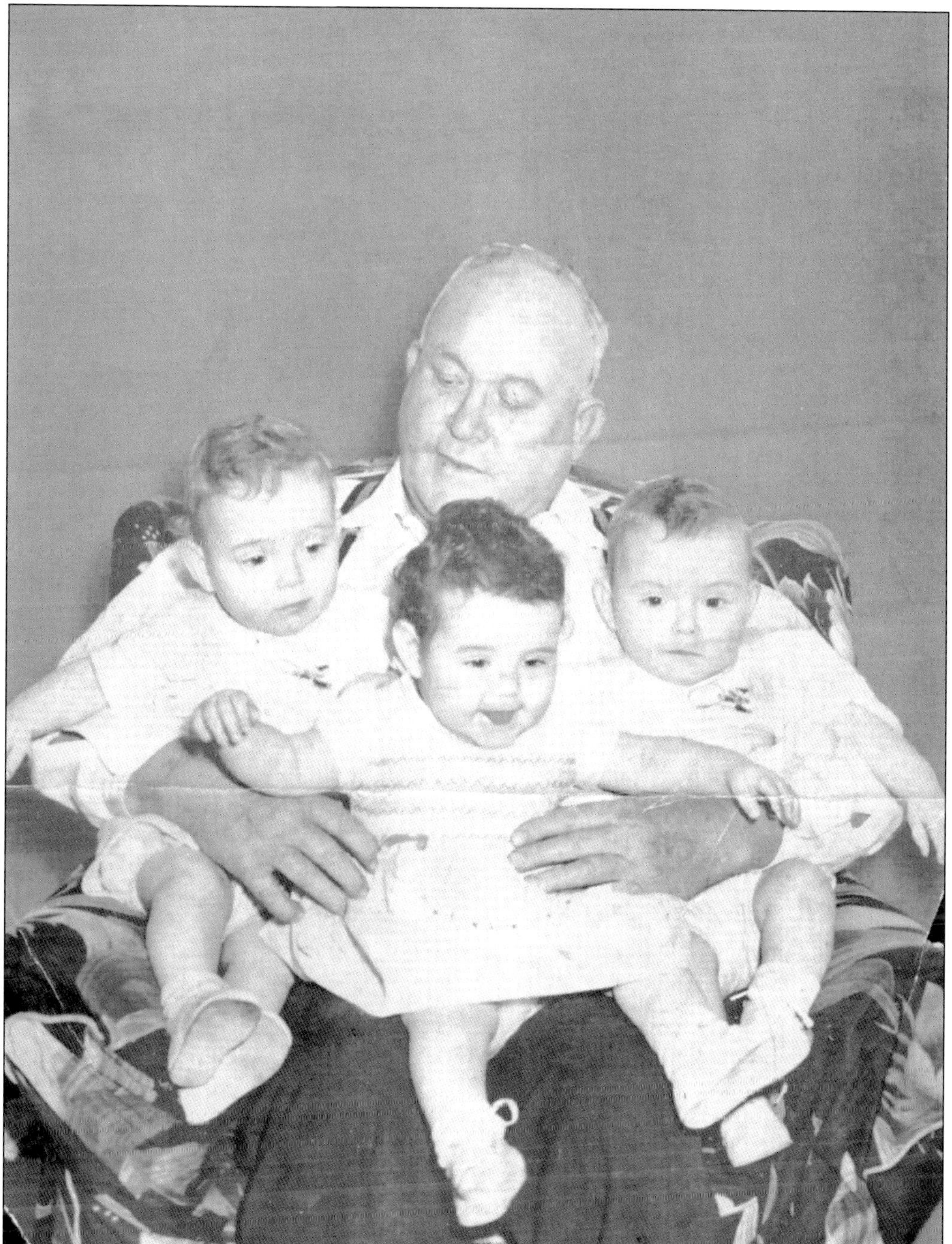

On May 30, 1952, Archie and Florence Hicks had the only triplets born in Forestville. In fact, the Hicks triplets were the first ever born in Sonoma County. Florence Hicks was Archie's second wife, after Hazel died. The triplets were named Archie M., Audra, and Alvin L. Hicks. After Archie closed the garage, he opened Hick's Bar, which is now the Forestville Club. Archie Hicks sold it to Dan Mori. Later owners were Martin Lorenzo, Harley Vanucci, and Chuck Furia; now Wayne Speer owns the Forestville Club. Archie, born in 1880, died two years after the birth of his triplets. (Courtesy of Lavon Speer Covington.)

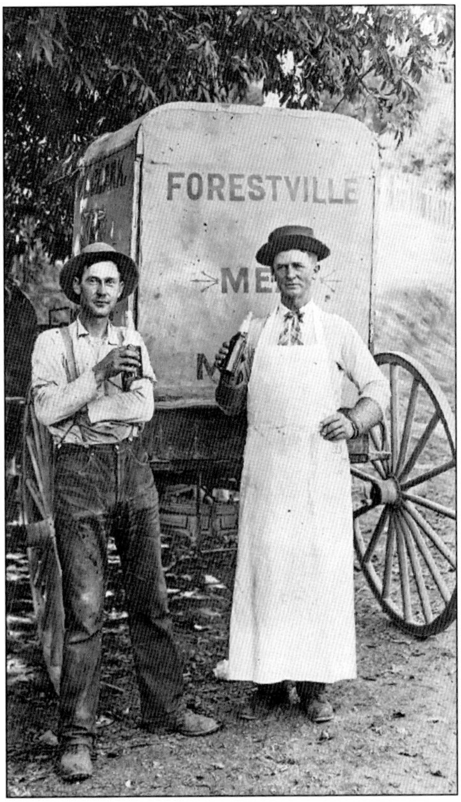

William Clark had a slaughterhouse where he butchered his customers' livestock for them, and his driver delivered the meat to their homes all around Forestville. This is William Clark (right) and his friend L. D. Yeager having some refreshments by William's butcher wagon. (Courtesy of the Dave Henry collection.)

William Clark often delivered meat to the hop-pickers camp and to the Trenton area. This picture was taken around 1910 in the Trenton area; the man with his hand on the horse is Jack Williams. (Courtesy of the Dave Henry collection.)

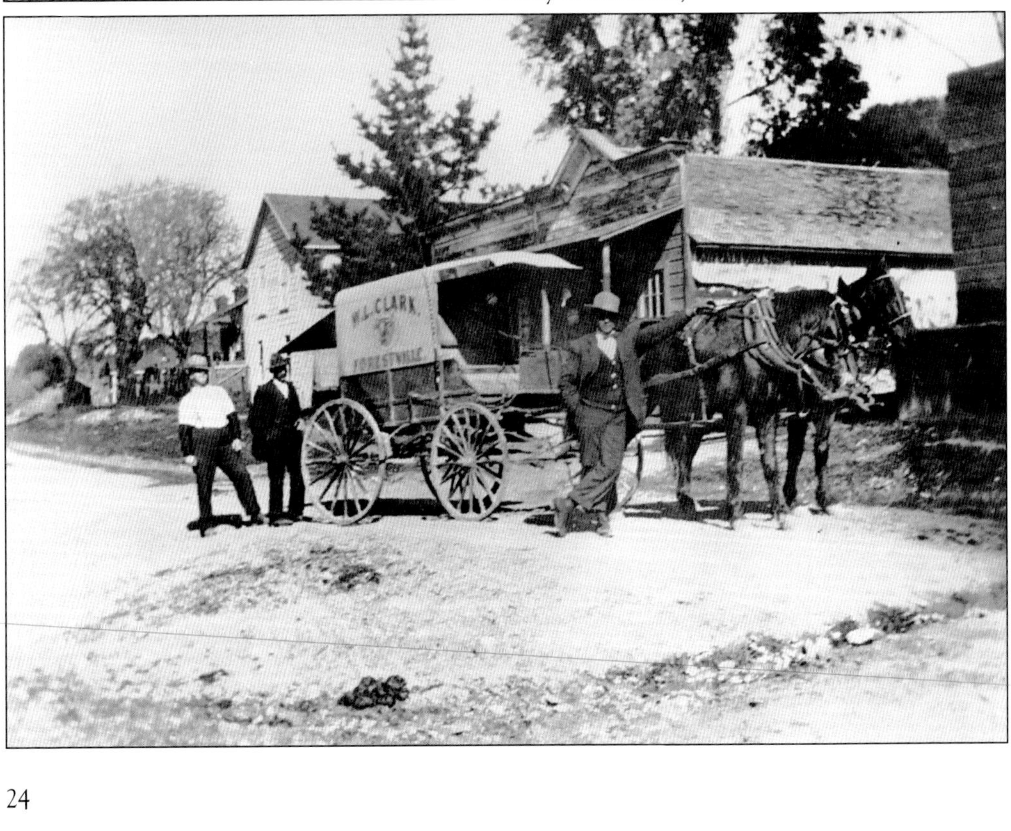

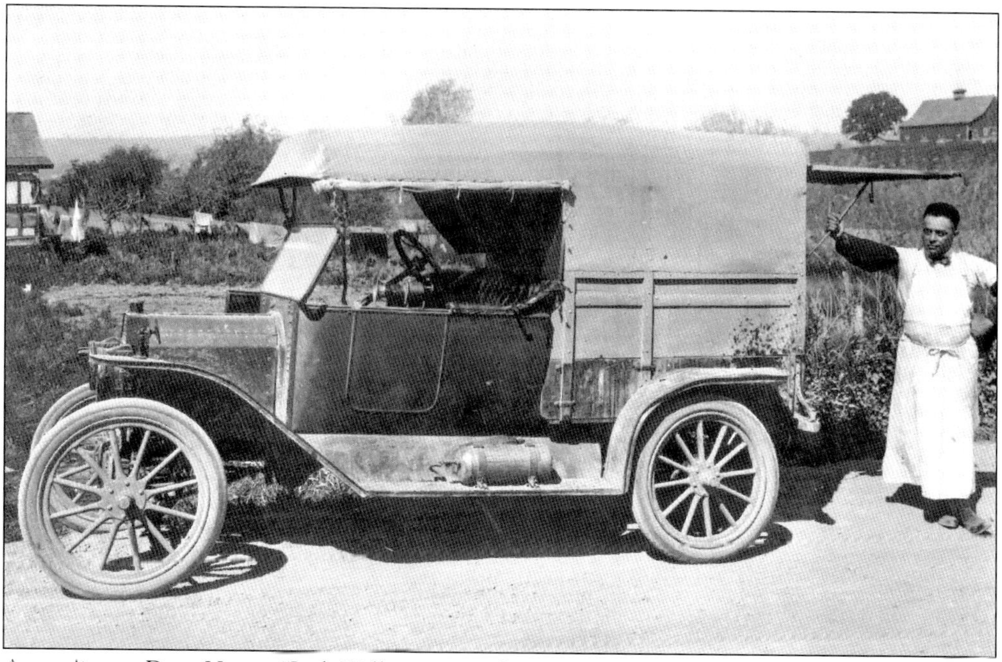

According to Dave Henry, "Jack Williams was a longtime employee and 'adopted son' of William Clark. He was the driver of the meat wagon. The Model T Ford was the butcher wagon that they used for meat delivery around May 21, 1920." The photograph was taken on Main Street in Forestville. (Courtesy of the Dave Henry collection.)

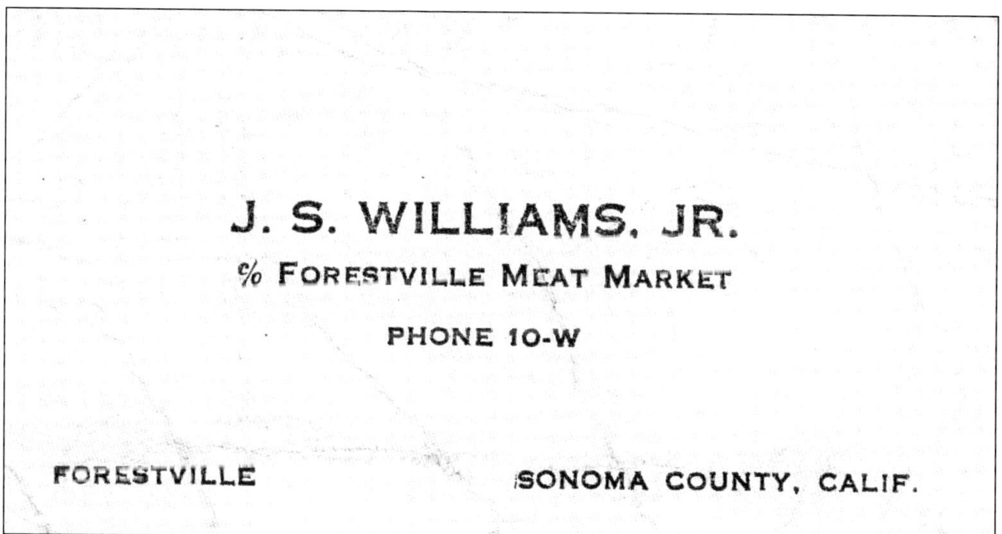

This is a business card that Jack Williams owned. Clark gave it to him for the meat business. Notice the telephone number—it is one of the first rural telephone lines in Forestville. (Courtesy of Ross Yeager.)

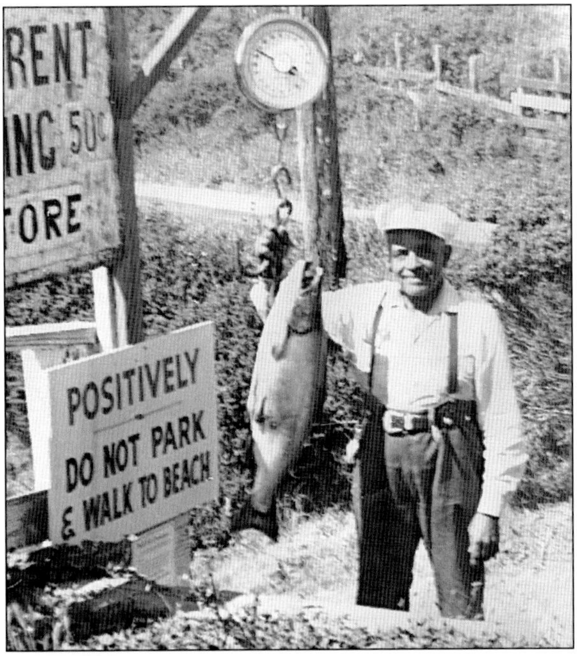

Jack Williams, who worked for Clark's meats, was an avid fisherman—one can see he was very good at it. He is also pictured in many of the Forestville sports activities. He was a very gregarious person who made friends easily. (Courtesy of the Bob Aldridge collection.)

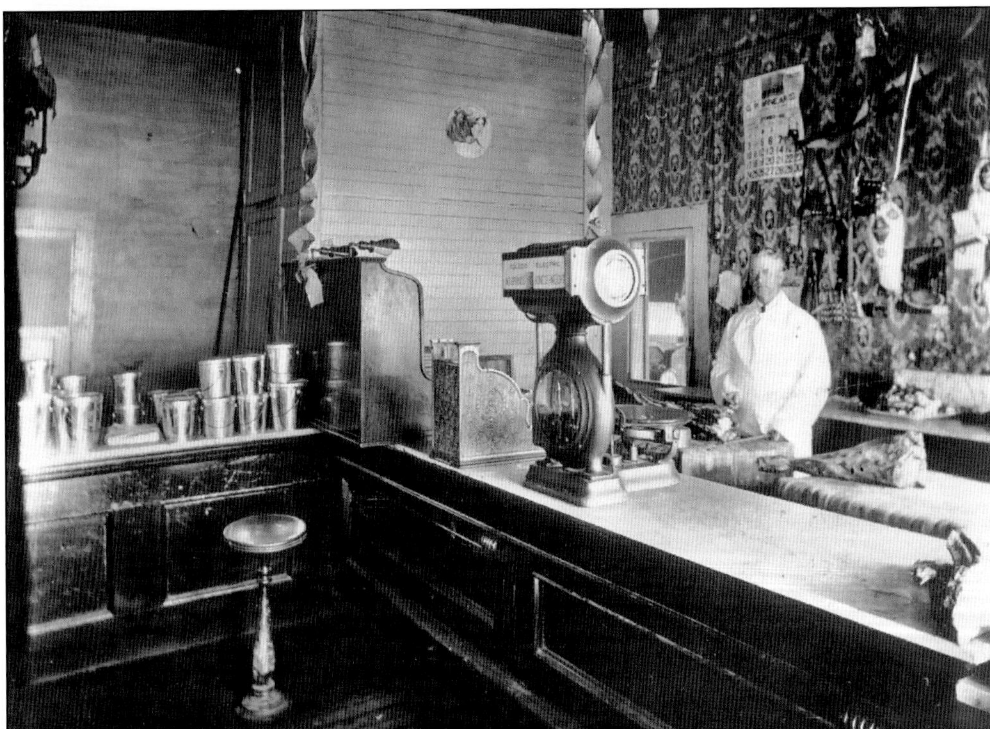

This is one of the earliest photographs of William Clark's butcher shop, taken in 1900. The shop continued to operate at the same site in the center of the block on the south side of Front Street between Covey Road and First Street for many years. At the left are buckets of lard for sale. Fly strips hung from the ceiling, suggesting conditions are much better these days at the local butcher shop. (Courtesy of the Dave Henry collection.)

William Clark was born in Windsor, California, on May 9, 1865, and learned how to run a business by working in his dad's store and post office as a child. To run a well-managed meat business, he needed three wagons delivering meats to households all over this part of the county. (Courtesy of the Dave Henry collection.)

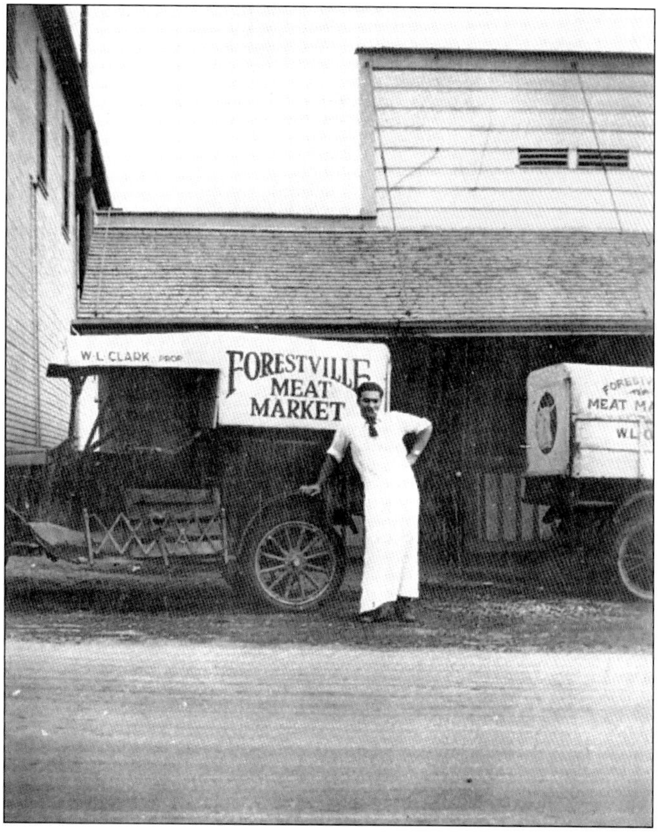

This picture of the Clark butcher shop was taken in 1925. From left to right are Jack Williams, William Clark, and Lloyd Clark (William's son). (Courtesy of the Dave Henry collection.)

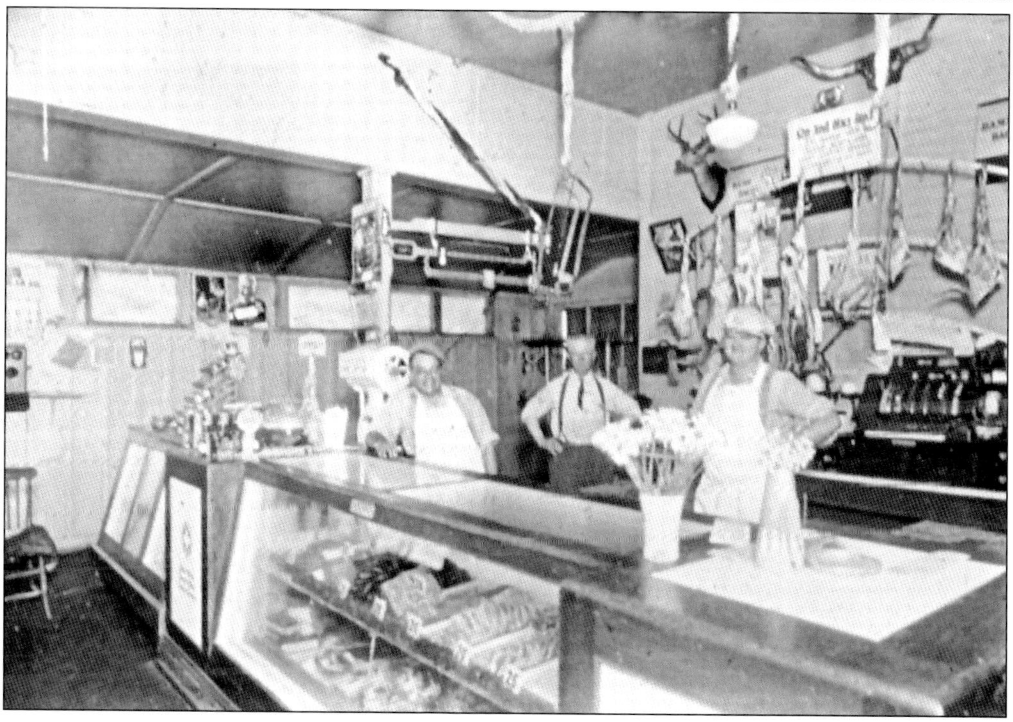

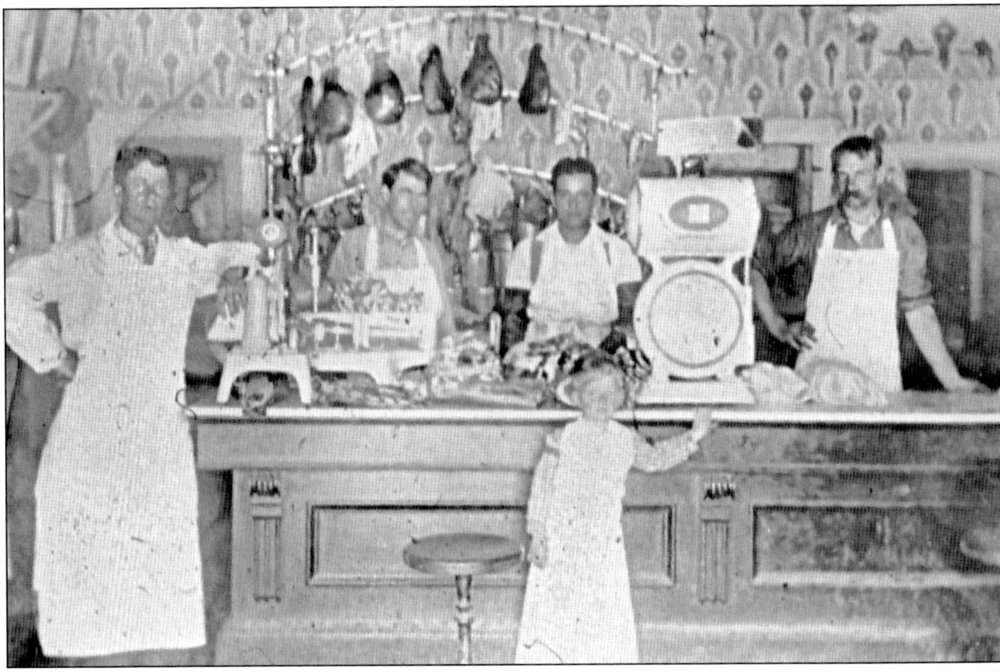

William Clark's father, W. S. Clark, was the postmaster in 1865 under Abraham Lincoln. He continued in this office until his death, running the post office and a store. W. L. Clark married Emma Jewett in 1890 and had six children, one of whom was Hazel, who later married Archie Hicks. The other children were Eva May, Gladys Ann, Wilma Stratton, Edna May (later a Ludolff), and Lloyd Smith. (Courtesy of the Dave Henry collection.)

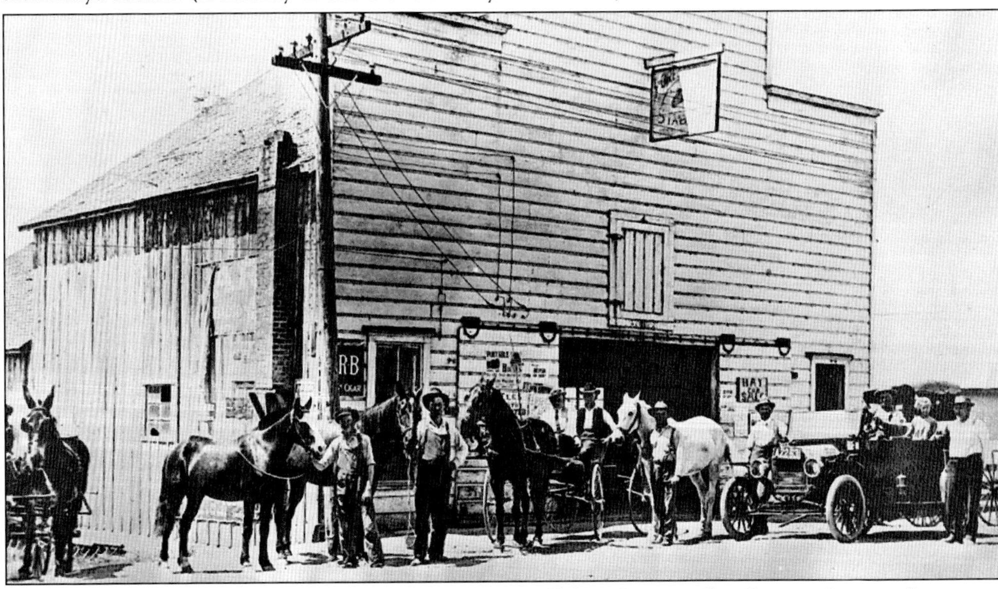

In 1914, the livery stable was a very important part of life in Forestville. As people stayed in town, they would store their buggy, and the liveryman would care for the needs of their horses. Shown in this picture is Ray Morrison on the left edge, and from left to right are I. B. Morris, Rosa Stampley, L. D. Yeager, Mark Rickett, Archie McGowan, John Evans, I. V. Morris Sr., Margaret Stratton, and Ed Evans. (Courtesy of the Dave Henry collection.)

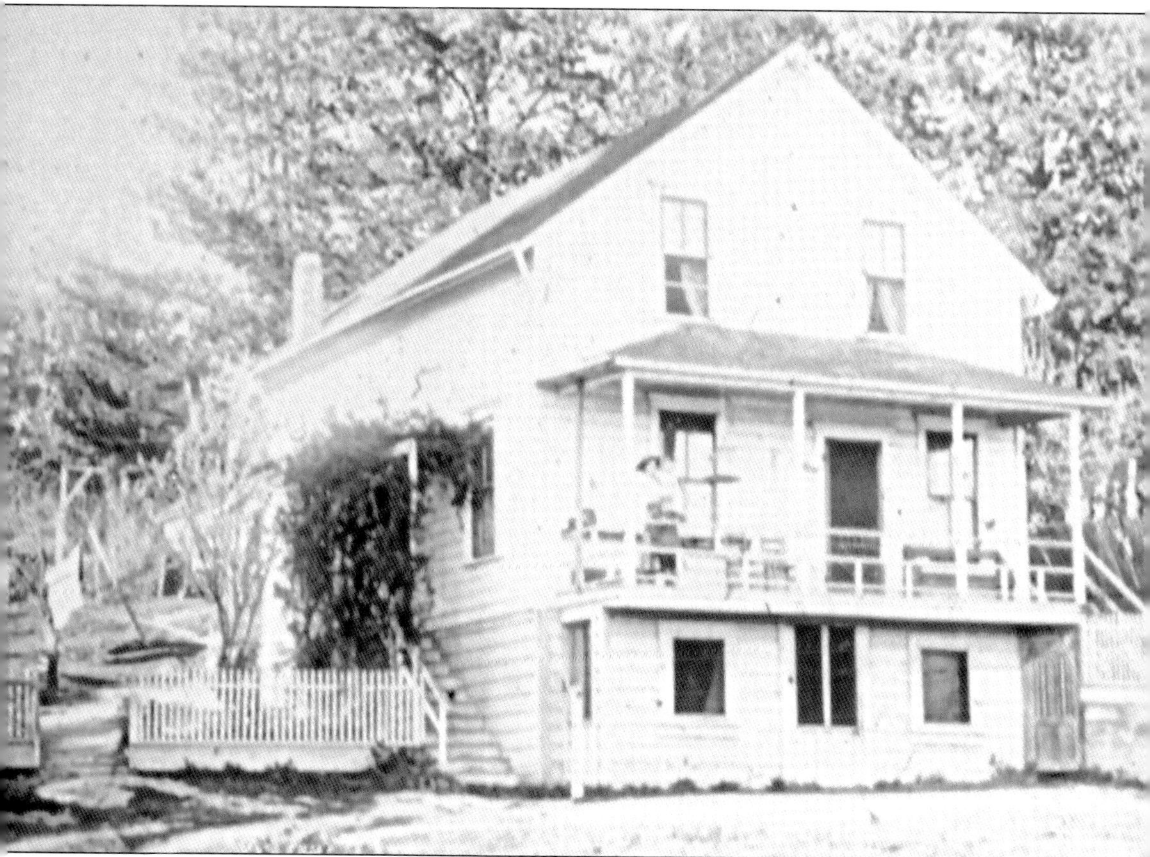

William Clark ran his first meat market and butcher shop from the ground floor of his three-story house. The upper two floors were the living quarters. Edna Clark Ludolff ran the market as a grocery store for many years after her dad stopped butchering. In the late 1800s, he moved his butcher shop across the street. Wilma remembered that he still operated the shop when she was a little girl. She married Floyd Arnett, who also had a meat market in his house. A parking lot was built in place of the house when it was demolished. (Courtesy of the Dave Henry collection.)

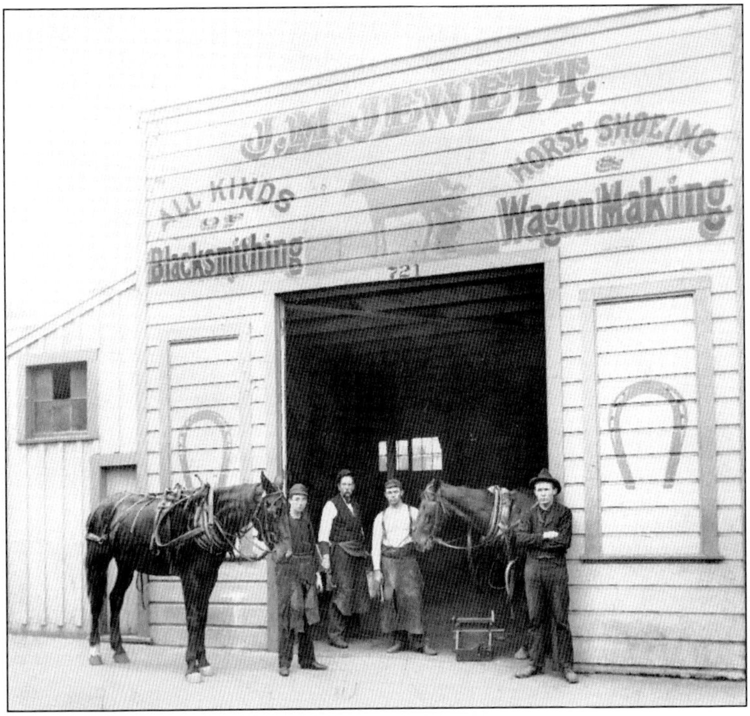

This picture is of J. M. Jewett's blacksmith and wagon-making shop in 1877. Jewett's blacksmith shop was located at 721 Front Street, or what is considered Main Street. (Courtesy of the Bob Aldridge collection.)

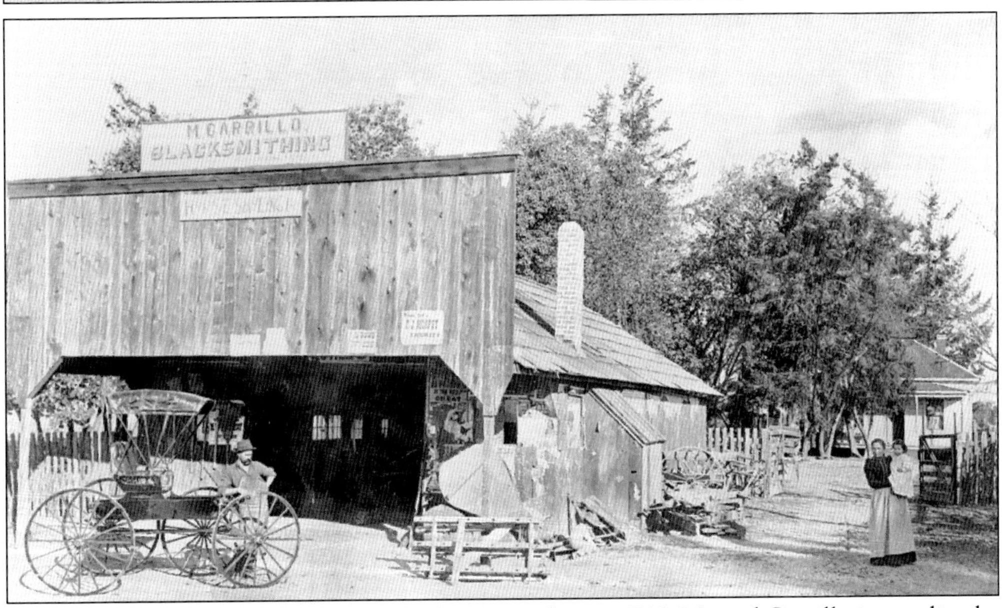

This picture of the Carrillo Blacksmith Shop was taken in 1910. Manuel Carrillo is standing by the carriage. Mrs. Martha Carrillo (she was a Mayer) is holding her son Gene at the right, and Lawrence is playing by the building near the lean-to; their son Earl is not in the picture. The small lean-to with the chimney is where the bellows were. The Carrillos lived about 3 miles from the center of Forestville near, Mr. Alderson's house. A. Carrillo Blacksmithing advertised that he did general repairing, and his specialty was horseshoing at $1.25 each. Carrillo was a descendant of the original Sonoma County Carrillos, who were some of the first to settle this county. (Courtesy of the Burton Travis collection.)

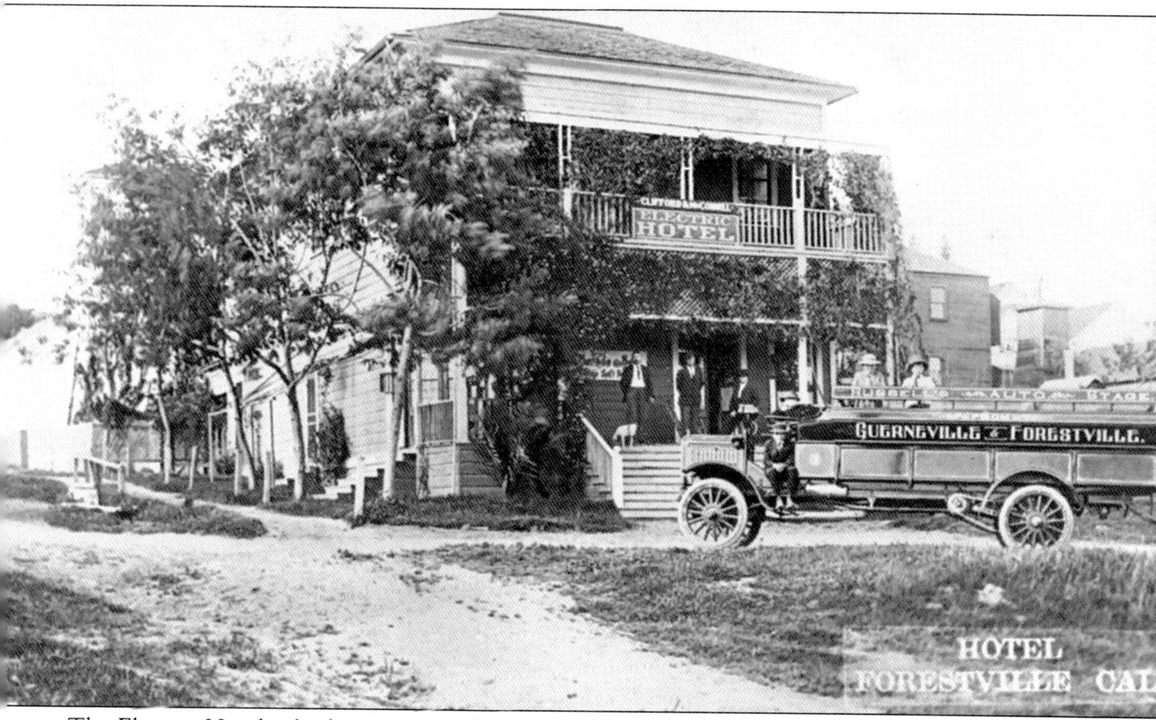

The Electric Hotel, which was originally the Johnson Hotel and located where Carr's Drive-Inn is today, moved across Main Street to Railroad Avenue at the P&SR railway station. Clifford and J. P. McConnell owned it when it was called the Electric Hotel. The blacksmith Charles Oliver said in an 1876 *Sonoma Democrat* article, "Mr. Foster at the Johnson Hotel bar on the hill was serving drinks to the thirsty for ten cents apiece or two for a quarter, so the more you bought, the more each drink would cost." One would think that is how the town was given the nickname Swindle Rig or Swindle Ridge. (Courtesy of Lavon Speer Covington.)

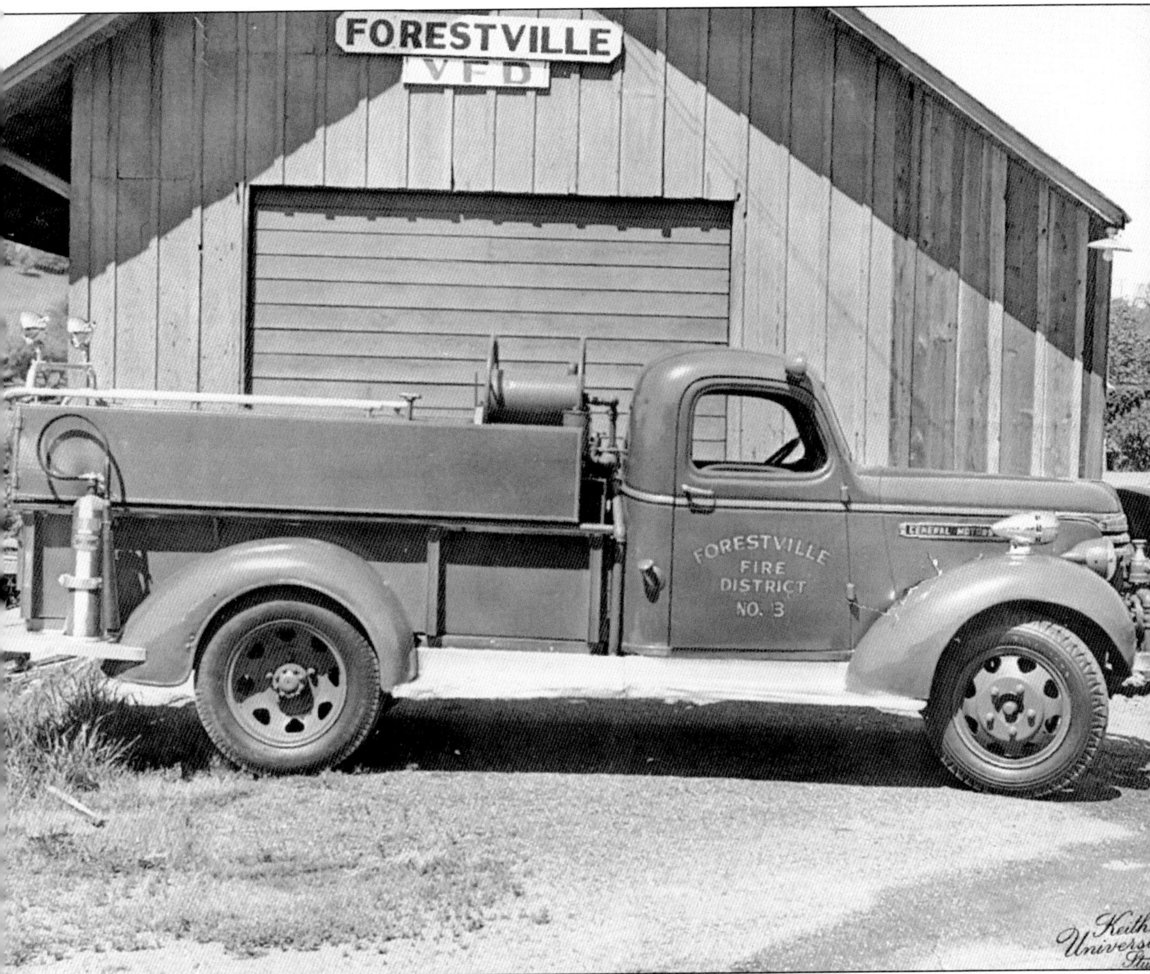

In 1938, Archie Hicks made the first fire truck out of an old Maxwell car using his own money. A little later, the Petri Winery let Ed Offutt make up a fire pump, which was a wine pump run by hand using a 50-gallon wine barrel for a water tank. Then came the next piece of firefighting equipment: a 20-gallon acid soda tank mounted on two cartwheels that were pulled by men. The town really needed a fire truck, so Tom Silk started a collection to raise enough for their first truck. They finally located a truck for $1,500 in Modesto, and Raford Peterson Jr. of the Wohler Ranch flew Cecil Edward down to Modesto to pick up the truck pictured here in 1948. The truck was a 1937 Ford Pumper. At one time there was also a small station at the Hacienda run by Mickey Fomin. (Courtesy of Darleen Speer.)

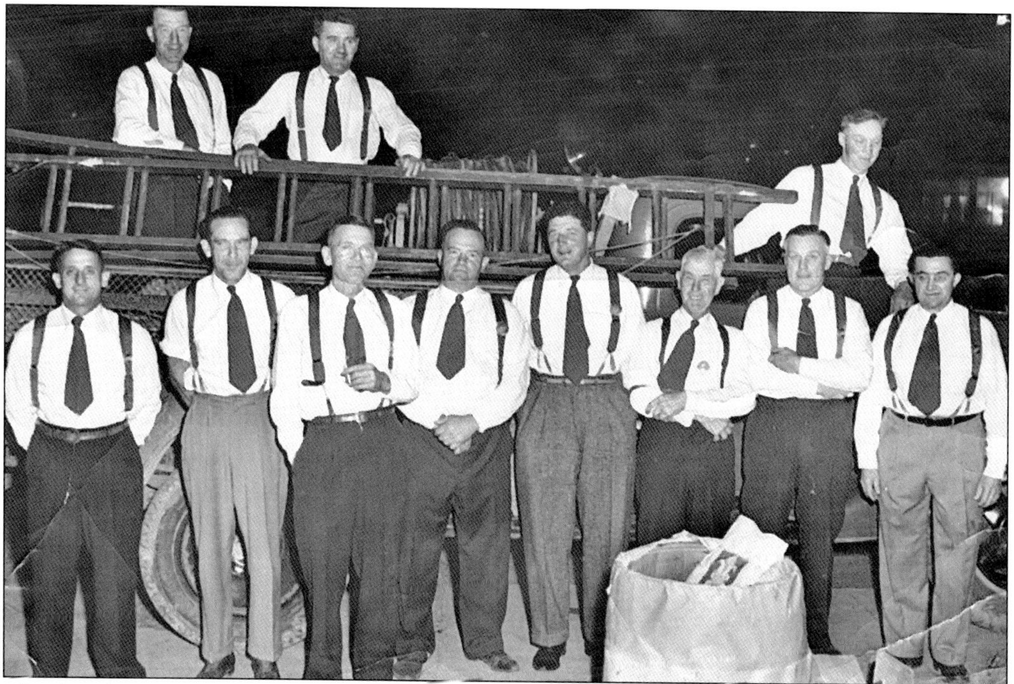

The fire department was organized in 1948. Until then, when there was a fire, the church bell would ring and everyone would come running to help put it out. This picture of the fire department board was taken in 1948. The fire department was reorganized in 1958 as a legal fire district. The first fire chief was Oscar Ludolff. Gary Duignan has been the fire chief since July 1970. Duignan is the longest-serving fire chief in Sonoma County. He was also the youngest fire chief in Sonoma County at the time he came to Forestville. The men standing in front of the fire truck include Reno Frigerio, Marvin Davis, Lou Allred, Mr. Goldbeck, Corn Van Keppel, and Oscar Ludolff. (Courtesy of Gary Duignan.)

According to Phill Marcucci, "William Hill, an upstate New York pioneer merchant and banker, founded the small town of Trenton in the early 1880s. He purchased 6,000 acres of the El Molino land grant where he planted 200 acres of vineyard and established the first winery in the Trenton area. The small town built itself around it. This picture was taken about 1900." (Courtesy of Phil Marcucci.)

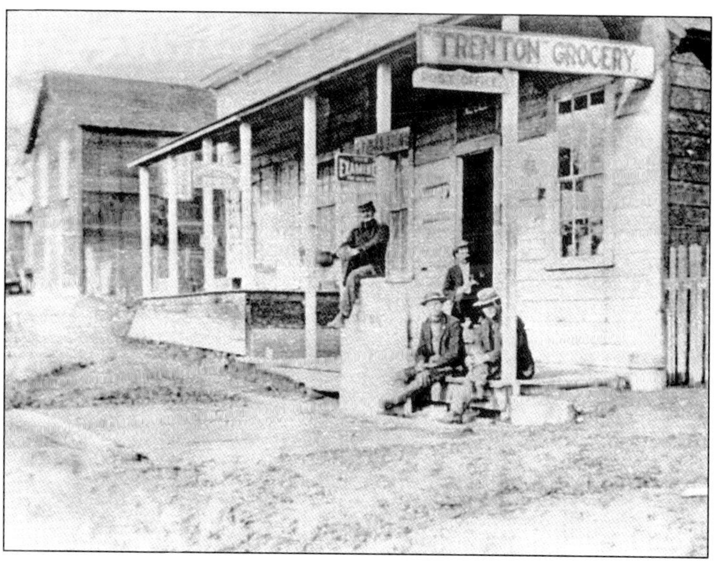

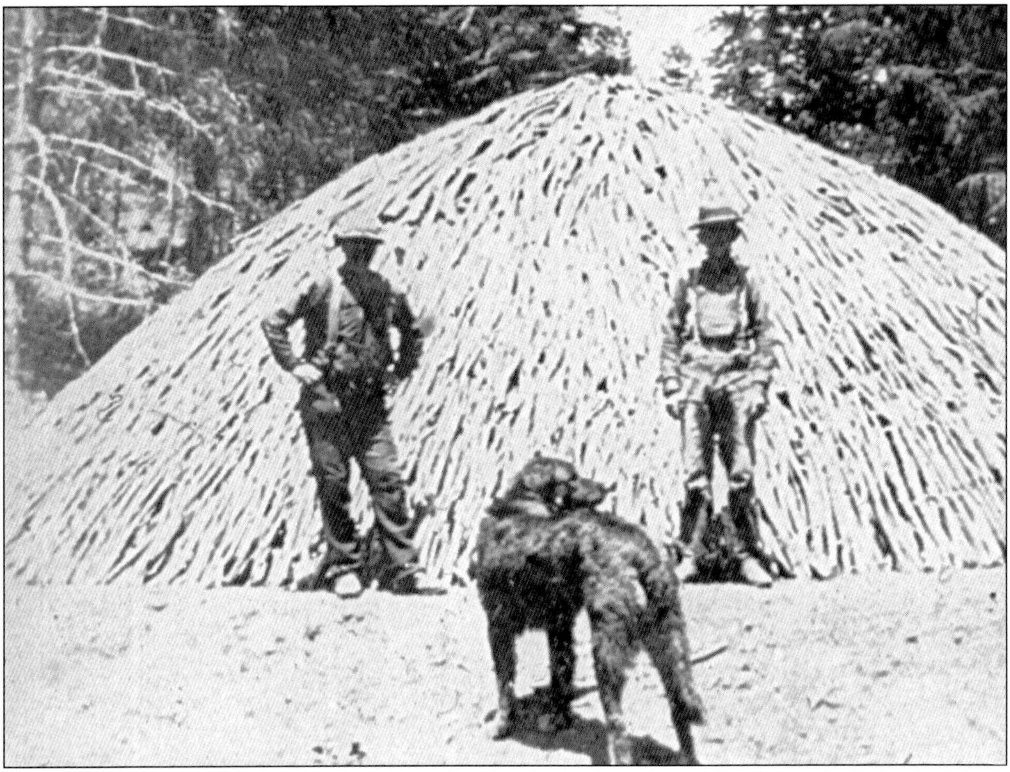

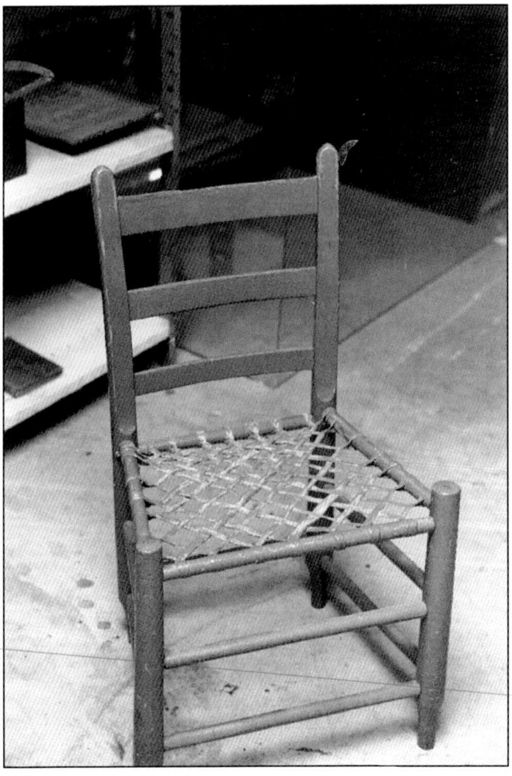

Mr. Dinnuci and his son Giusto are pictured here with their charcoal business. Tommy Ross writes in his journal about taking his wagon to the "Italians" and picking up charcoal to take to Petaluma to sell. (Courtesy of the Dave Henry collection.)

Pictured here is a Faudré rawhide chair. People still collect these chairs, and Forestville citizens especially value them. They marketed the chairs as far away as Arizona. The price of each chair was determined by the scarcity of lumber and how far it needed to be shipped by wagon. It is amazing that they were built so well they can still be used more than 100 years later. (Courtesy of Hal Wood.)

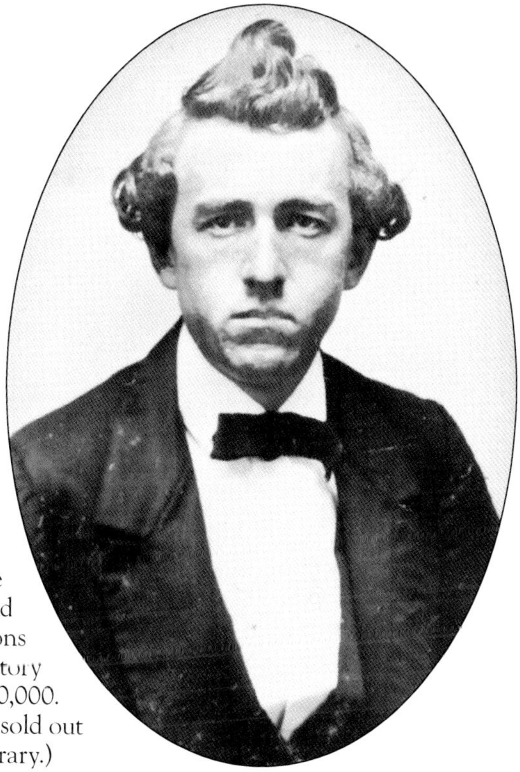

Forestville was well known for its rustic chair factory, which started around 1877 and was owned by Stewart W. Faudré. Maj. Isaac Sullivan was the first to build rustic chairs out of rawhide strips and oak, chestnut, or ash wood. Faudré came from Kentucky and married Martha C. Jose from Illinois. He was a minister of the Methodist church and raised four sons, two of whom are pictured here. The chairs were sold all over the states of Nevada and California. They were loaded on four-horse wagons at 200 to 400 a load. It is estimated that the factory brought into Sonoma County not less than $250,000. After Faudré had sold about 30,000 chairs, he sold out to S. P. Nowlin. (Courtesy of the Bancroft Library.)

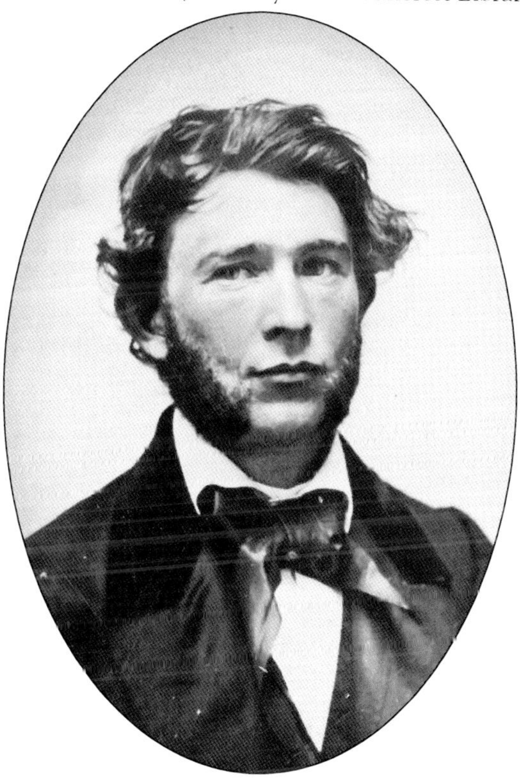

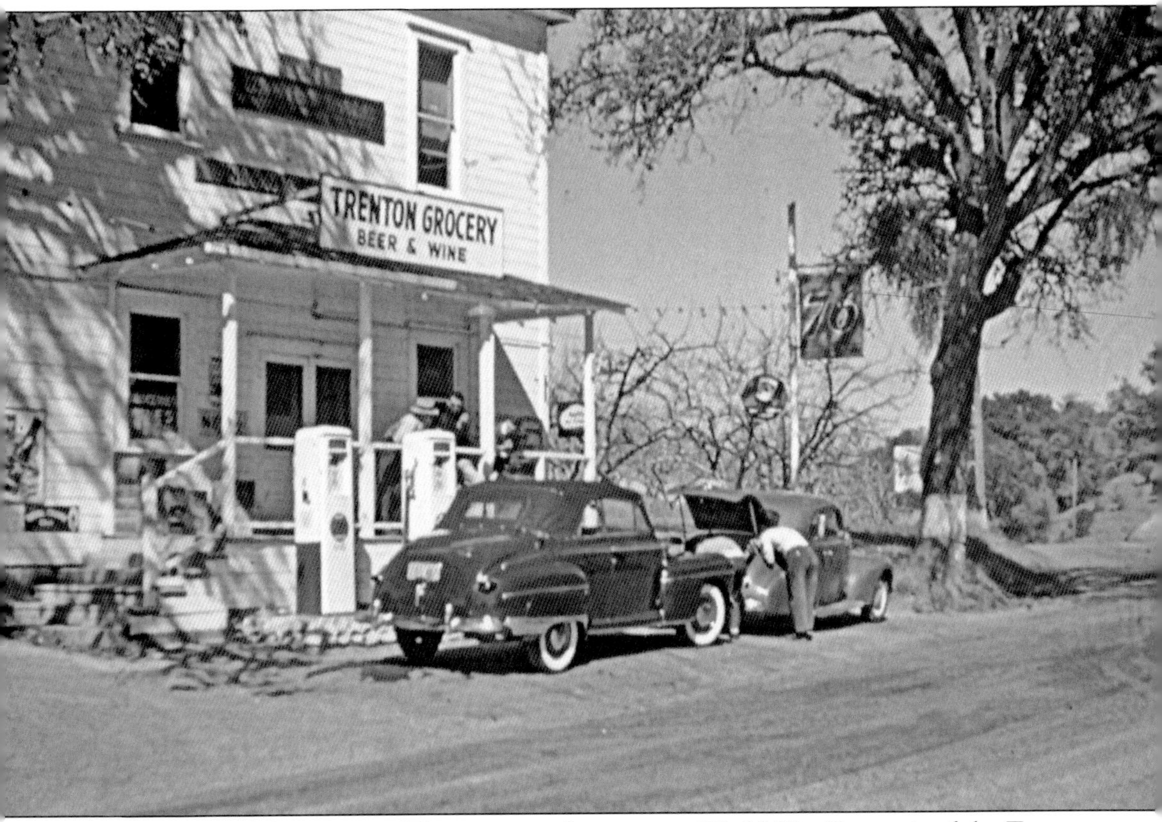

According to Phil Marcucci, "This picture taken in post–World War II years is of the Trenton grocery store located at the intersection of Laguna, Woolsey, and Trenton roads. Many residents used this location on a Sunday morning as a spot to shop and talk with friends. At this time the store was owned and managed by Silvio and Clara Cia who lived in the back of the store and shared the top floor with the local Vine Hill Druid Chapter. All that remains of this view today is the large valley oak tree." The Albianis owned the store and then later sold it to the Cias. (Courtesy of Phil Marcucci.)

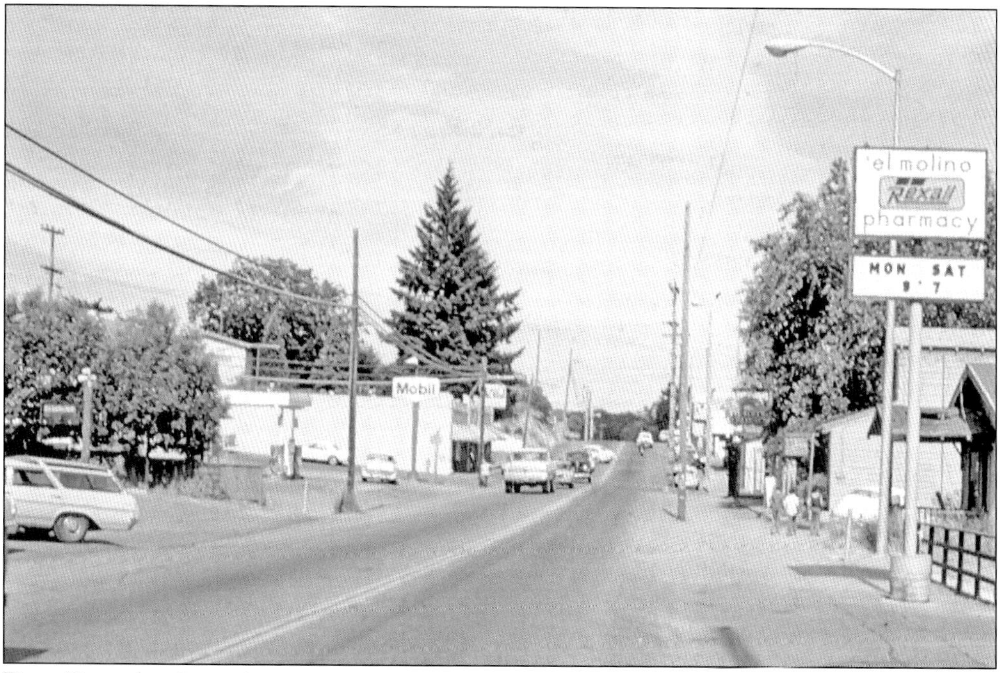

Dave Henry has been the pharmacist and owner of El Molino Pharmacy for 37 years, since 1970. In 1988, Dave Henry was citizen of the year, a well-deserved accolade. Dave has collected the most comprehensive archive of Forestville historical pictures. He continues to give a "dog and pony" show of local history to inform the town of its past. On September 24, 2007, the pharmacy closed, but Henry will be remembered for making customers feel like family. In 1999, Cindy Vaughn, an employee of the pharmacy, was honored along with Dave and Kay Henry for their work helping people with AIDS. (Courtesy of Kay Henry.)

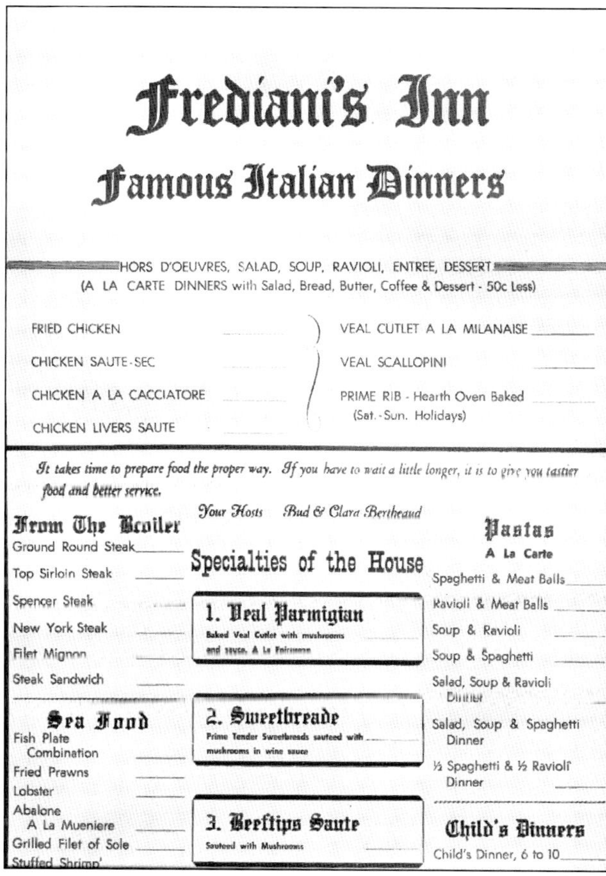

Frediani's Inn

Famous Italian Dinners

HORS D'OEUVRES, SALAD, SOUP, RAVIOLI, ENTREE, DESSERT
(A LA CARTE DINNERS with Salad, Bread, Butter, Coffee & Dessert - 50c Less)

FRIED CHICKEN
CHICKEN SAUTE-SEC
CHICKEN A LA CACCIATORE
CHICKEN LIVERS SAUTE
VEAL CUTLET A LA MILANAISE
VEAL SCALLOPINI
PRIME RIB - Hearth Oven Baked (Sat.-Sun. Holidays)

It takes time to prepare food the proper way. If you have to wait a little longer, it is to give you tastier food and better service.

Your Hosts Bud & Clara Bertheaud

From The Broiler
Ground Round Steak
Top Sirloin Steak
Spencer Steak
New York Steak
Filet Mignon
Steak Sandwich

Sea Food
Fish Plate Combination
Fried Prawns
Lobster
Abalone A La Mueniere
Grilled Filet of Sole
Stuffed Shrimp

Specialties of the House
1. Veal Parmigian
Baked Veal Cutlet with mushrooms and sauce, A La Fairmann
2. Sweetbreads
Prime Tender Sweetbreads sauteed with mushrooms in wine sauce
3. Beeftips Saute
Sauteed with Mushrooms

Pastas
A La Carte
Spaghetti & Meat Balls
Ravioli & Meat Balls
Soup & Ravioli
Soup & Spaghetti
Salad, Soup & Ravioli Dinner
Salad, Soup & Spaghetti Dinner
½ Spaghetti & ½ Ravioli Dinner

Child's Dinners
Child's Dinner, 6 to 10

Most people who are new to Forestville will not know of the wonderful restaurant that was located on Highway 116 south of town, Frediani's Inn. It was created and run by the Frediani family. They served authentic Italian food. (Courtesy of Fred Bertheaud.)

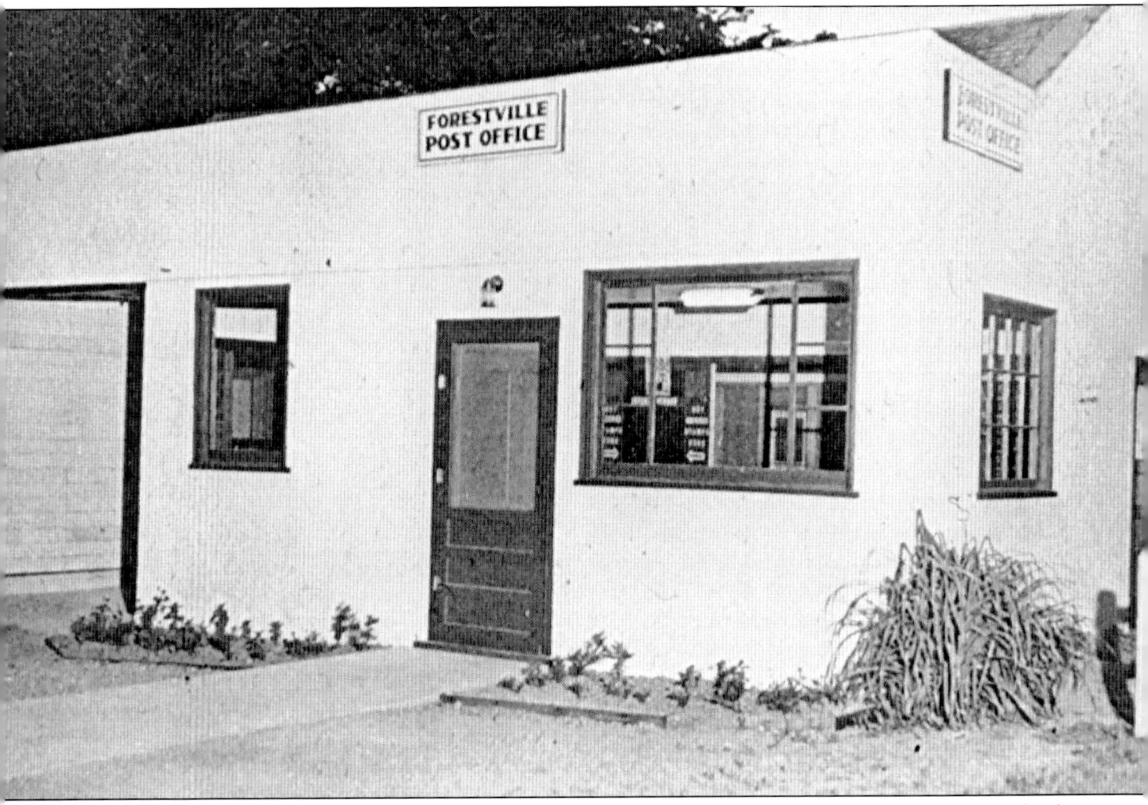

On January 30, 1872, John Oliver was appointed the first postmaster of Forestville. He had a blacksmith shop where he built little pigeonholes originally made for bolts and nuts. In 1881, the post office was in Clark's store on Main Street. In 1900, Tom Silk became the postmaster. Ida Silk became postmaster when a civil servant test was required, and it was George Athey who moved the post office in 1946 to just west of the bank, which is where this picture is located. In 1961, the post office moved to the location that is presently Sequoia Properties. (Courtesy of the Dave Henry collection.)

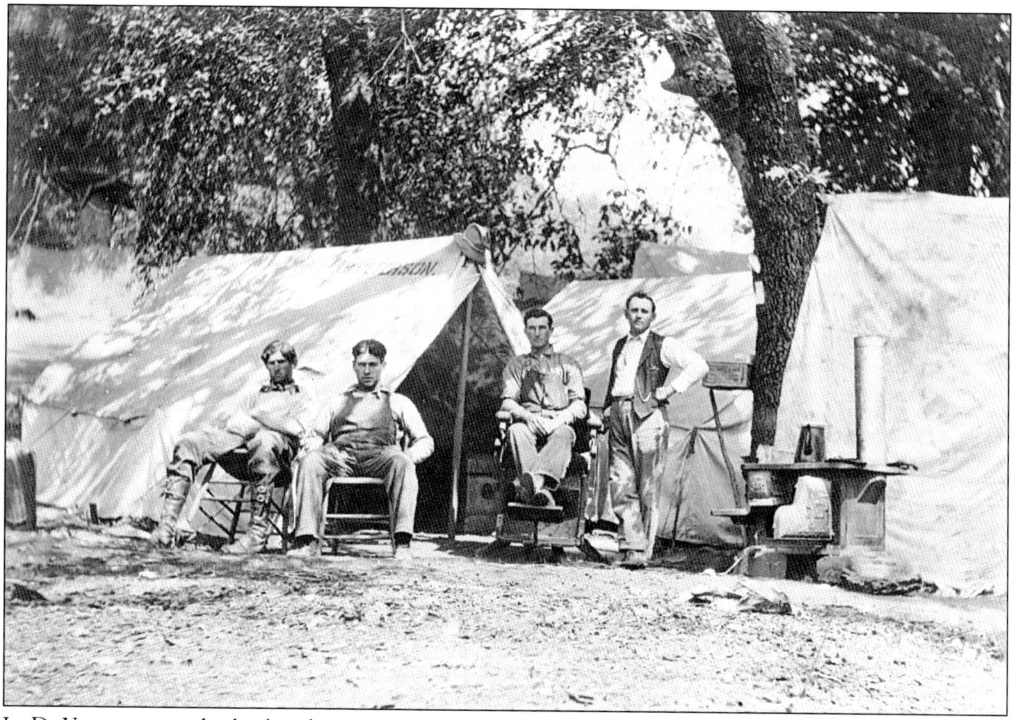

L. D. Yeager owned a barbershop in town. He was a very enterprising person, because when the hop fields were at their busiest, he would set up a barbershop in the hop fields on the Peterson Ranch, also known as the Wohler Ranch. (Courtesy of Ross Yeager.)

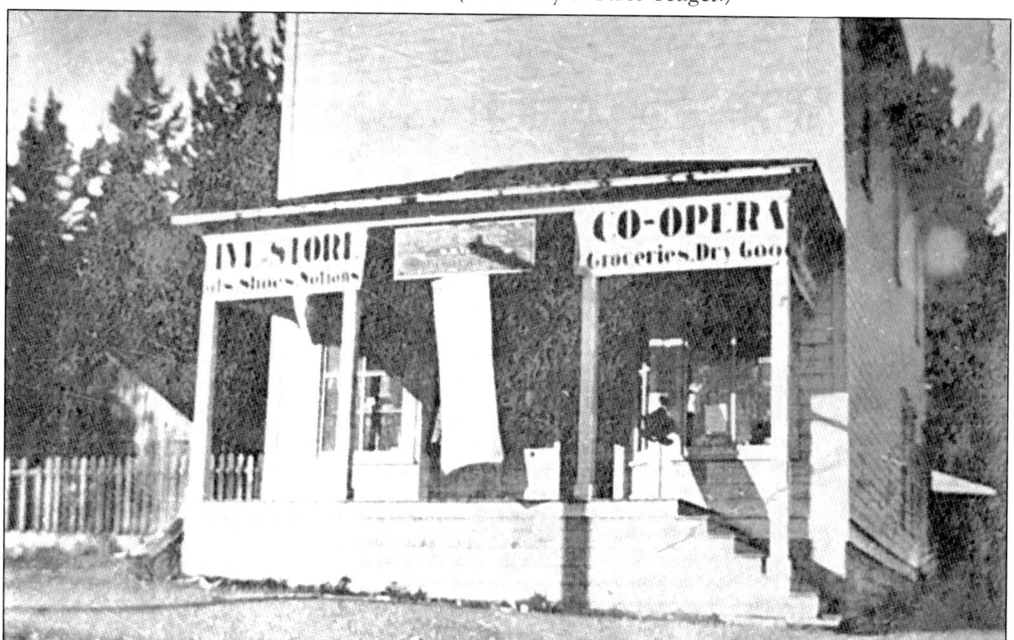

The Co-Op Store was part of the Forestville Rochedale Company; people bought shares in the company and could buy food or house wares at a low price. This store was incorporated on December 19, 1903. (Courtesy of the Dave Henry collection.)

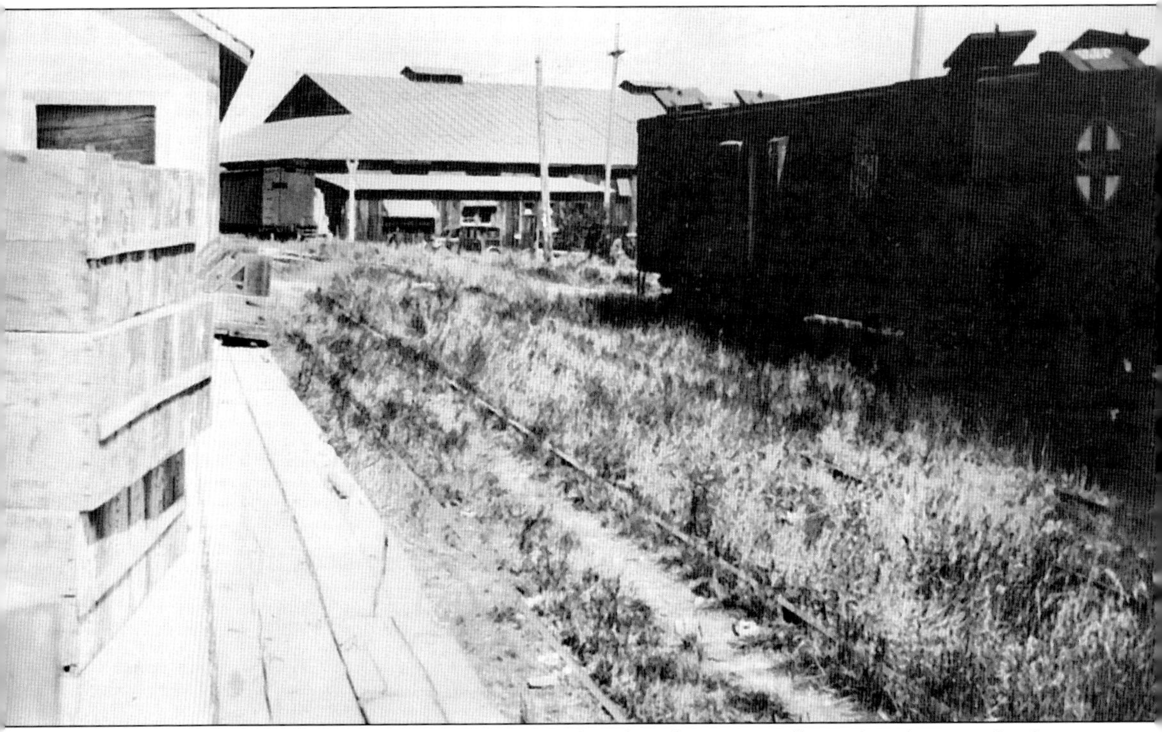

Many families in the Forestville area were employed at the Forestville packinghouse, which was the Gravenstein Apple Co-Op. Bert Travis was well remembered as managing the packing plant after World War I. He credited his ability to be organized during his senate race with his work at the Forestville packinghouse. (Courtesy of the Dave Henry collection.)

Three

EARLY SETTLERS

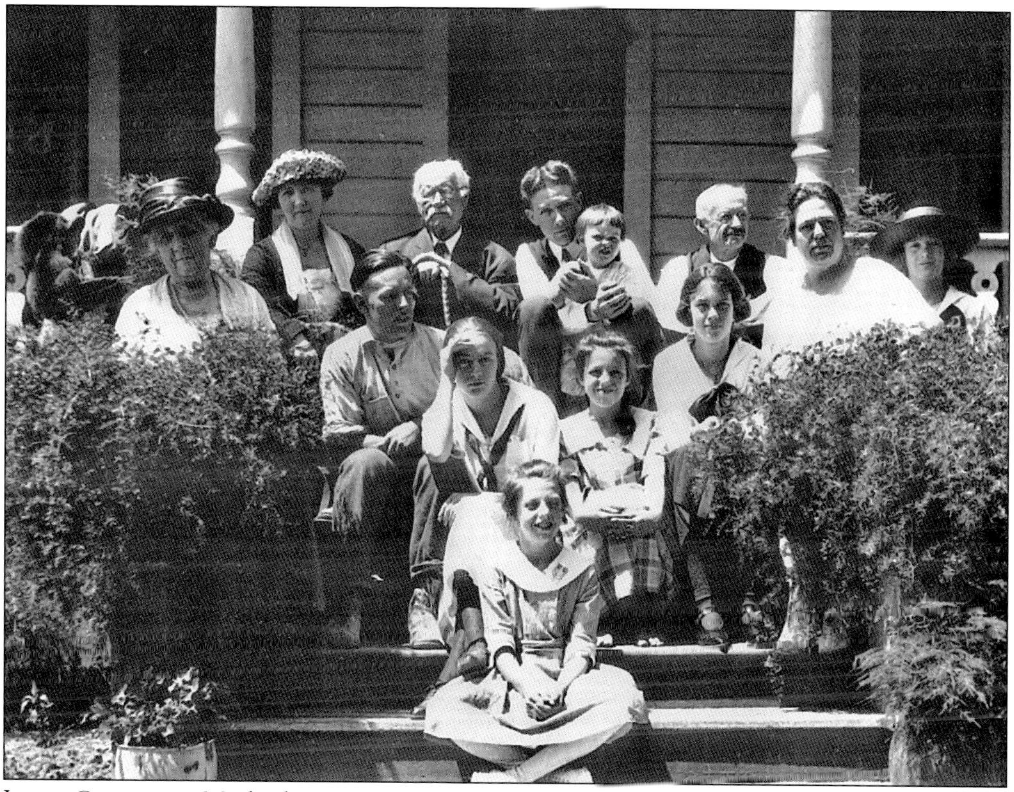

James Case was a Methodist minister who retired from preaching to work the Case Ranch. Pictured from left to right are (first row) Hellen Case; (second row) Westwood Case, Ruth Case, Frances Case, and unidentified; (third row) Jesse Watt, unidentified, grandpa W. W. Case, Walter Case holding baby Verna, Jane L. Case, unidentified, and Fannie Case. Today the Case Ranch still stands, with Diana Van Ry and Allan Tilton running it as a bed-and-breakfast. It is located on 7446 Poplar Drive in Forestville. (It is a registered Sonoma County landmark.) (Courtesy of Diana Van Ry.)

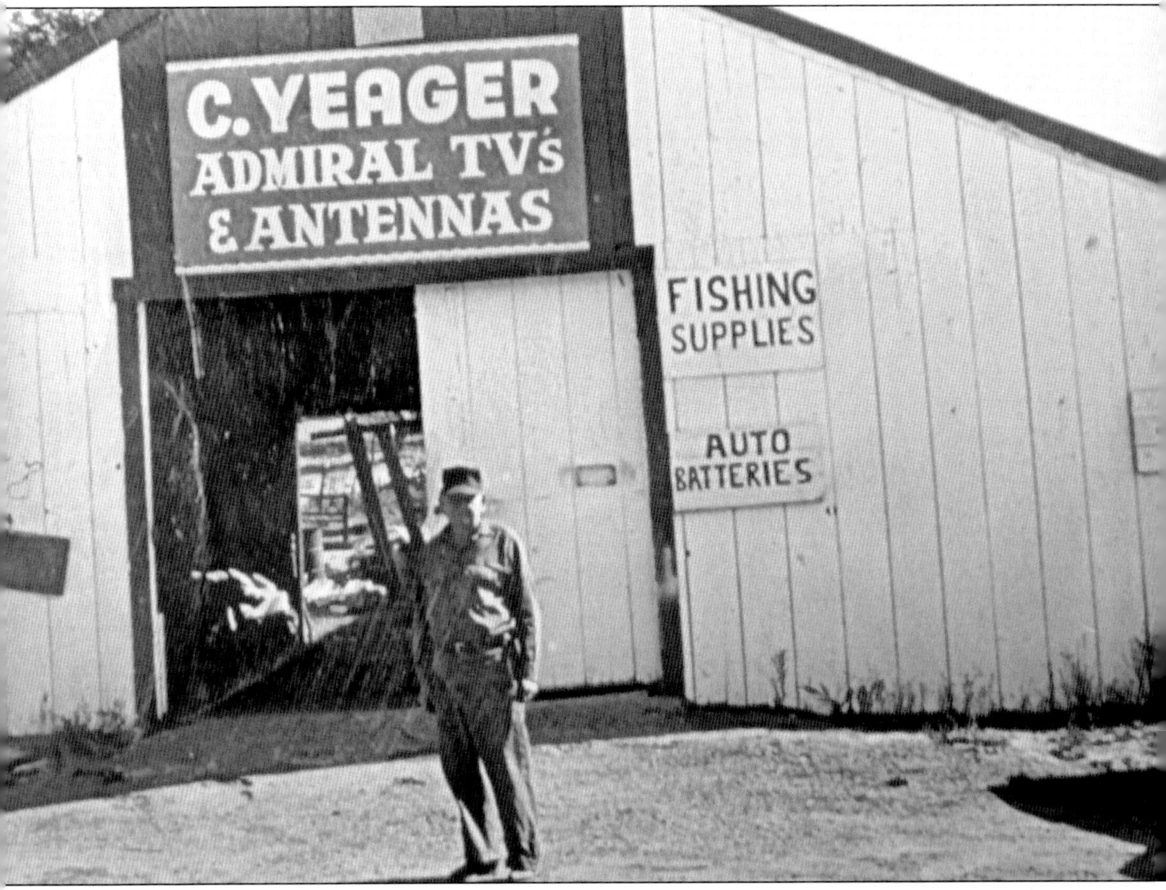

Clinton Yeager ran this garage, where he was the authorized Ford mechanic and supplied parts for Ford Model Ts. He also sold Admiral televisions, radios, and fishing supplies. Clinton loved to fish, and if it was a good day for steelhead, he would hang up a sign that said "gone fishing." "He sometimes went door to door selling any extra surf fish he caught," remembers Linda Burke. In recent years, his grandson Wayne Yeager owns the garage. Clinton, or "Clint" as he was better known, is the man in this picture. (Courtesy of Ross Yeager.)

In the early years, Clinton Yeager ran his auto repair shop from his garage in the back of his house off Mirabel Road. The picture here shows Clinton and a customer in his little garage. He was an expert at working on Fords, so there are a couple Model T cars in this picture. (Courtesy of Ross Yeager.)

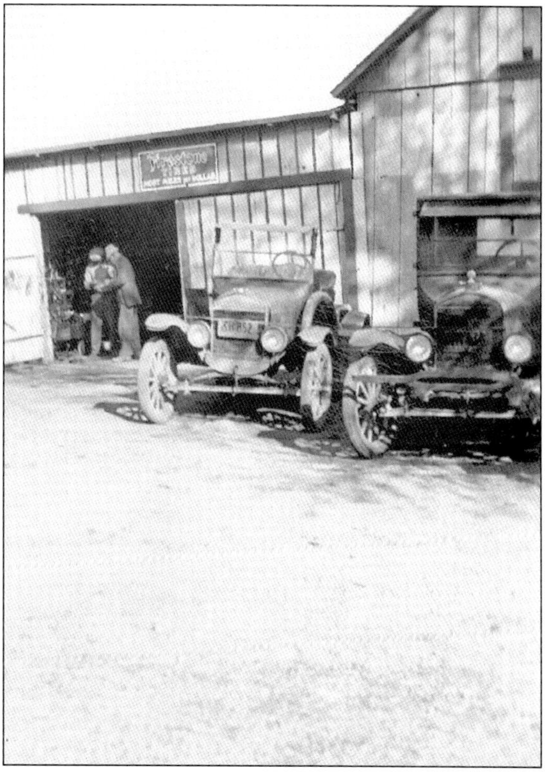

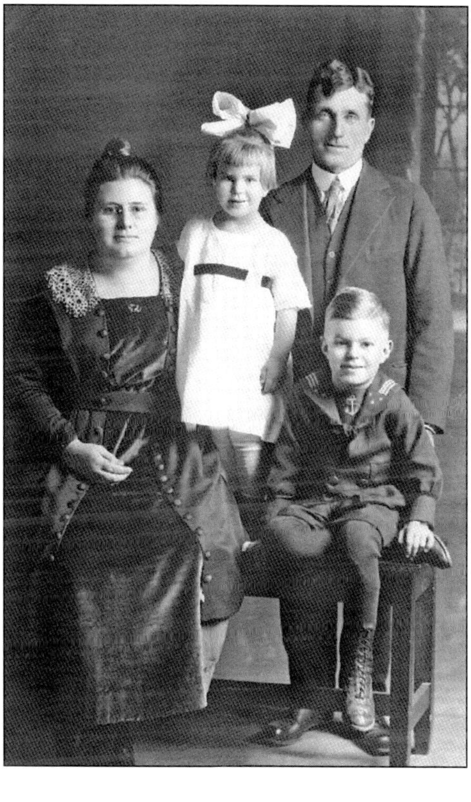

In 1913, John Van Keppel bought 30 acres of land and married Clara Kimes. The house he lived in was previously owned by the Jewett family and was built in the 1900s. He rebuilt the original house in 1927, and Van Keppel Road was named after him. Pictured from left to right are Clara, Alice, John, and Jack. Their other two children, Virginia and Bob, were born later. (Courtesy of Virginia Van Keppel Hughes.)

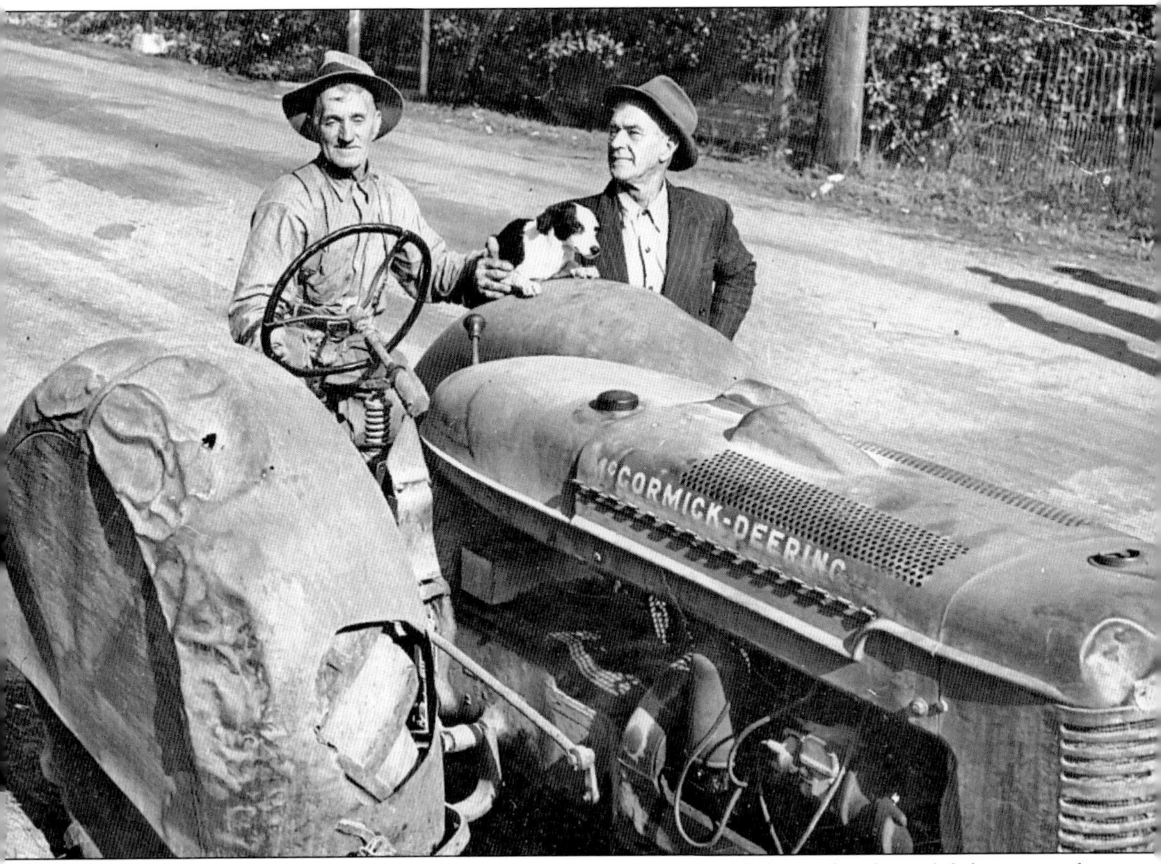

"The sound of tractors in the fields was the sound of spring and the cycle of new life begun each year here in Forestville," Virginia Van Keppel Hughes remembers. This photograph of John Van Keppel seated on his tractor and Cornelius Van Keppel with John's dog Rowdy was taken in 1940. The young brothers came to Forestville around 1910 from Bennett Valley. Cornelius came first and bought 30 acres on Mirabel Road, and later John bought his 30 acres on what became Van Keppel Road. They married sisters Clara and Daisy Kimes. (Courtesy of Virginia Van Keppel Hughes.)

Hendrick Van Keppel (right) was born in 1914. The son of John Van Keppel and brother of Virginia Van Keppel Hughes, he was an industrial designer who became a world-famous furniture maker. His furniture was displayed in the Museum of Modern Art in New York City. He was a genius at merging technology and nature. His furniture was used outside as well as inside, being built with such materials as perforated steel, yacht lines, and redwood. He owned a business in Beverly Hills on Rodeo Drive called Van Keppel Green. People like Frank Sinatra and movies like *Giant* used his furniture. In the 1940s, his furniture made the front cover of *Life* magazine. This picture of Hendrick riding a horse (below) symbolizes his love of the simple country life in Forestville growing up. (Courtesy of Virginia Van Keppel Hughes.)

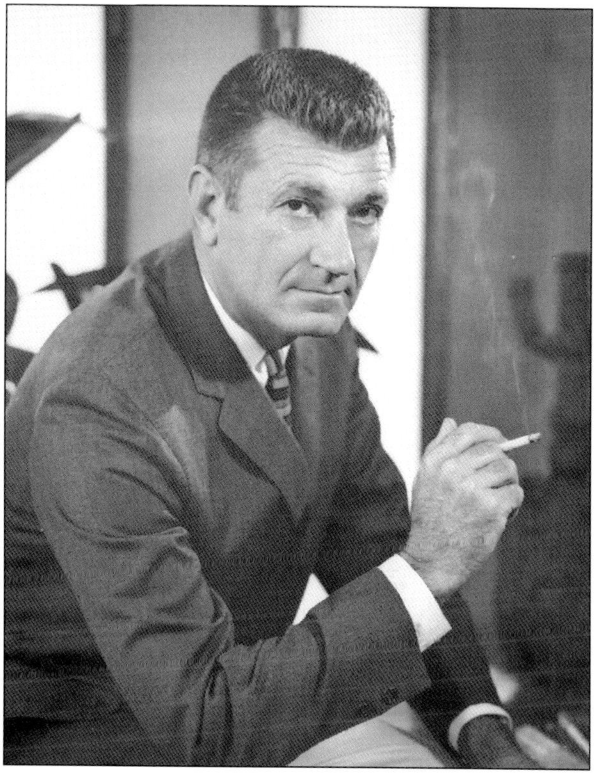

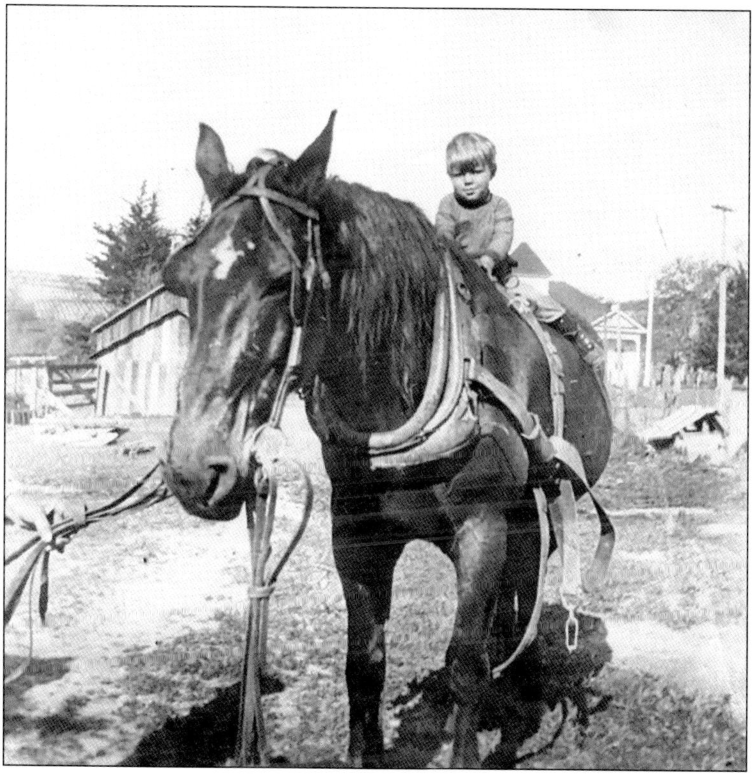

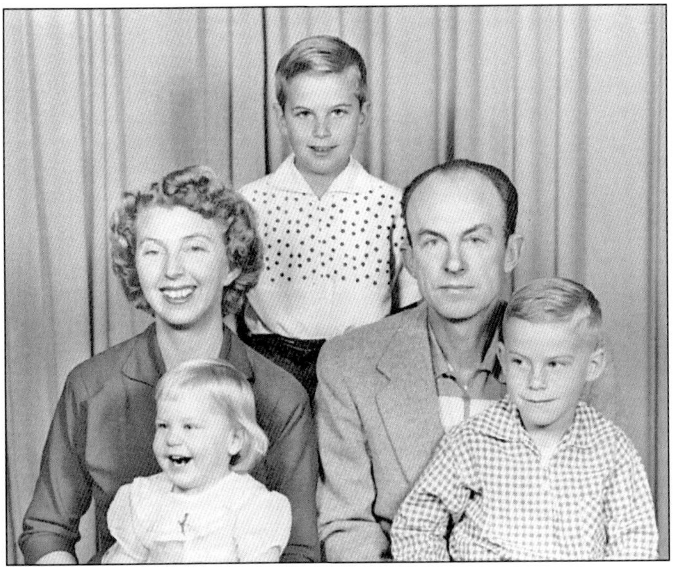

This picture of the Louis E. Hughes family was taken in the 1950s. Louis Hughes was a captain in the merchant marines during World War II. He bought land between the Travis Ranch and the Van Keppel Ranch. After settling into Forestville, he married Virginia Van Keppel and had three children. He was an owner of Benelli's Market along with Joe Pearson. From left to right are Virginia, LuAnn, Louis L., Louis E., and John L Hughes. (Courtesy of Virginia Van Keppel Hughes.)

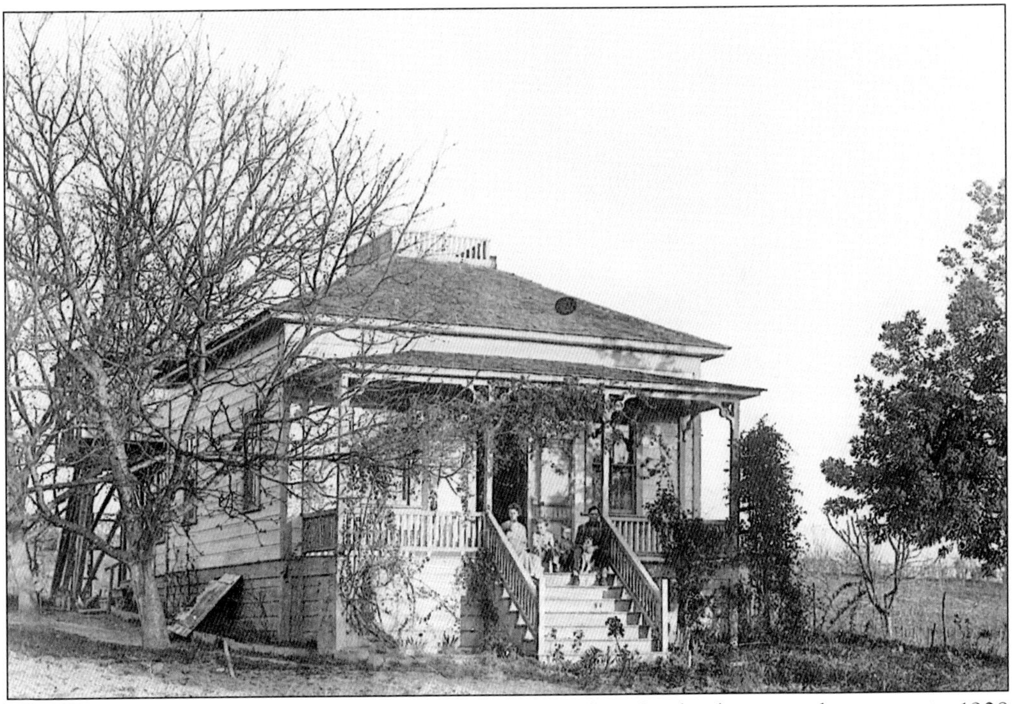

According to Lavon Speer Covington, "James F. Speer bought this house and property in 1908 from J. R. Thomas. He was asked to come to San Francisco from Pennsylvania to help rebuild San Francisco after the 1906 earthquake. He decided he didn't want to raise his children in the city, so he came to Forestville and bought this property. He commuted back and forth to the city to work. In the picture from left to right are Maude Speer holding Paul, James Jr., Howard, and James Speer Sr." (Courtesy of Lavon Speer Covington.)

On Halloween night in the early 1920s, Howard and Paul Speer decided to get into some mischief by hoisting some underpants belonging to the daughters of the local deputy sheriff Walter Kimes up the flagpole at the grade school. Kimes became aware of the prank and fired birdshot at them, hurting both boys. When they told their older brother, Jim, he then approached Sheriff Kimes asking why. Kimes then fired at Jim but was out of buckshot, so he hit him on the side of the head with the gun, shown on this picture. When their father heard of this, he loaded them into a car and headed for the Santa Rosa police station. Kimes was put in jail and fined $2,500. (Courtesy of Lavon Speer Covington.)

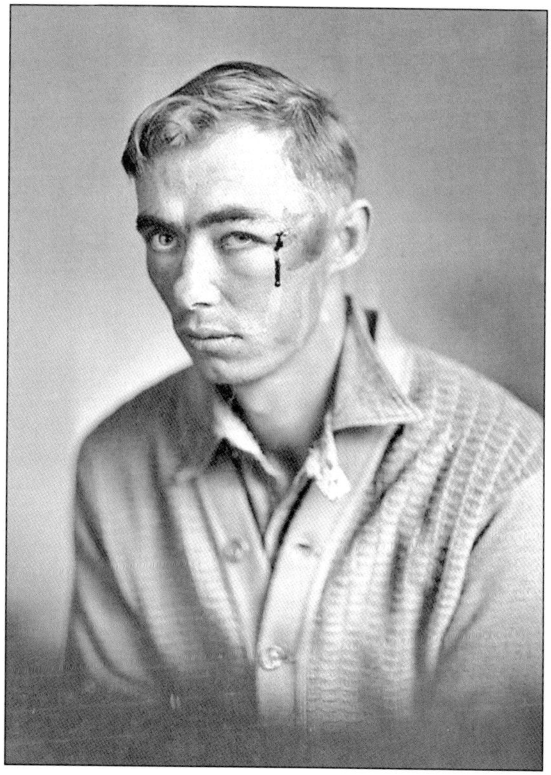

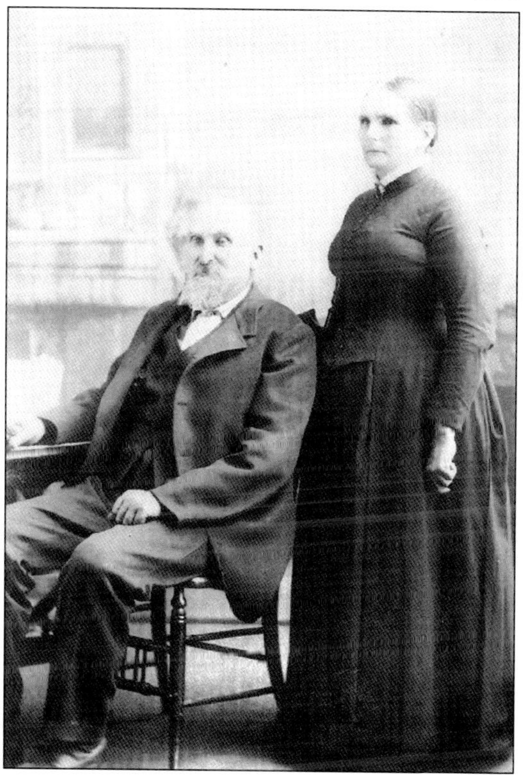

Uriah and Sarah Covey bought the property on Trenton Road, known today as the Sunshine Camp. Uriah Covey's son, William Covey, bought the house across from El Molino High School from Tom Lynton around 1919. Covey Road was named after Uriah Covey. (Courtesy of Bill Smith.)

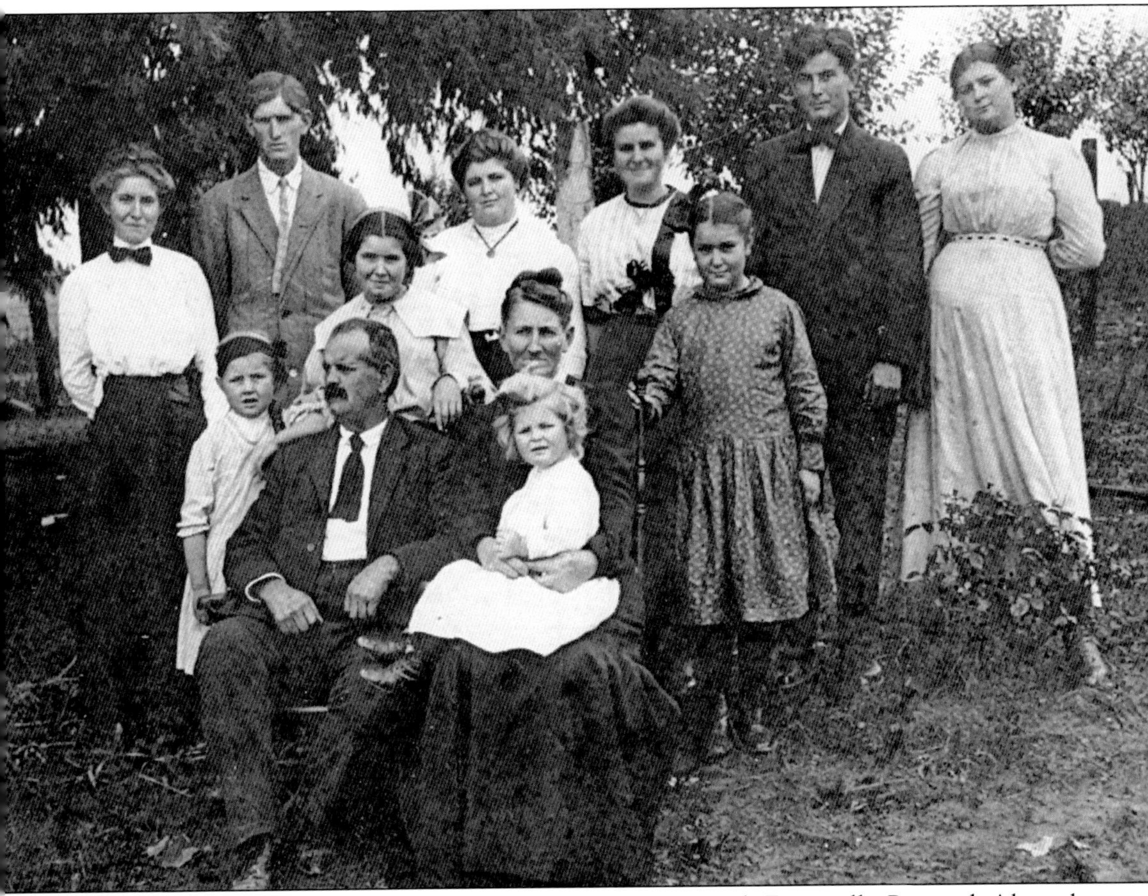

A family of pioneers, the Kimes family was well respected in early Forestville. Patriarch Alvarado L. Kimes (March 20, 1858–July 29, 1934) was a housepainter. His wife, Alice Ross Kimes (June 22, 1869–May 4, 1941), was a descendant of the Ross family. Avarado and Alice were married December 25, 1887. They are pictured here with their children in 1910. From left to right are (first row) Alvarado, Alice, and Lois (on her mother's lap); (second row) Gertrude, Florence, and Jessie; (third row) Daisy, Walter, Mabel, Clara, Ed, and Esther. (Courtesy of Virginia Van Keppel Hughes.)

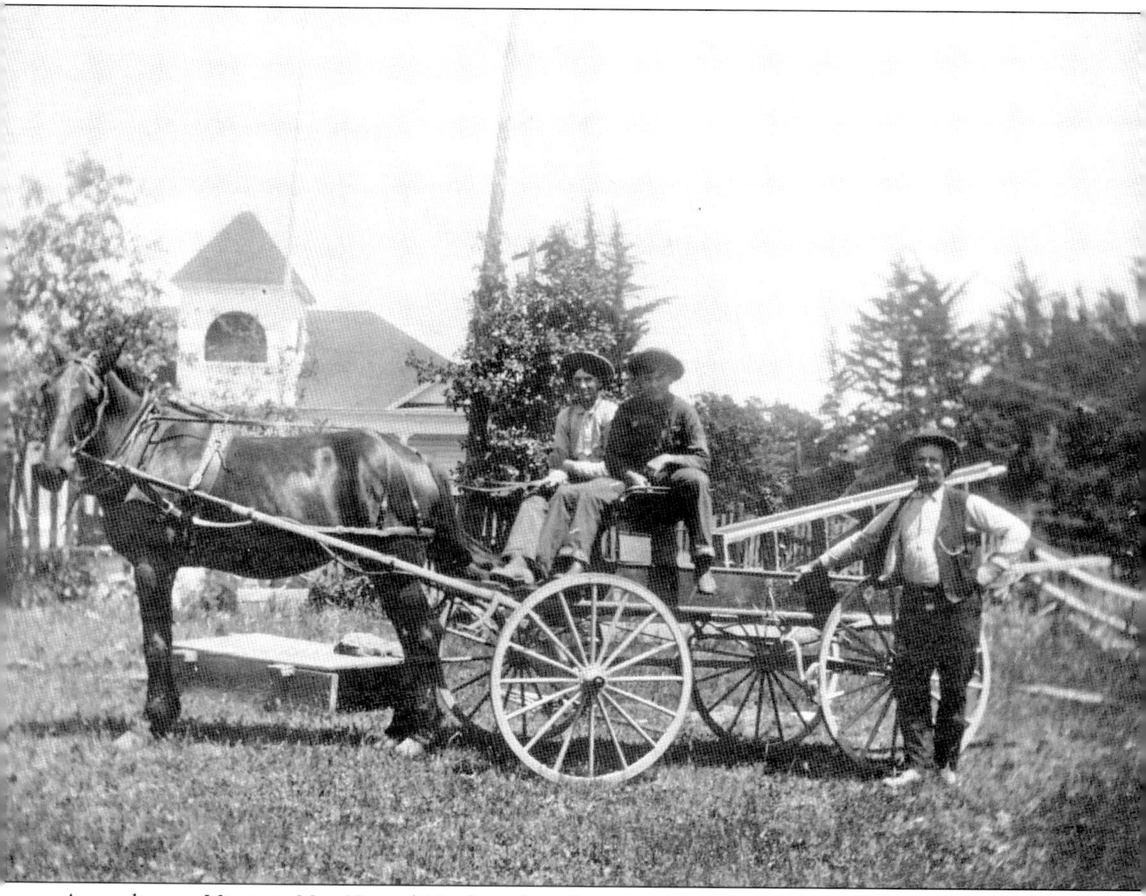

According to Virginia Van Keppel Hughes, this photograph was on a postcard dated February 1, 1909, with a 1¢ Ben Franklin stamp on it. It is addressed to Blanche Meredith in Healdsburg's rural area. It states, "Dear Friend" and is signed by Walter Kimes. Walter and Blanche eventually were married, so this is most likely a budding romance. Walter explains he had this picture taken of "Old Duke and their paint wagon." Apparently they did house and barn painting. The distinctive building in the background is the Forestville Elementary School, built in 1899. (Courtesy of Virginia Van Keppel Hughes.)

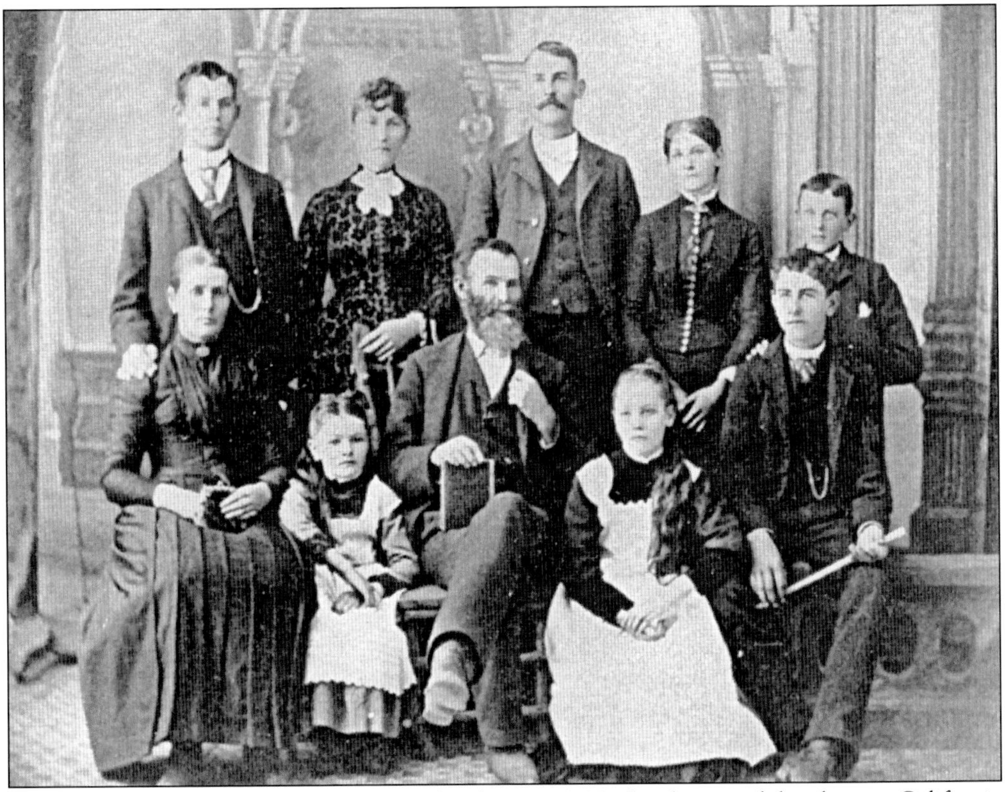

William Tommy Ross came to California when he was 13. His family crossed the plains to California by ox team and on foot. After they settled on Ross Road, they did general farming and delivered charcoal, later concentrating on fruits and hops. They were one of the most memorable families who settled the area. In the picture above are William Thomas Ross, Sarepta Turner Ross, and their nine children, from left to right: (first row) Sarepta, Sadie, William Tommy, Hattie, and Arthur; (second row) Edward, Alice, Charles, Minnie, and Harry. (Courtesy of Virginia Van Keppel Hughes.)

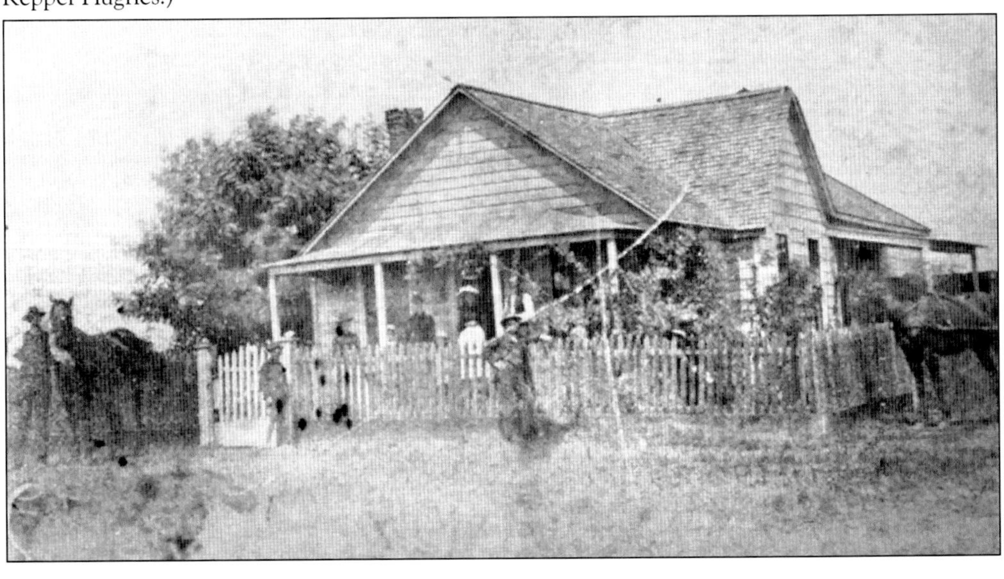

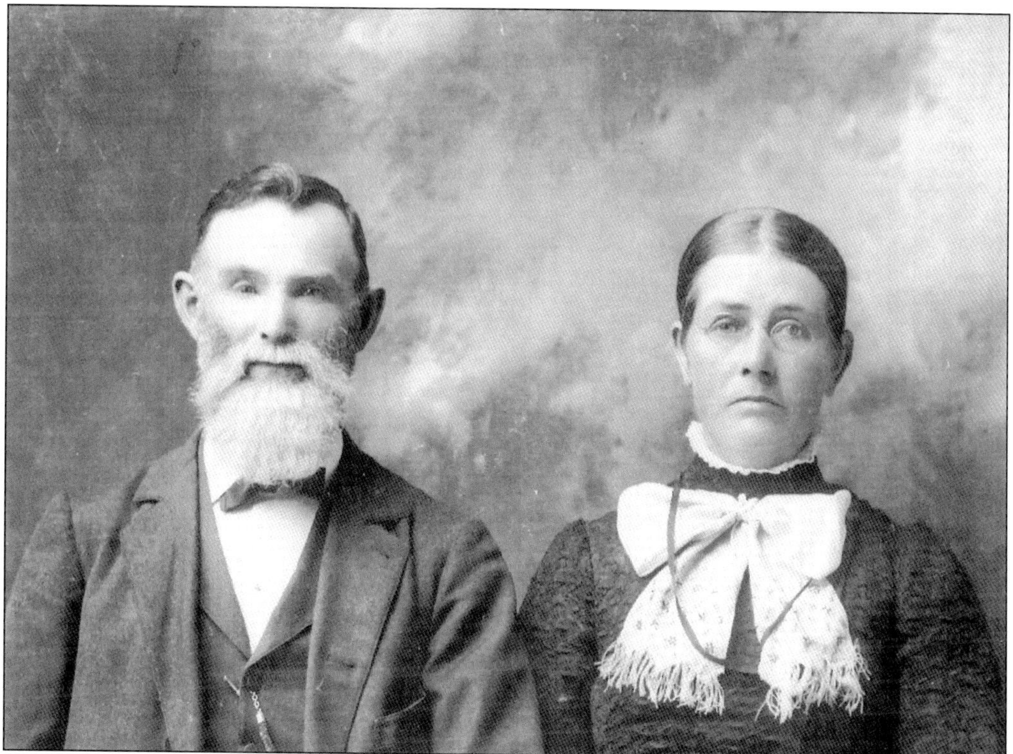

William Thomas Ross was born May 22, 1842, in Harrison County, Indiana. He lived until April 5, 1906. He married Sarepta Ann Turner on December 15, 1864. She was born October 10, 1848, and lived until February 3, 1923. Ross Station Road is where they settled in Forestville. Both Tommy and Sarepta kept daily journals about their life in Forestville. Tommy wrote about going hunting with Jasper O'Farrell, the well-known surveyor. They worked hard and went to church many times a week. (Courtesy of the Dave Henry collection.)

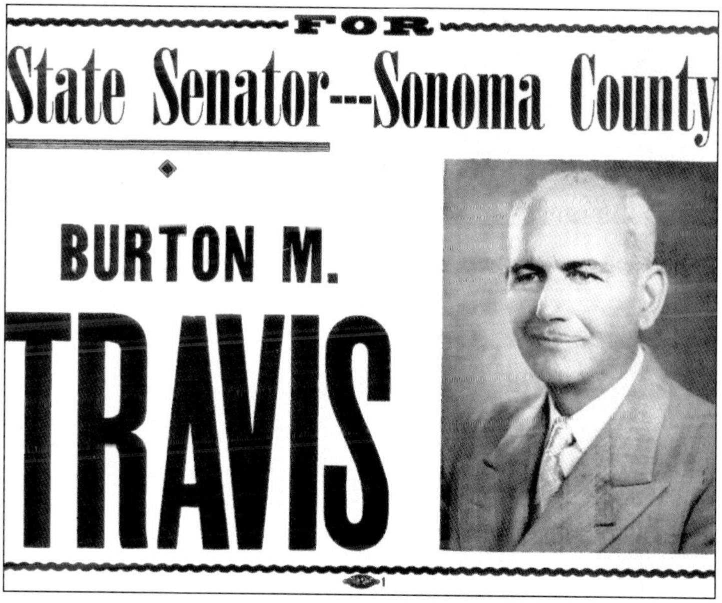

Burton Travis ran in the Democratic primary for state senator. His candidacy came about as the result of his and a friend's curiosity as to how people become candidates. As a test of the system, he followed the prescribed steps and was surprised to find himself a candidate. When he lost the election, he said it was "democracy at work," because he thought the other candidate was a better choice. (Courtesy of the Dave Henry collection.)

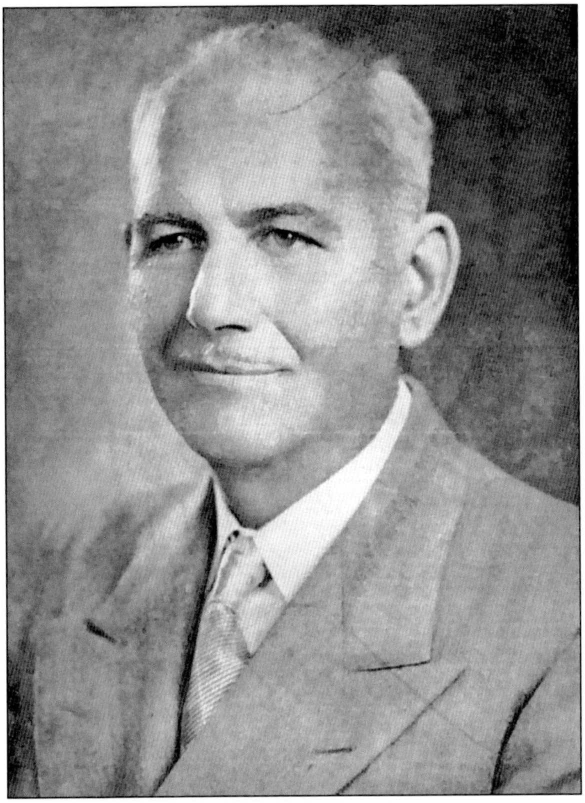

Burton Travis was very interested in local history and was active in the Sonoma County Historical Society. He wrote *The History of El Molino Rancho and Forestville Town*, which was finished by his son, Russell B. Travis. The work he most liked and was best at was managing the fruit-packing house. He ended up spending most of his life farming, which he disliked, to benefit his growing family. (Courtesy of the Dave Henry collection.)

During World War I, Burt Travis worked in a submarine yard in San Francisco. During World War II, he was farming; he had an *Application for War Ration Book* in 1943. In 1942, the Office of Price Administration issued ration books to Americans to help in the war effort. Tire and automobile rationing had already begun, and now Americans were asked to ration sugar. In January 1943, *War Ration Book Two* was issued. This time it had four pages of blue and four pages of red stamps. Book three was issued in October 1943 and contained brown stamps used for dairy foods. (Courtesy of the Bob Aldridge collection.)

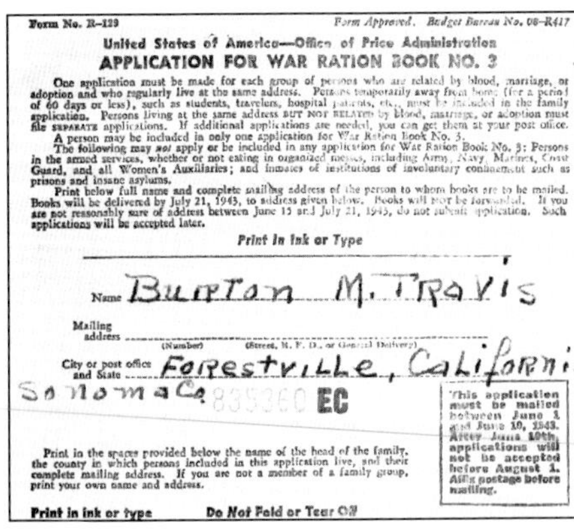

Form No. R-129 *Form Approved. Budget Bureau No. 08-R417*

United States of America—Office of Price Administration

APPLICATION FOR WAR RATION BOOK NO. 3

One application must be made for each group of persons who are related by blood, marriage, or adoption and who regularly live at the same address. Persons temporarily away from home (for a period of 60 days or less), such as students, travelers, hospital patients, etc., must be included in the family application. Persons living at the same address BUT NOT RELATED by blood, marriage, or adoption must file SEPARATE applications. If additional applications are needed, you can get them at your post office.

A person may be included in only one application for War Ration Book No. 3.

The following may *not* apply or be included in any application for War Ration Book No. 3: Persons in the armed services, whether or not eating in organized messes, including Army, Navy, Marines, Coast Guard, and all Women's Auxiliaries; and inmates of institutions of involuntary confinement such as prisons and insane asylums.

Print below full name and complete mailing address of the person to whom books are to be mailed. Books will be delivered by July 21, 1943, to address given below. Books will NOT be forwarded. If you are not reasonably sure of address between June 15 and July 21, 1943, do not submit application. Such applications will be accepted later.

Print in ink or Type

Name BURTON M. TRAVIS

Mailing address (Number) (Street, R. F. D., or General Delivery)

City or post office and State FORESTVILLE, CALIFORNIA

SONOMA CO. 835360 EC

This application must be mailed between June 1 and June 10, 1943. After June 10th, applications will not be accepted before August 1. Affix postage before mailing.

Print in the spaces provided below the name of the head of the family, the county in which persons included in this application live, and their complete mailing address. If you are not a member of a family group, print your own name and address.

Print in ink or type Do *Not* Fold or Tear Off

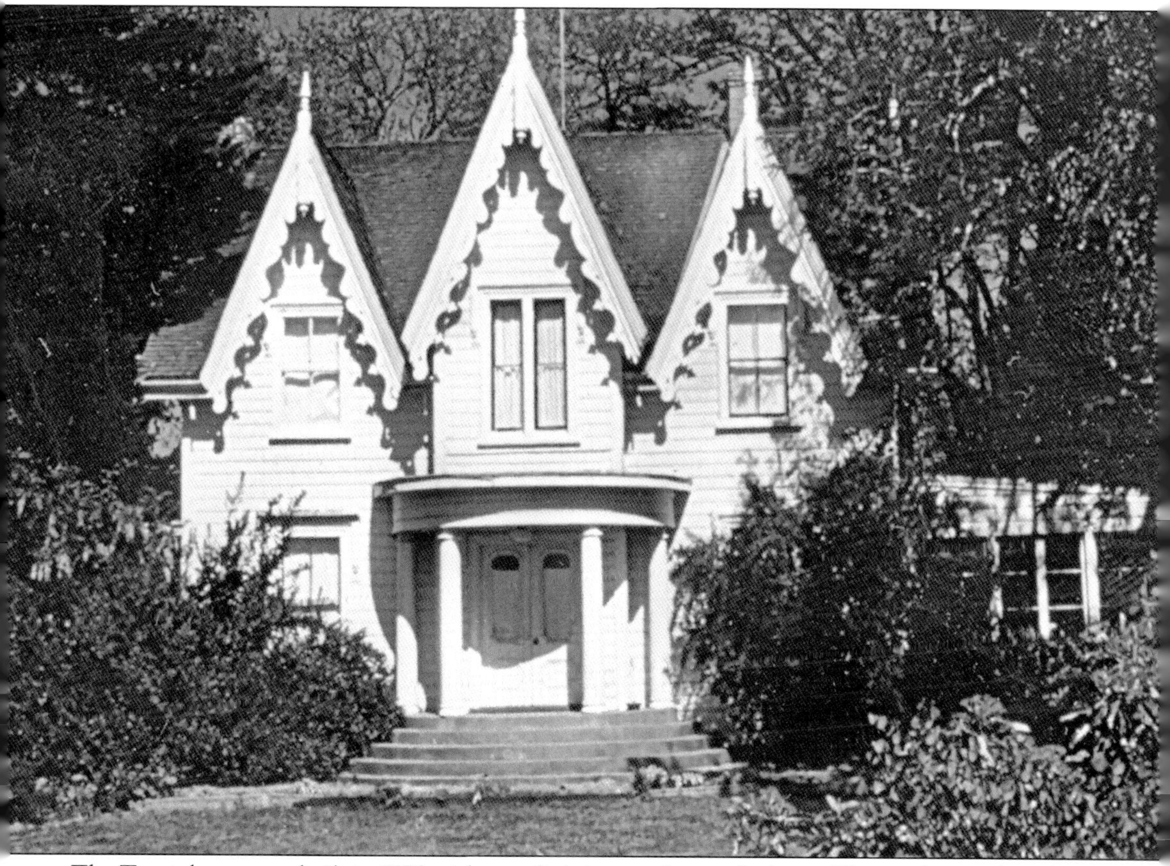

The Travis house was built in 1873 with an adjoining road named after it. The road started on the curve of Highway 116 as a long, lovely lane that ran down the hill north of the school, through a meadow, and up the knoll to the Travis house. It was the most beautiful house in Forestville, built by Mr. A. Shoemaker in carpenter Gothic style, but unfortunately it is now gone. The land is filled with vineyards, and some of the creeks have disappeared. Burton Travis married Edna Pearl Russell from the Russell family, who owned the hotel, livery stable, and motor-stage service to Guerneville. (Courtesy of the Burton Travis collection.)

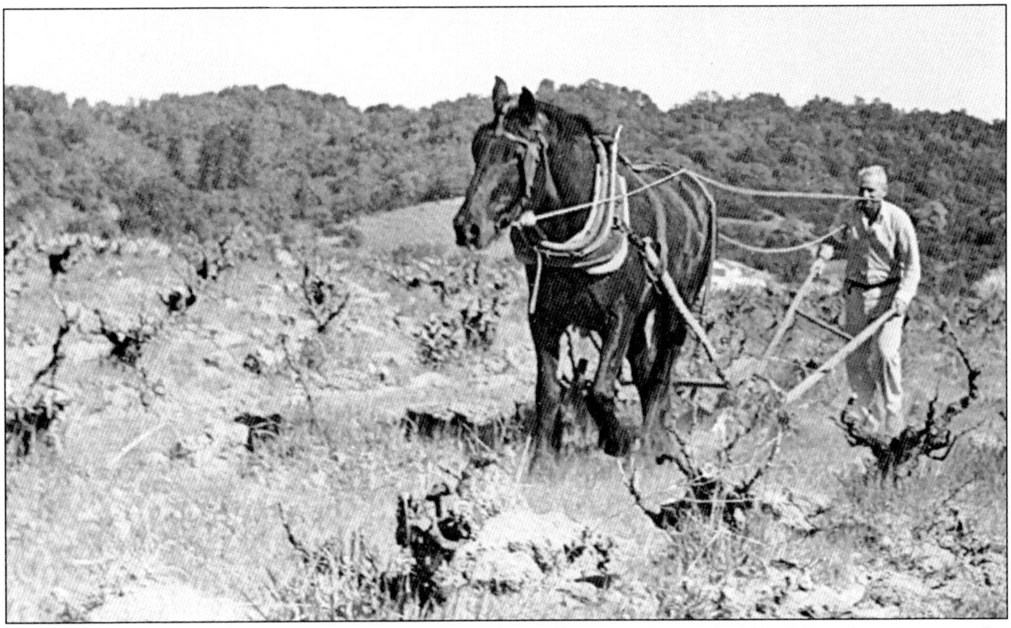

Burton Travis was a well-known Forestville rancher from 1927 until 1972. He is best known for his active interest in education and for being on the Forestville School Board for 15 years as well as the Analy Union High School Board for 27 years. The library at the Analy High School was named after him in 1964. (Courtesy of the Dave Henry collection.)

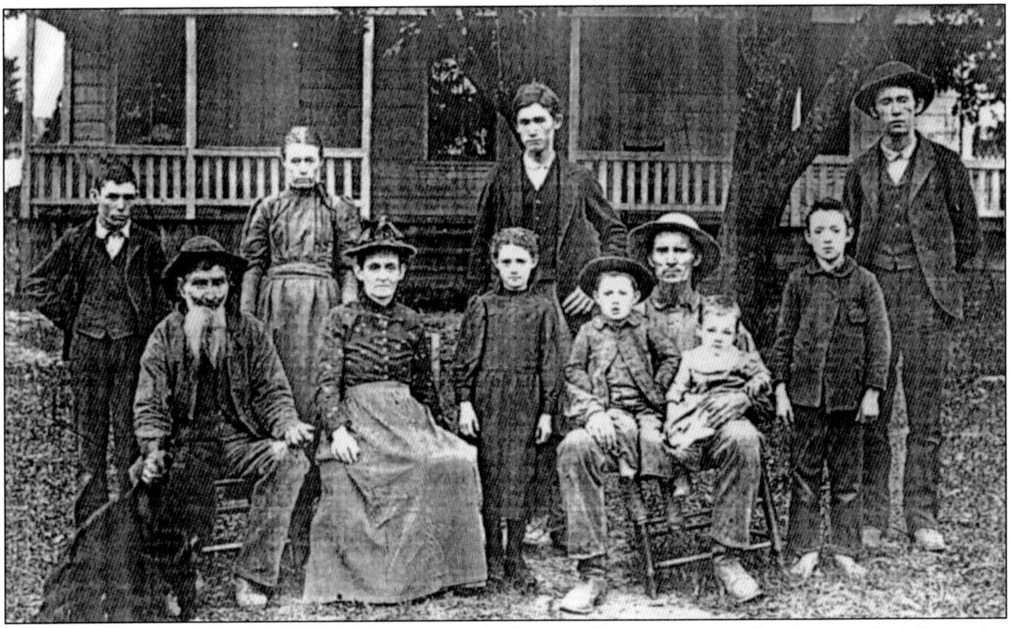

Davis Road is named after Levi Davis, an early Forestville settler. His land extended from the Russian River along Mirabel Road. Raising carp in pools was one of Levi Davis's early business pursuits. The pools were located either near the river or up on Mirabel Road close to Davis Road; the exact location isn't known. This picture was taken in 1893 on Mirabel Road. The house was probably built in the mid-1800s. His grandson Sydney Davis demolished the house and built the current house. Many of Levi Davis's descendants live in Forestville. (Courtesy of Ron Davis.)

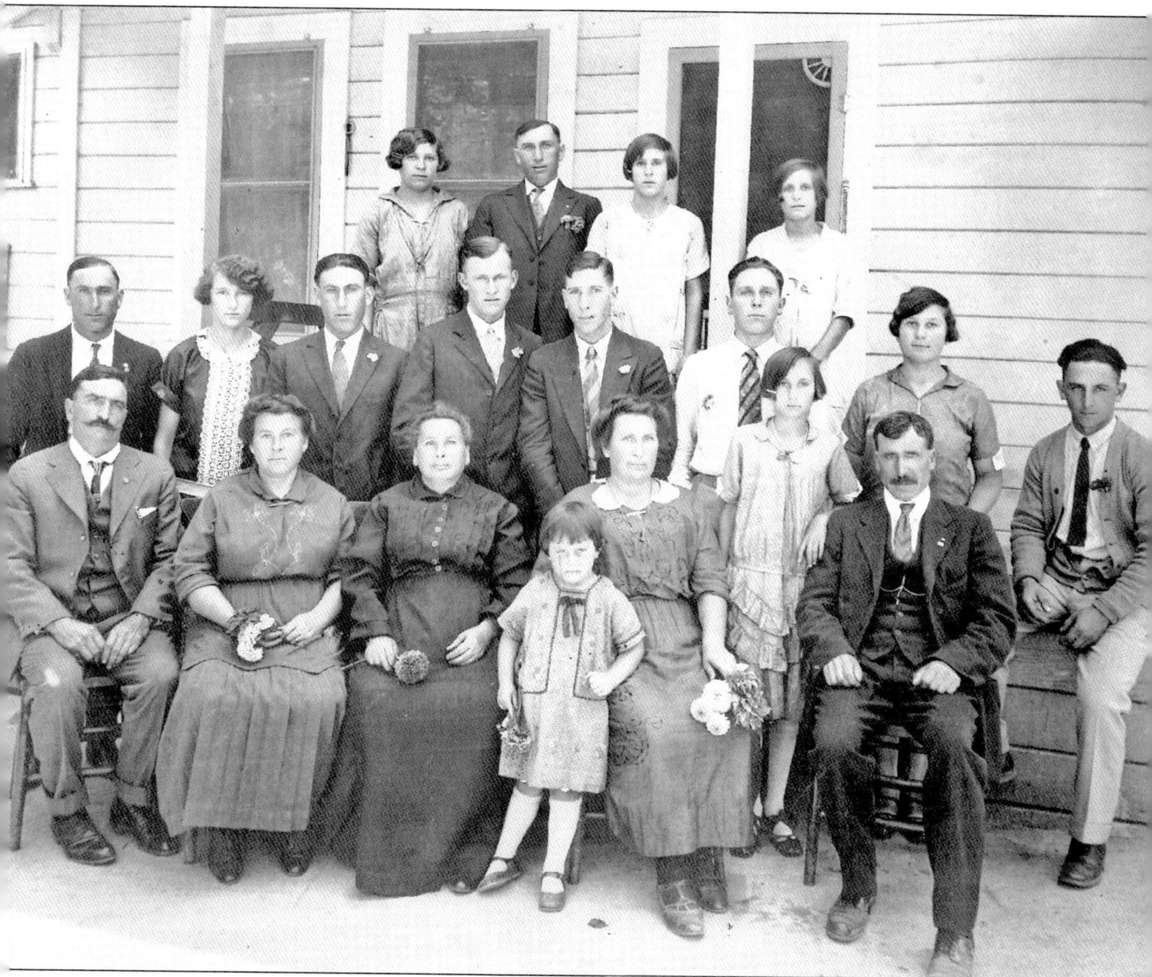

Giusti Ranch, known as "La Collina," meaning "on the hill" in Italian, was founded by Angelo Giusti in the 1870s. The Giusti Ranch was originally covered in oak trees. The Giusti family, being among the first settlers on this land, constructed the road themselves. The land was cleared for farming. Some of the original crops included olives, grapes, prunes, cherries, and apples. This picture was taken in the 1920s in front of the Giusti home. From left to right are (first row) Massimo Mancini, Julia (Giusti) Mancini, Elizabeth Giusti (Angelo's wife), Lena Cinquini, Eda (Giusti) Cinquini, Elizabeth Mancini, Dominico Cinquini, and Pete Cinquini; (second row) Tony Giusti, Eva Mancini, Michele Giusti, Angelo Mancini, Frank Cinquini, Henry Cinquini, and Carlotta Mancini; (third row) Flora Cinquini, Frank Giuisti, Mary Cinquini, and Jennie Cinquini. (Courtesy of Angelo Giusti.)

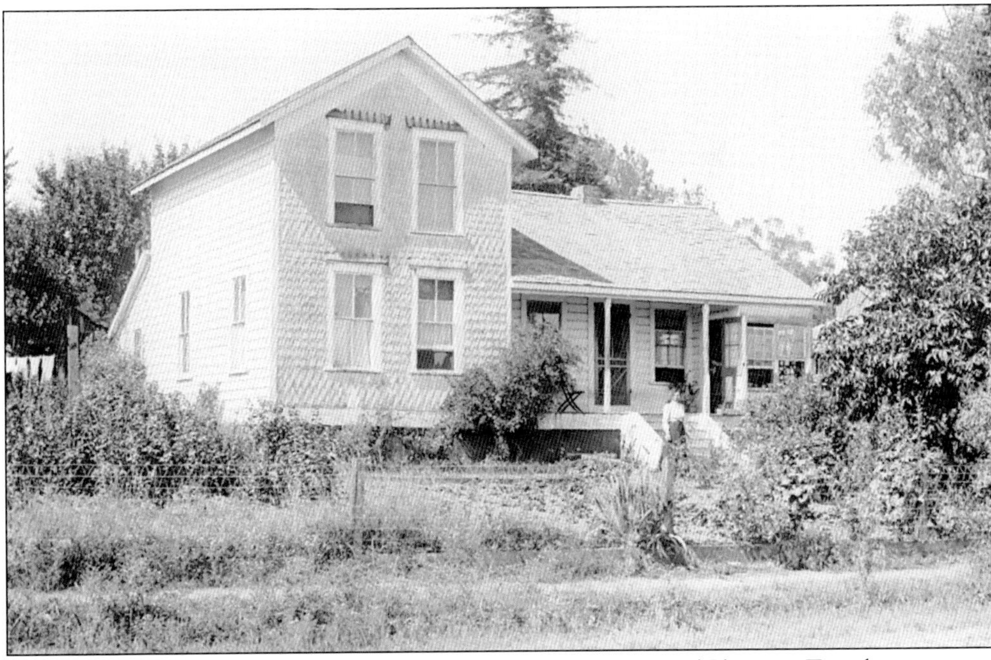

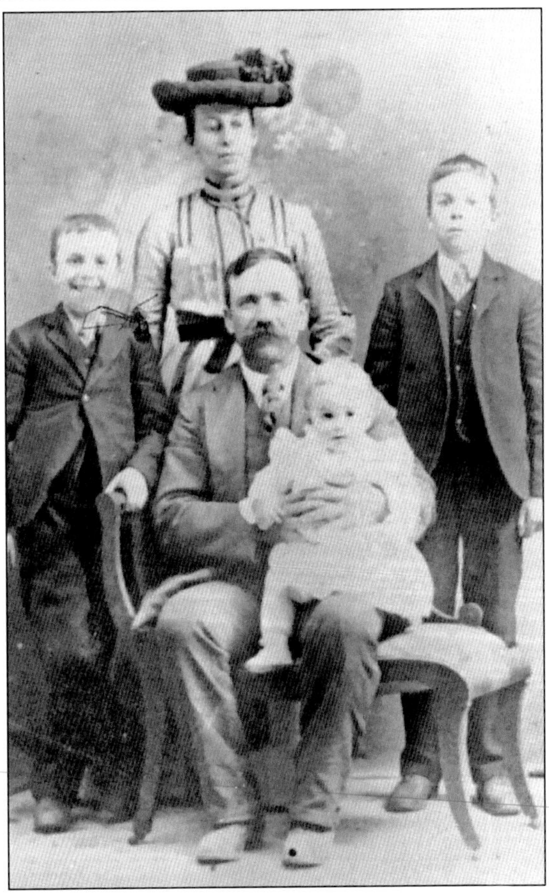

Warren and Florence Templeman, recall, "Robert Templeman arrived in Forestville in 1885. He and Linda Bushnell of the Vine Hill District were married in 1890. After running a general store in Fish Mill near Fort Ross, he came back to Forestville in 1903 and bought the home at the corner of Highway 116 and First Street, which was owned by Samual Legg. Robert was born and raised in Scotland, where people lived in little villages and went out to their small farms in the country to work during the day. Robert followed the custom and bought a ranch on what is now Templeman Road and went out each day with his horses and wagon to work on the property. He lived in Forestville until he died in 1947. They raised three sons, Robert Jr., Clarence (Scotty), and Kenneth. After 1947, Kenneth built and ran a service station on the spot where the Templeman home used to be. Clarence bought and ran the ranch on Templeman Road, Robert Jr. moved to San Rafael. Pictured standing from left to right are Scotty, Linda Bushnell Templeman, Robert Jr., and Robert Sr. holding Kenny." (Courtesy of Warren Templeman.)

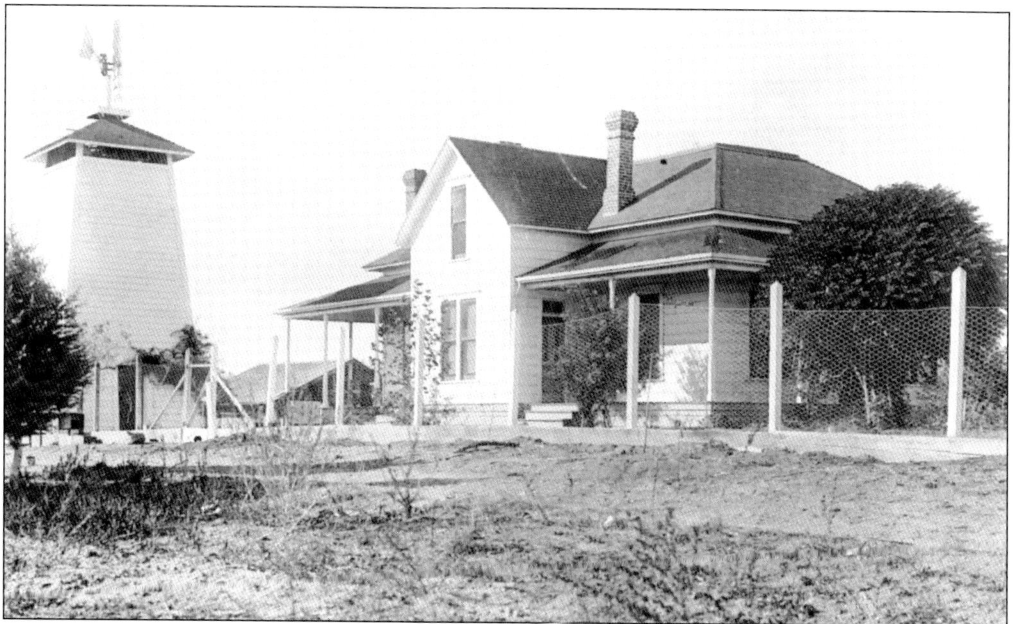

The Nolan house, built in 1897 on 250 acres, was originally referred to as the Richilieu-True property. Catherine Dibble first married James Richilieu, whose daughter Edith married Albert Nolan. Albert Nolan was the principal of Forestville School and later the Daniel Webster School for bad boys in San Francisco. (Courtesy of the Dave Henry collection.)

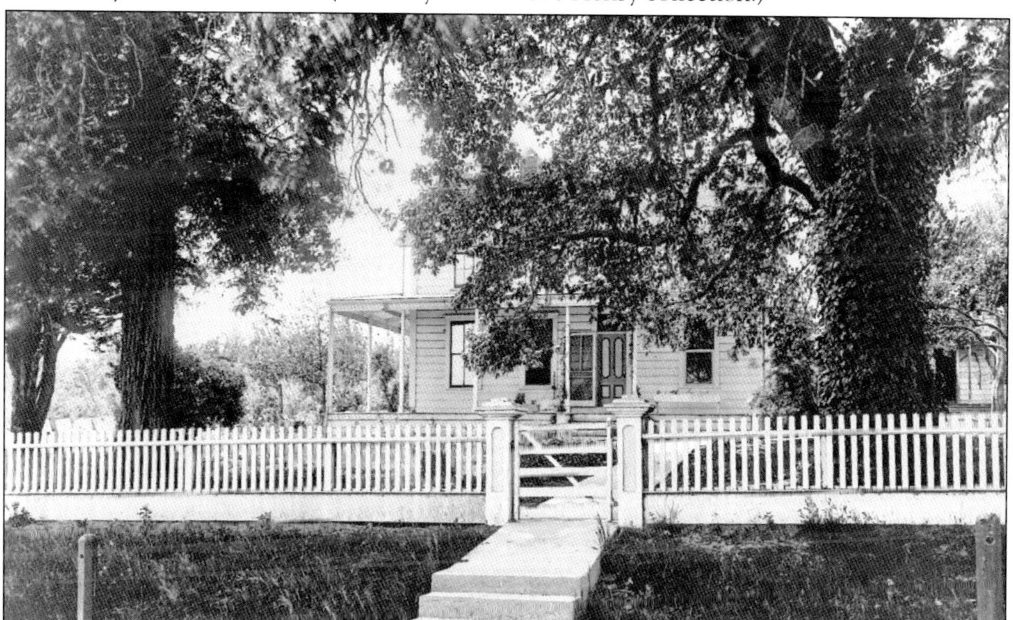

This house has been known as the C. C. Wakeland house and is now called the Century House, a beautiful reminder of Forestville's past. C. C. Wakeland was the brother of J. J. Wakeland, who lived down the road from his brother. J. J. Wakeland never forgot his obligations to the community, according to Burton Travis. He was born in Morgan County, Indiana, on July 6, 1866. He was a teacher, then a farmer, and finally a contractor who built many of the best homes around. (Courtesy of the Dave Henry collection.)

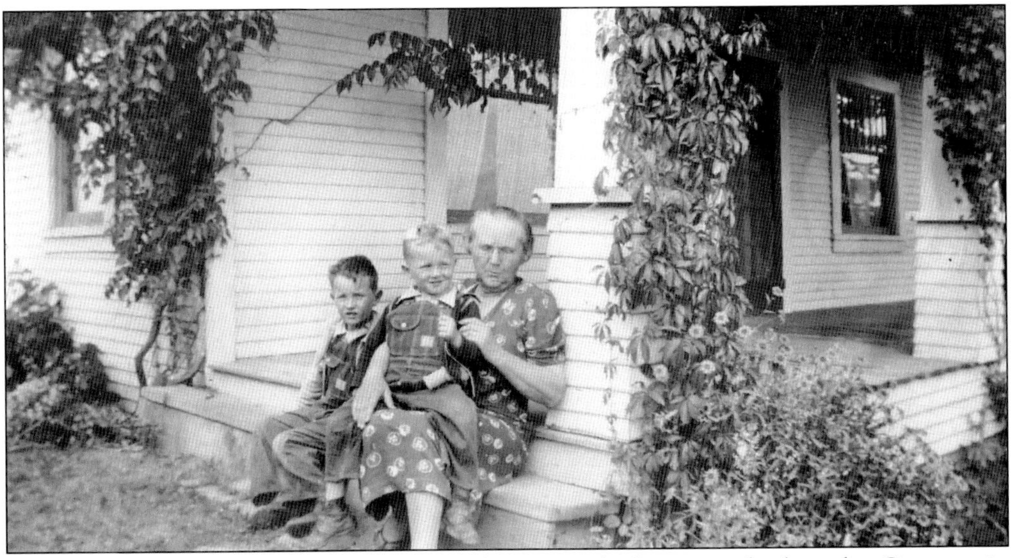

John Anderson remembers, "The family owned 16 acres, which was mostly planted in Gravenstein and Jonathan Red apples. They supplemented their income with 200 egg-laying chickens and by picking hops. There also was an abundant vegetable garden and lovely flowers. It was the good life (or so it seemed to their grandchildren). AV's father, Leroy Sisson Anderson arrived in Forestville in 1865. He was a teamster with eight oxen and hauled redwoods from Guerneville to Petaluma, a two-day trip, from 1867 to 1877. In 1877, the railroad came in and put all the teamsters out of business. He then purchased acreage in Pocket Canyon and later in Forestville. Cousin Joe Williams currently owns the family property. This picture of the front porch is Edna Anderson with her two grandchildren John and Mike in 1940. The family picture from left to right is of 'AV' (Albert Vaness) Anderson, wife Edna, and children Fred and Hilda (about 1906)." (Courtesy of John Anderson.)

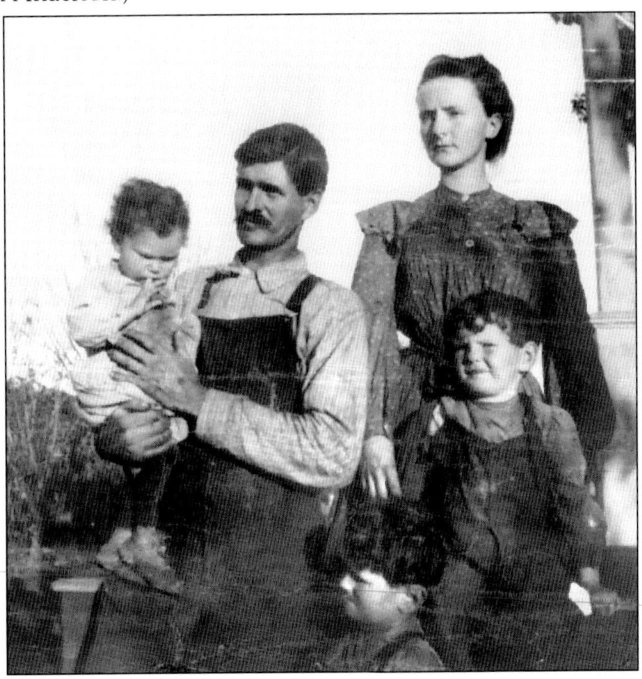

John Z. Johnson and his wife, Mary Ann Yeager Johnson, bought 350 acres from the original El Molino land grant. In 1875, they built the house that is now used for the elegant Farm House Inn and restaurant run by Joe and Catherine Bartolomei. Joe and Catherine are great-grandchildren of Domenic Giovanetti, who was a neighbor of the Johnsons. John Z. Johnson came by ox team to the gold fields in California in 1849, trying to establish his wealth, but it didn't work out, so he turned to farming and returned to his home state of Virginia to be married to Mary Ann Yeager. On the ranch, they raised hops, orchards, and alfalfa, and it was also a dairy farm. The NWP Railroad ran in front of the house where River Road is today. The Johnsons had two children, Daniel Webster and Rebecca. Daniel Johnson married Emma Banks and then became a farmer, painter, machinist, and photographer. (Courtesy of Joe Bartolomei.)

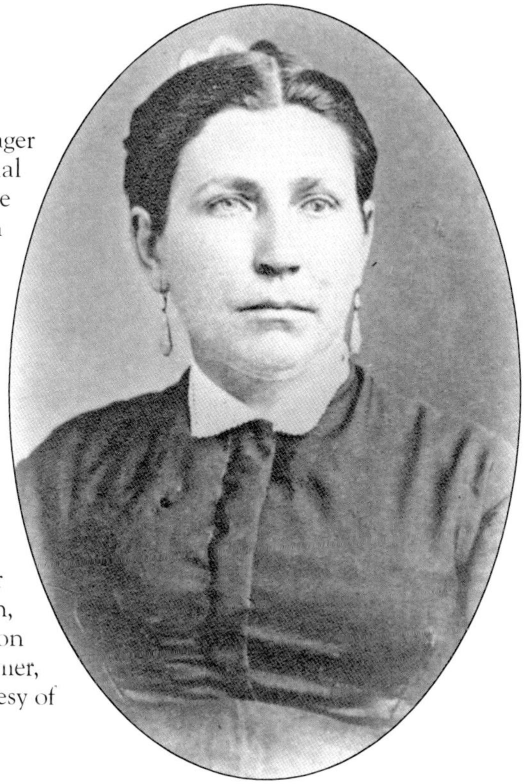

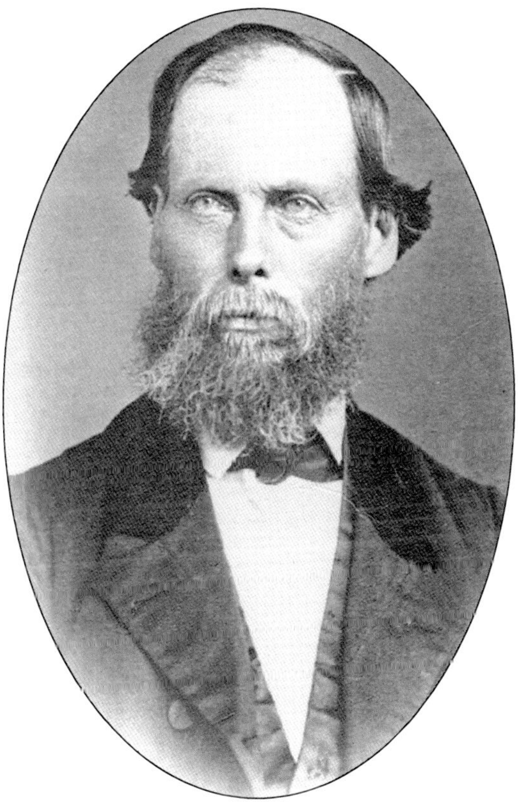

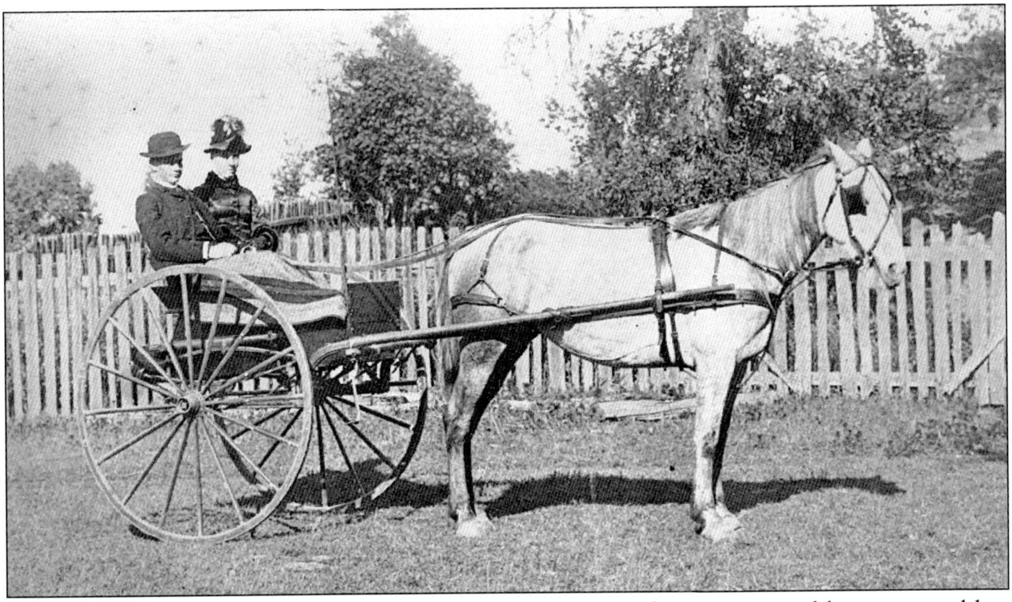

The well-known Forestville photographer Daniel Webster Johnson captured his sister and her husband in this photograph. His sister is Rebecca Johnson Malone, who married James Malone II in 1888. They are sitting in a carriage on their farm. James Malone was a well-known engineer and electrician in Santa Rosa. (Courtesy of the Bob Aldridge collection.)

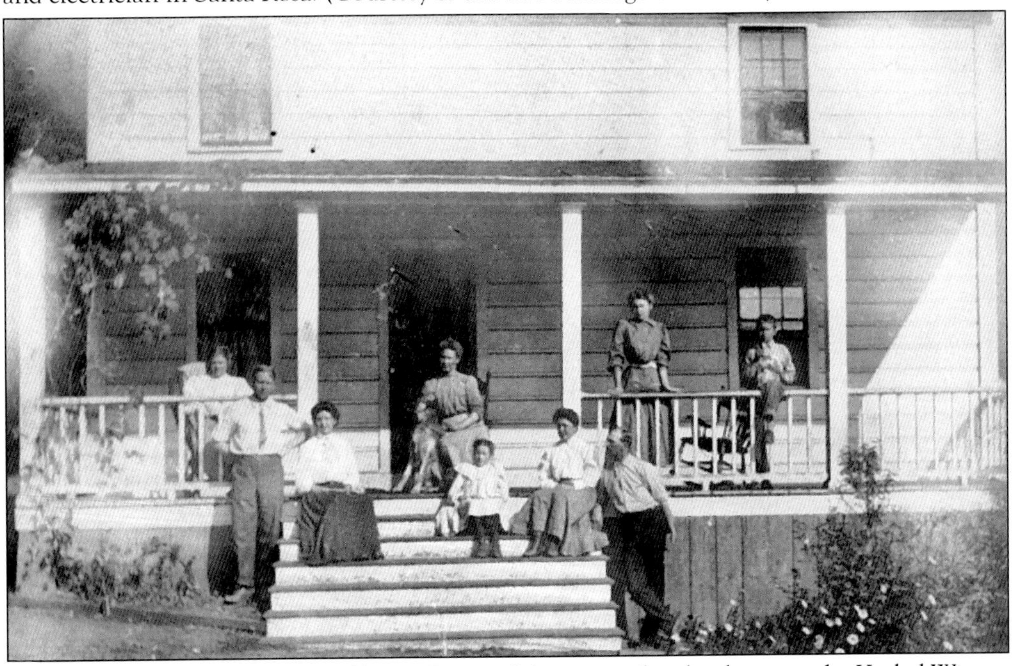

Anthoney McPeak came from Callaway County, Missouri, to buy land next to the Korbel Winery in 1857. He sold the land to the Korbel brothers and bought 1,694 acres at Hilton, where he built a home and raised the largest sheep ranch in this section of the country. He later developed a summer resort known as the Cosmos Farm. He married Melissa Bell in 1864, and together they raised nine children. Unfortunately, several of their children died before reaching adulthood. (Courtesy of the Dave Henry collection.)

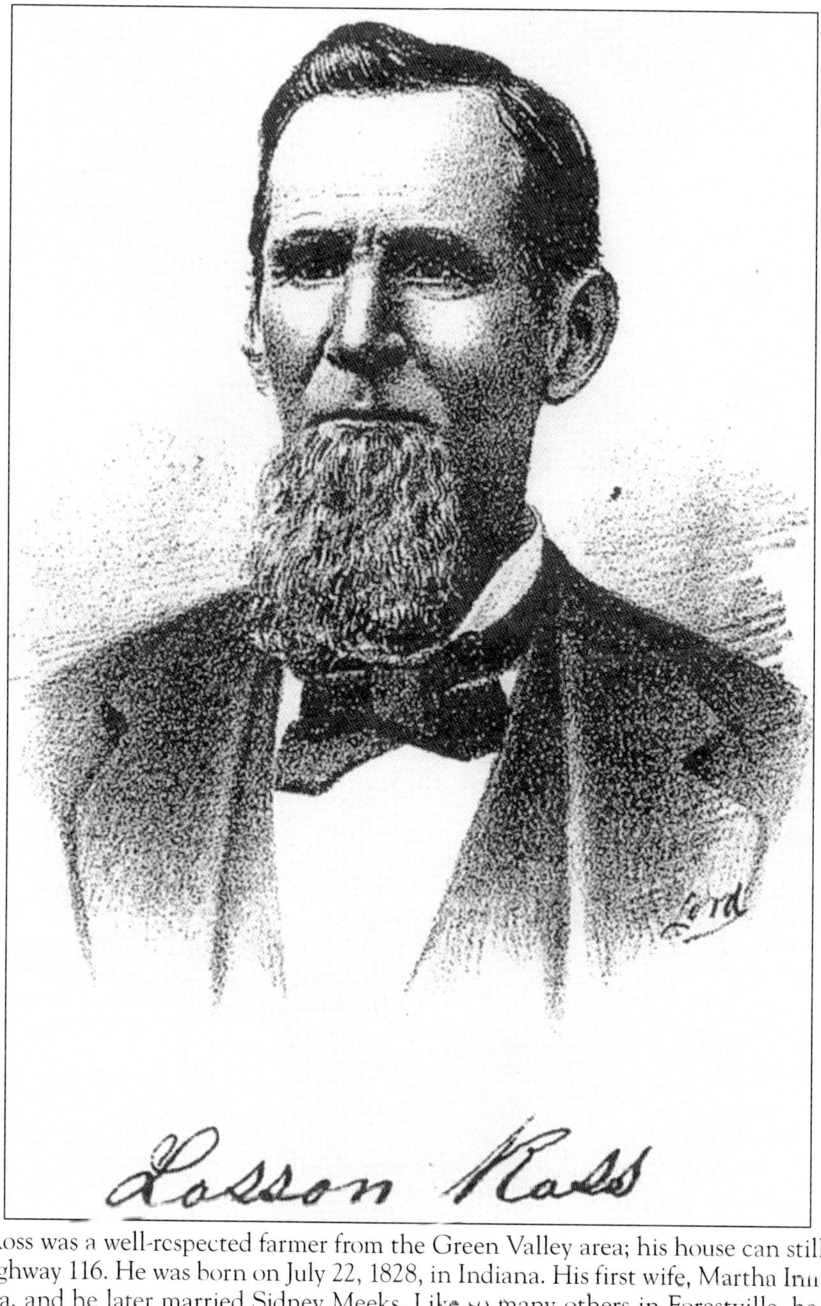

Losson Ross was a well-respected farmer from the Green Valley area; his house can still be seen along Highway 116. He was born on July 22, 1828, in Indiana. His first wife, Martha Inman, died of cholera, and he later married Sidney Meeks. Like so many others in Forestville, he traveled to the gold fields by ox team but later decided to become a farmer. He developed an incredible peach orchard and a peach called Ross cling. He also grew hops and had one of the most complete hop-drying houses. His two-story house was considered one of the most substantial and complete during his day according to the *History of Sonoma County*. The Paul Hobbs Winery is currently restoring the house and vineyards. Losson Ross was chosen by his constituents to represent them in the Democratic county conventions. He was a member of the Methodist church. He and his wife had seven children, and he was the brother of William Tommy Ross and James Ross of Forestville. (Courtesy of Forestville Historical Society.)

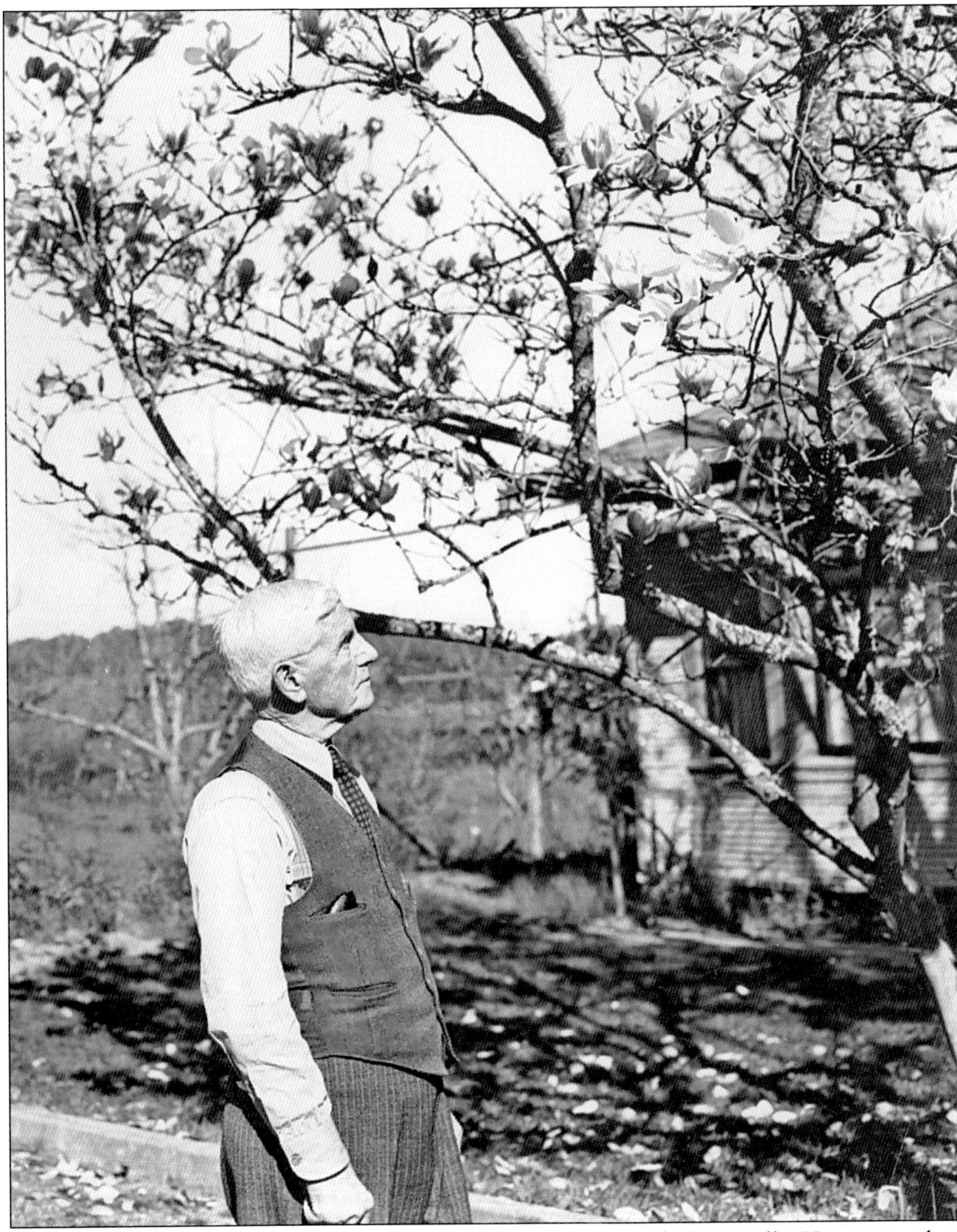

Tom Silk was one of the most interesting people that lived in early Forestville. He was involved in just about everything—banking, running a variety store, serving as postmaster, sports teams, and horticulture, as this picture shows. He is standing in front of his home. (Courtesy of Lavon Speer Covington.)

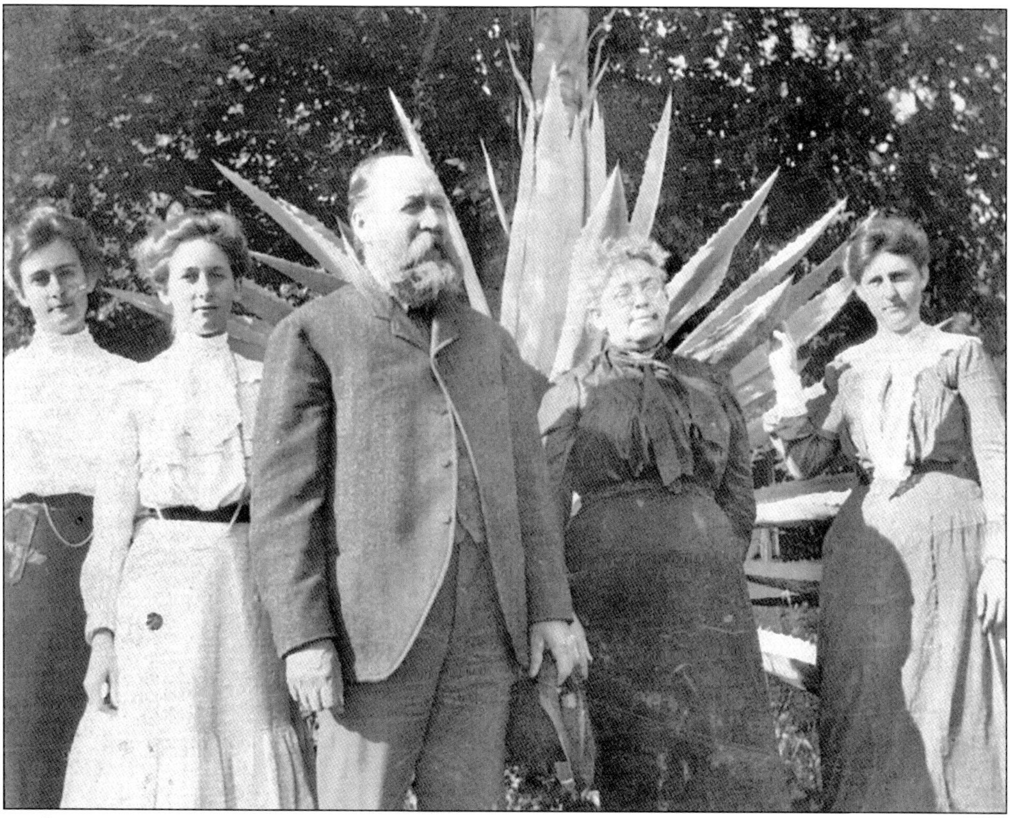

Nathaniel Griffith moved to the Vinehill area of Sonoma County in 1883. He bought 80 acres after leaving a job as a mining engineer in Nevada. He was known as the "Grandfather of the Gravenstein apple." A friend of his, Luther Burbank, suggested that Sonoma County had the best climate to grow Gravenstein apples. Nathaniel Griffith had three incredible daughters and a son who died at an early age. In this family portrait from left to right are Alice, Nellie, Nathaniel, Ida (her maiden name was Fleming), and Grace Griffith. (Courtesy of Jeani Martini.)

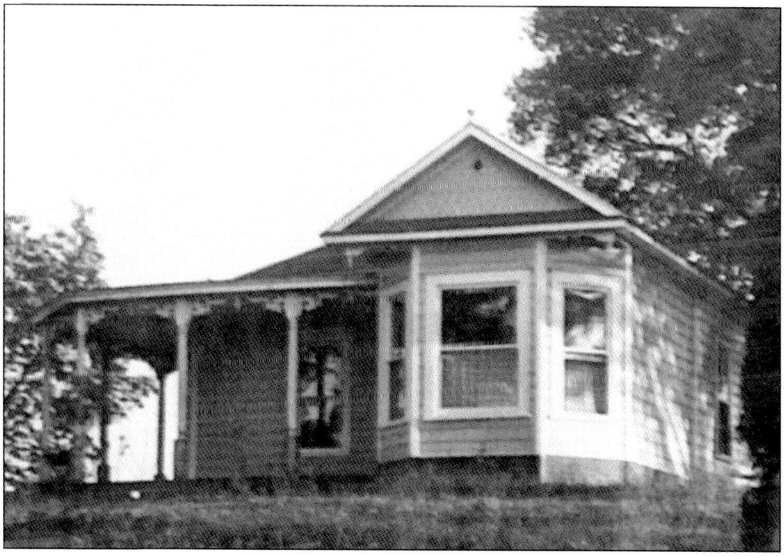

This is the Nathaniel Griffith home. He planted more than 400 redwood trees along the creek on his property. (Courtesy of Bodega Bay Heritage Galley.)

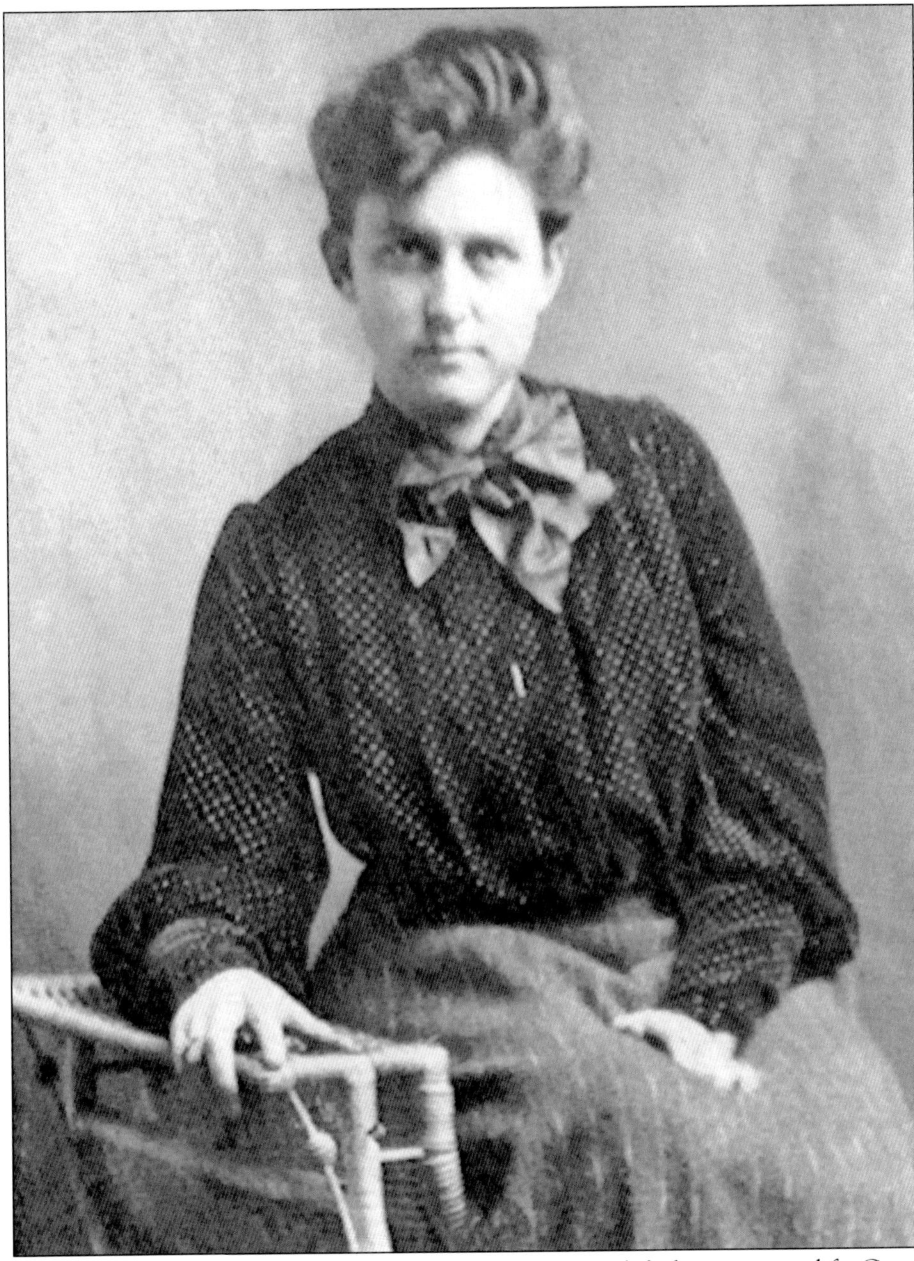

Grace Griffith is pictured here, but each of the Griffith sisters left their print on life. Grace was an artist, gifted enough to be elected to England's Royal Society of Artists. Her artwork can be seen at the Bodega Bay Heritage Gallery. She painted watercolors of Luther Burbank's gardens. She married Charles Allison. Nell was a well-known poet who at one time dated Robert Ripley of *Ripley's Believe It or Not* fame. She married Ned Wilson and settled in Kenwood. One of her poems, "Blood Donors Prayer," was published in Eleanor Roosevelt's syndicated column. She also published her poems in *Readers Digest, Better Homes and Gardens*, and *Good Housekeeping.* Alice was a naturalist who found happiness in her father's redwood grove. Luther Burbank proposed to her, but she was too independent to accept and didn't marry until she was 75 to neighbor Jess Ingle. (Courtesy of Bodega Bay Heritage Gallery.)

Four

MAKING SPIRITS

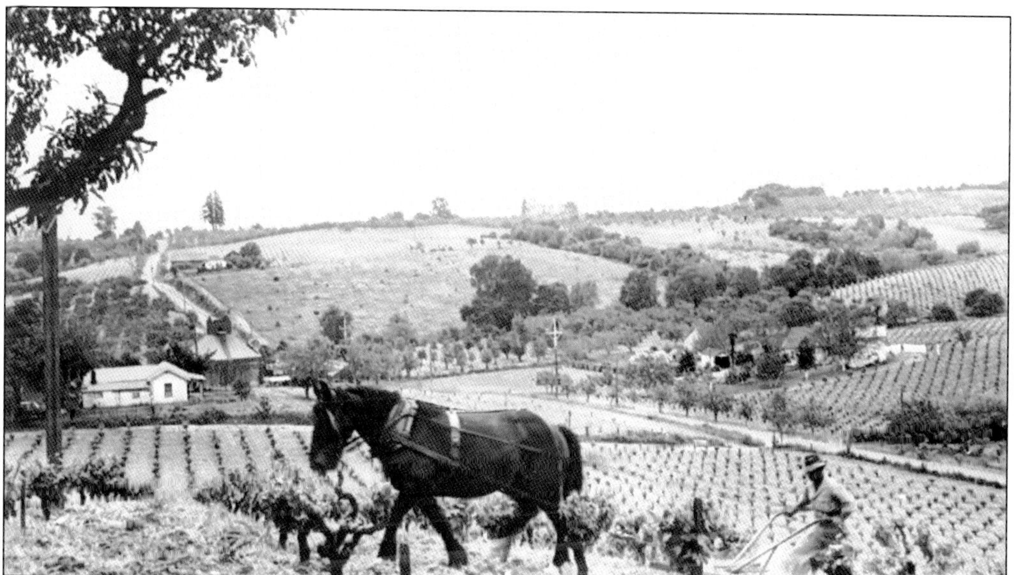

Phil Marcucci remembers, "In the late 19th century, Italian immigrants came to the North Bay bringing their prized grapevines from Italy. They planted vineyards all over Sonoma County, including the Russian River Valley, where the climate is ideal for grape growing. The area was known as the 'Golden Triangle' and also part of the 'Russian River appellation,' an area of fertile soil to grow vineyards. Joe Vannucci's son Clarence is pictured here plowing a vineyard for his father in the spring of early 1940s in the Trenton Road area. The photograph is facing southwesterly with Laguna Road at the bottom right corner of the photograph running uphill toward the Martini and Prati Winery." (Courtesy of Phil Marcucci.)

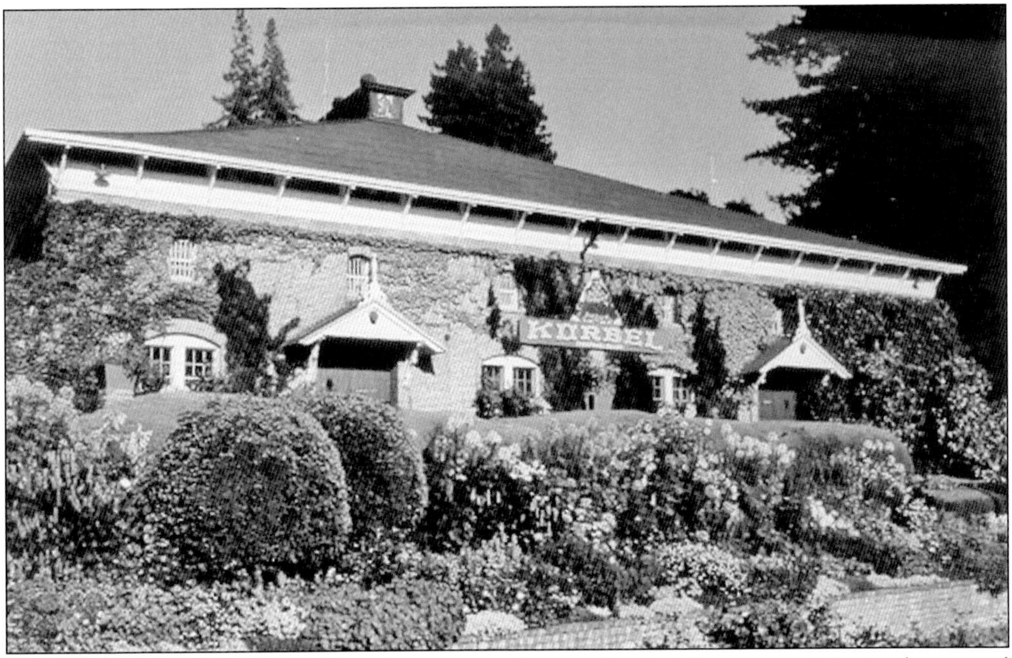

In the mid-1800s, three Korbel brothers set out for new land with opportunities in the rugged Sonoma County, California, countryside by emigrating from Czechoslovakia. Their endeavors consisted of a sawmill first and then a dairy. They also started growing wheat, prunes, beets, corn, alfalfa, and a few varieties of grapes. When the lumber boom slowed down, they began farming in the rich sandy river soil. Their interest turned to making champagne by growing pinot noir grapes. (Courtesy of Korbel Winery.)

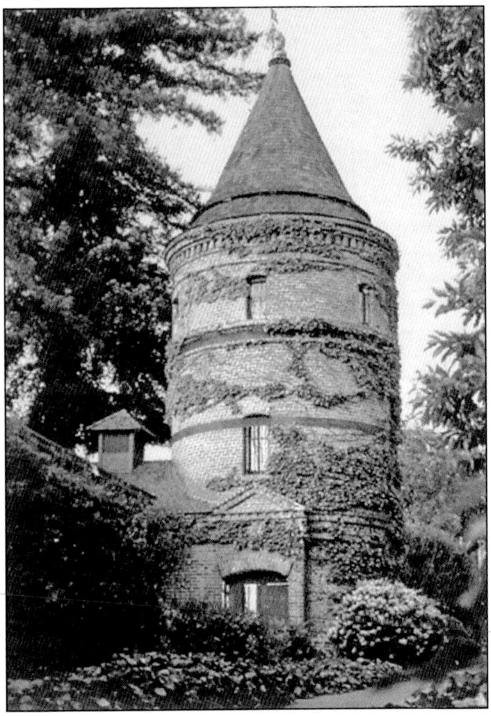

In 1882, the Korbel winemaking started with an output of 20,000 to 30,000 gallons of wine. Frank Hasek from Prague became their champagne master. Prohibition tested the family's ingenuity, but sadly bothers Francis, Joseph, and Anton all passed away before the repeal of 1933. Since 1954, the Adolf Heck family has continued the tradition of fine champagne making and brandy production. Brandy Tower is pictured here. Gary Heck has been the president and chairman since 1982. (Courtesy of Korbel Winery.)

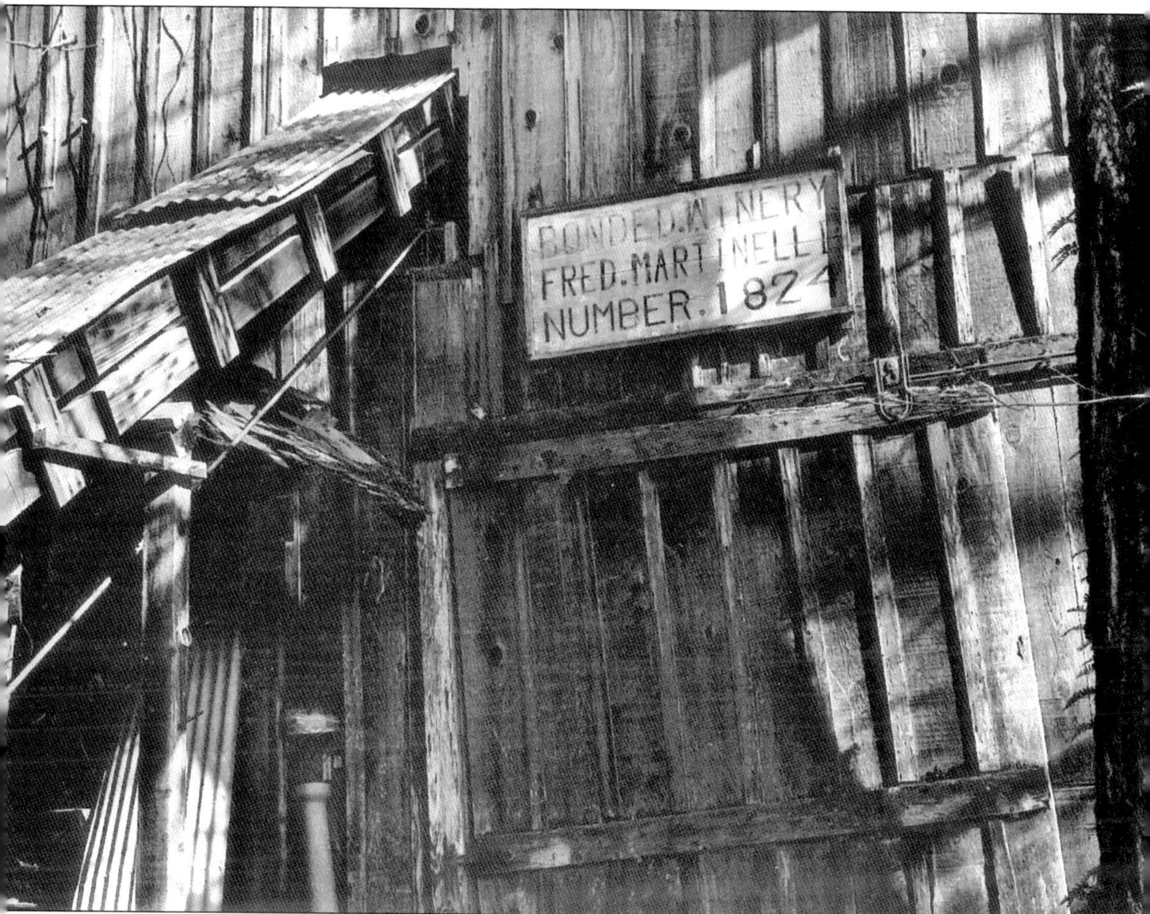

"By 1902 Giuseppe, Luisa, Fred, and Bing had all the hills planted in grapes. The vineyards extended from the Butler place to the Banfield place, to the very top of the hill. The bottom of the big hill is now known as Jackass Hill. The upper part to the top is now all in timber. The flat land was planted in prunes, apples, hay, and corn. The grapes planted were zinfandel, Muscat, Burgundy, sauvignon vert, and golden chaisler. Lino Martinelli was born in the new house in 1907," wrote Eve Martinelli. The original winery on the Martinelli Ranch closed in 1952 when Fred protested federal regulations requiring the use of stainless-steel tanks in place of the traditional oak barrels. Lee Martinelli and wife Carolyn developed the winery located on River Road in Fulton. They continue to run the winery with the help of their children, Julianna, George, and Lee Jr. (Courtesy of Sherry Martinelli.)

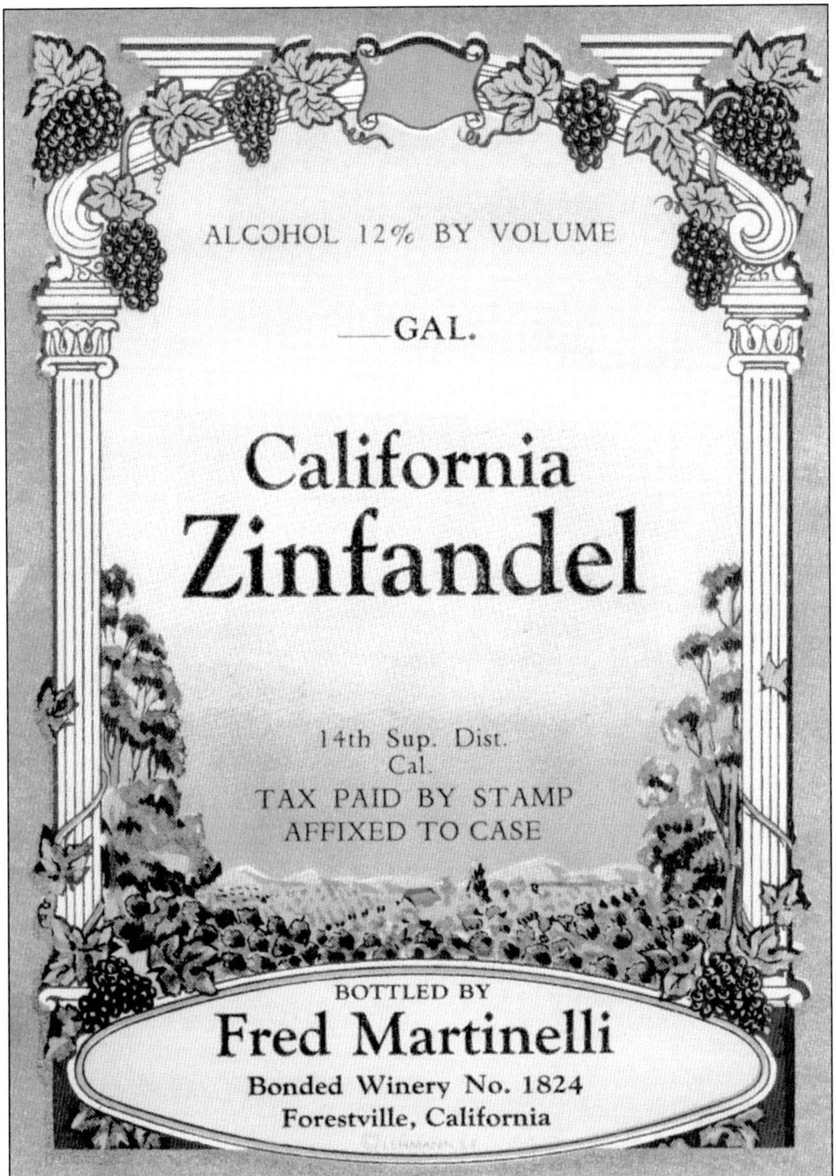

In 1885, at the ages of 19 and 16, Giuseppe Martinelli and Luisa Vellutini eloped from their small village in Tuscany, Italy, making their way to California. Luisa initially worked at San Francisco's Italian Grand Hotel while her husband traveled to Forestville and found work grafting zinfandel grapevines for the Maddocks family. Giuseppe became friends with neighbor Dominic Giovanetti and was allowed to build a small cabin on the property. Luisa joined her husband, and they started their family. The first two children were born in the cabin, Fred (1889) and Domingo (1891). Giuseppe and Luisa also worked cutting wood, picking hops, and making charcoal in an effort to generate enough money to buy property. On Sundays, the young couple hiked the valley in search of property with plenty of water, flat land, and hills. In 1902, they were able to purchase a large parcel on a handshake and a promissory note from George and Ida Call. Later on, cash ($2,625) in the form of gold bars replaced the handshake. The land had once been part of the El Molino land grant. (Courtesy of Sherry Martinelli.)

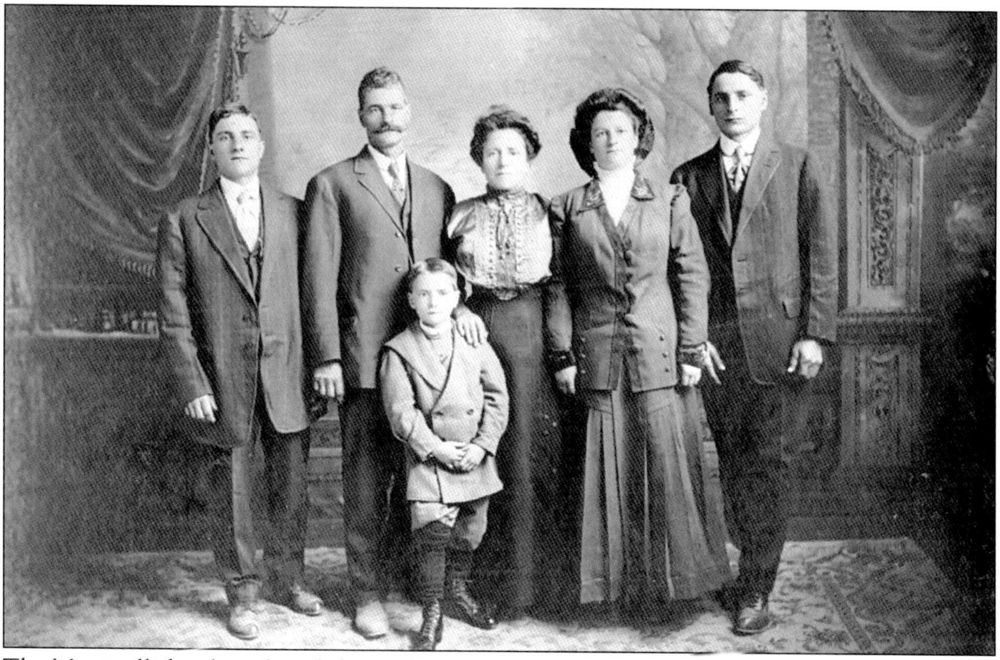

The Martinelli family is, from left to right, son Bing, father Giuseppi, wife Luisa (Gigi), daughter Eda, son Fred, and Lino, the youngest son in front. Fred was born in 1889, his wife was Natalina, and they had Eva and Evo. Bing was born in 1892, his wife was Pia, and they had Joe and Emily. Lino was born in 1907, and his children are Lee and Joyce. Eda was married to Lelio Allesandro, and they had no children. (Courtesy of Sherry Martinelli.)

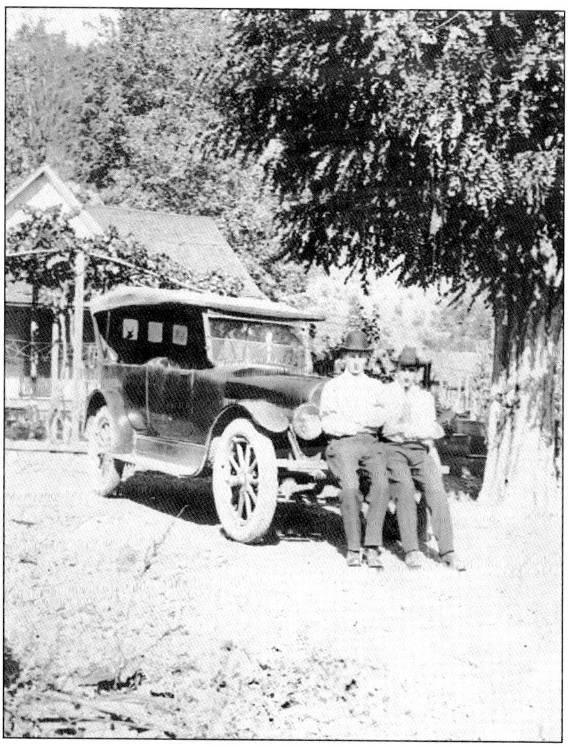

Fred and Bing Martinelli sit in front of their new car, a 1916 Hudson Super 6. Their mother, Luisa (Gigi), was worried her two sons wouldn't find good Italian wives, so she saved $1,000 to send for two women from Italy. While crossing the Atlantic, the two women were entertained by the ship's musicians. They fell in love before they reached New York and married the musicians. Mother Gigi didn't give up, she sent her son Bing to Italy to find brides. He met two eligible sisters, Pia and Natalina Lencioni. Bing was a good match for Pia, and they quickly married; however, due to legal restrictions he could only return to America with his wife. Fred Martinelli made the next trip to Italy and, being a good talker, was able to make arrangements to marry Natalina and return to the United States. (Courtesy of Sherry Martinelli.)

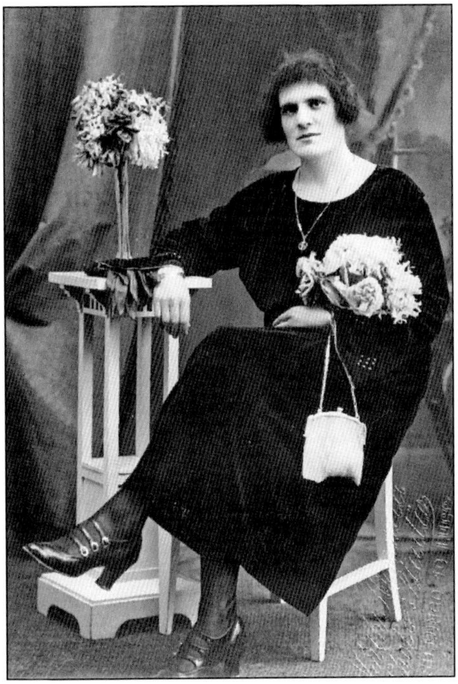

Fred Martinelli was married only a few short years when Natalina Lencioni Martinelli died on October 3, 1926, after her second child's birth. Aunt Pia, although grieving for the loss of her sister and caring for her newborn son, Joe, became instant "mom" to Eva and Evo. (Courtesy of Sherry Martinelli.)

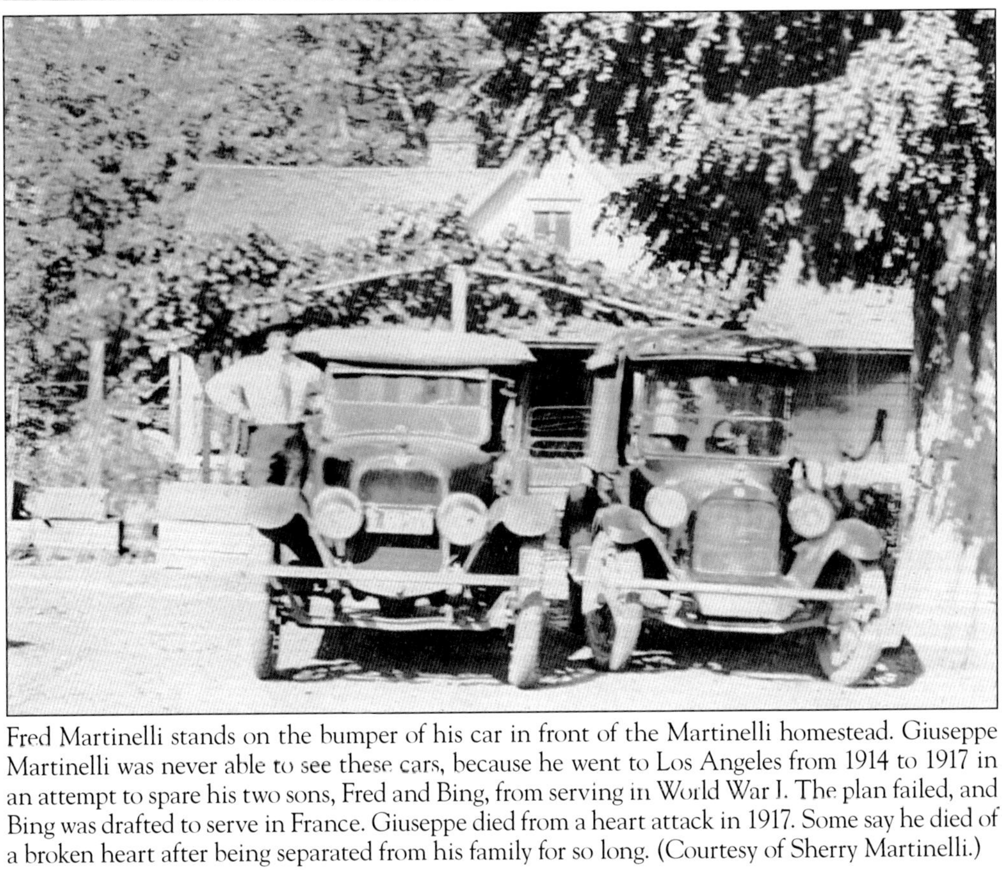

Fred Martinelli stands on the bumper of his car in front of the Martinelli homestead. Giuseppe Martinelli was never able to see these cars, because he went to Los Angeles from 1914 to 1917 in an attempt to spare his two sons, Fred and Bing, from serving in World War I. The plan failed, and Bing was drafted to serve in France. Giuseppe died from a heart attack in 1917. Some say he died of a broken heart after being separated from his family for so long. (Courtesy of Sherry Martinelli.)

This 1902 picture shows the valley planted in grapes from the adjoining Butler Ranch to the hilltops on the other side of the valley. During Prohibition, the valley was called Still Valley, and Luisa Martinelli tried to fend off the federal government inspectors with her shotgun. Generally local winemakers were warned of an impending raid and would pay off the local sheriff; however, on one occasion, Gigi refused and spent some time in the county jail. The two new brides, Pia and Natalina, arrived from Italy and were horrified to find out their new mother-in-law had violated the law and was in jail. (Courtesy of Sherry Martinelli.)

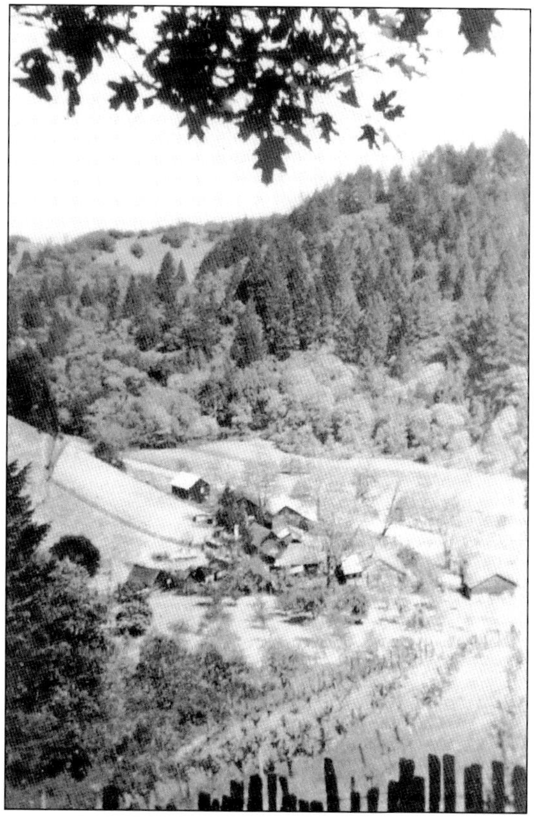

The Martinelli women did more than raise children and clean house. This picture is of Luisa baking bread in the Dutch oven, which was the custom among farm women in the area, as well as cutting wood and hunting deer, squirrels, and birds for food. Sons Bing and Fred ran the winery, and in later years young son Lino assisted with the vineyard and winery work. (Courtesy of Sherry Martinelli.)

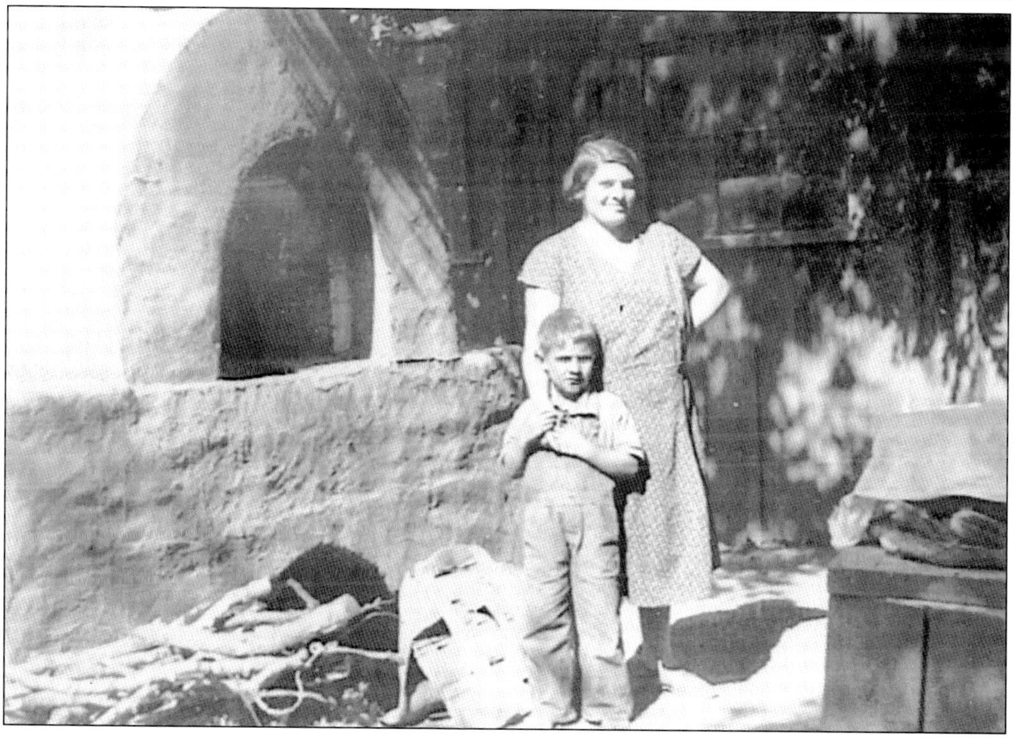

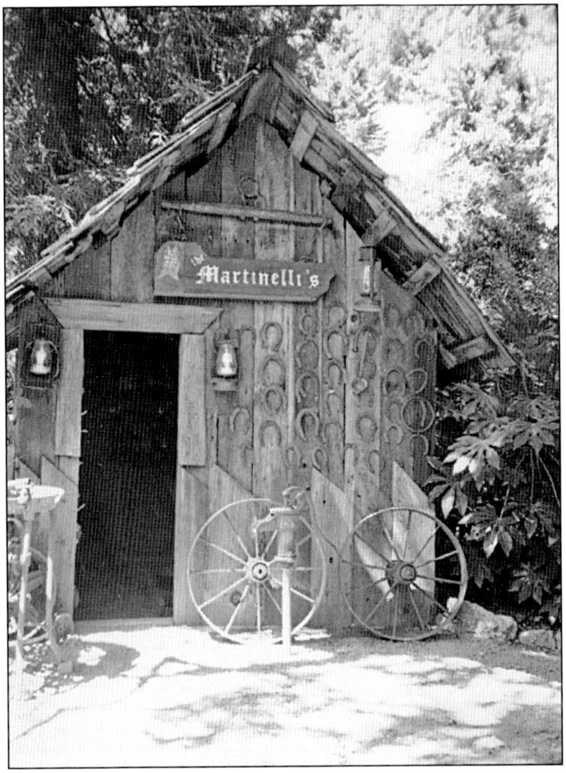

This shed houses the large grindstone wheel for sharpening farm tools. It still stands today. (Courtesy of Sherry Martinelli.)

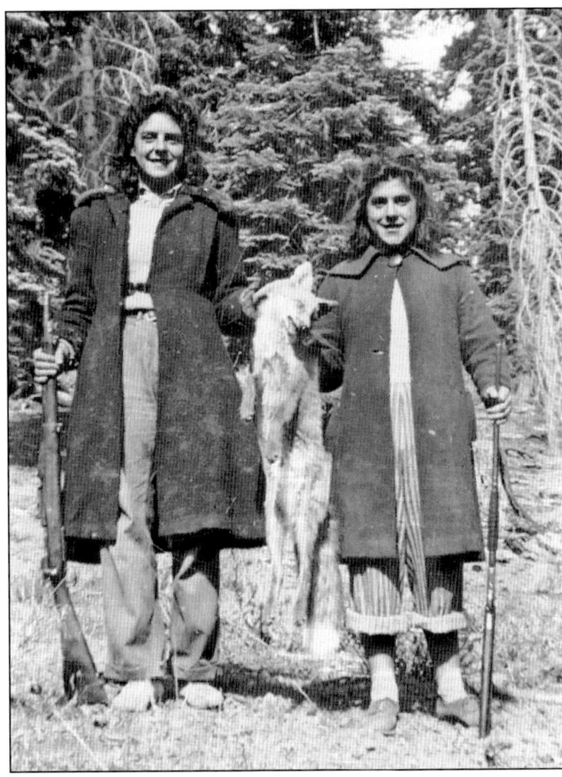

It looks like Eva Martinelli (left) and Mary Dagnello have just shot a fox. They were known to be good hunters. (Courtesy of Sherry Martinelli.)

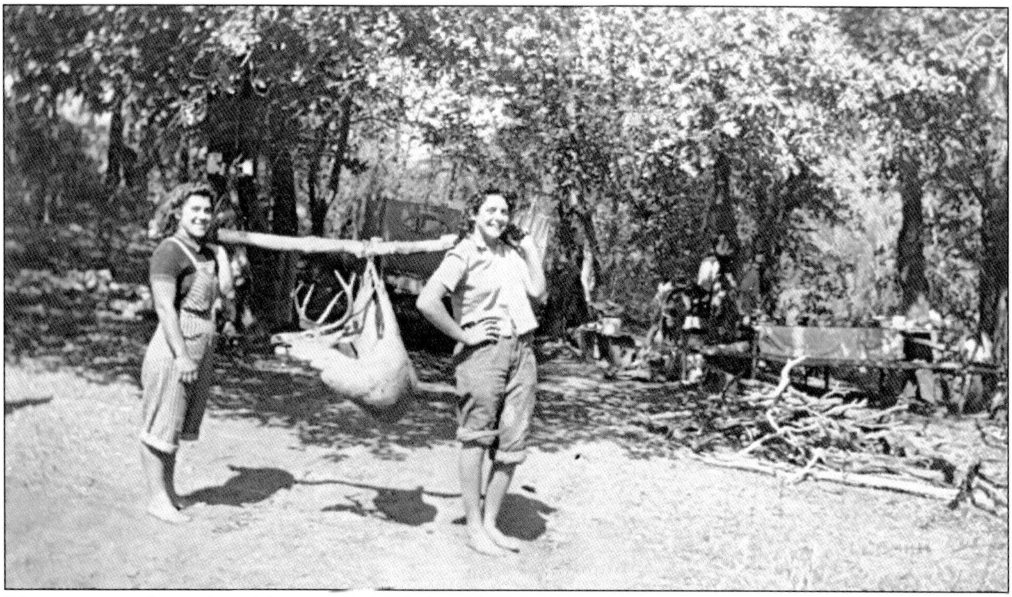

This picture shows Eva Martinelli (right) and Mary Dagnello on a family deer-hunting trip. The Martinelli women are very strong. Eva was a pioneer woman with many skills, such as carpentry, gardening, deer hunting, skin diving, and oil painting. (Courtesy of Sherry Martinelli.)

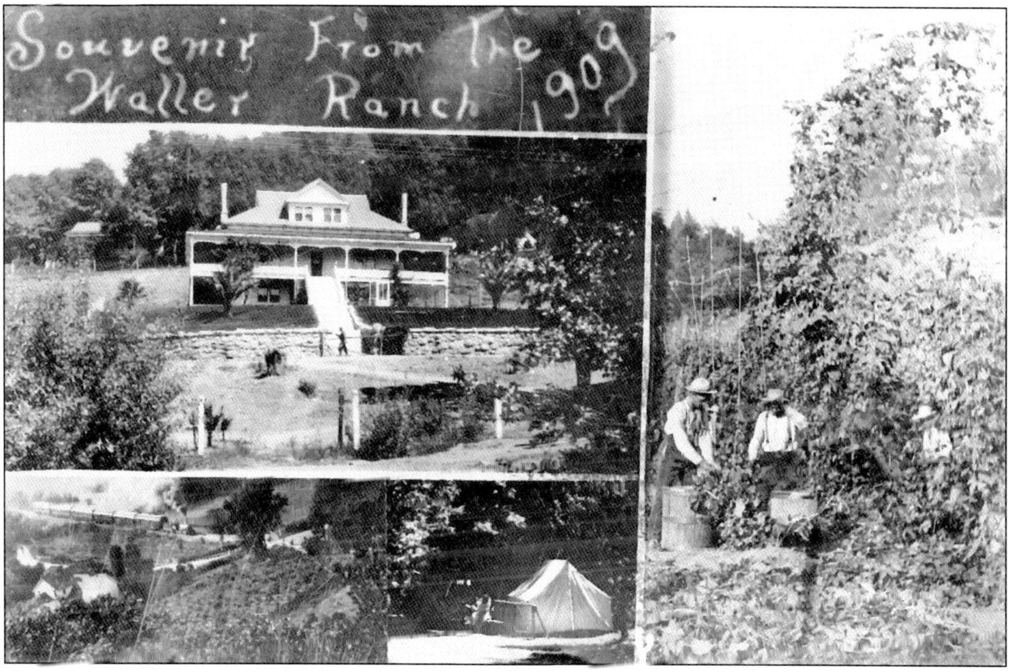

"Captain Cooper gave 1,500 acres of the El Molino land grant to each of his daughters, Anita and Amelia, for love," said Harry Lapham, the Sonoma County archivist who located these deeds during his 1982 county records search. Anita Cooper married Herman Wohler on September 29, 1859. They never had children to pass the Wohler Ranch on to. (Courtesy of the Dave Henry collection.)

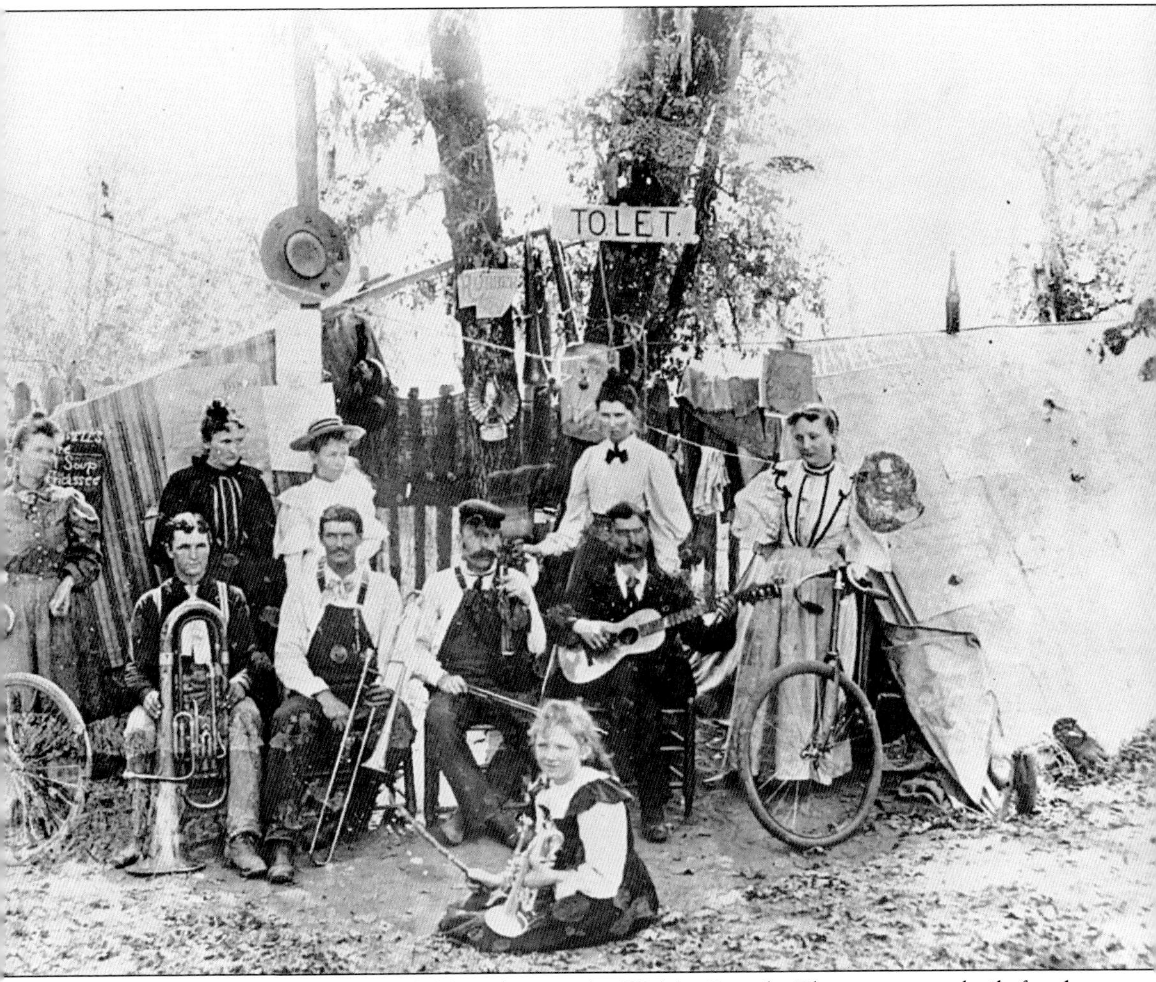

This band was playing for the field workers at the Wohler Ranch. The tents were built for the local pickers and new immigrant workers to live in during the harvest. Many new arrivals from as far away as Lucca, San Pellegrinetto, or Fornovolasco, Italy, came to pick and start a new life in America. Immigrants would work and save to buy their own land and start again. Many romances brought new families together listening to the music and staying in the tents. (Courtesy of Lavon Speer Covington.)

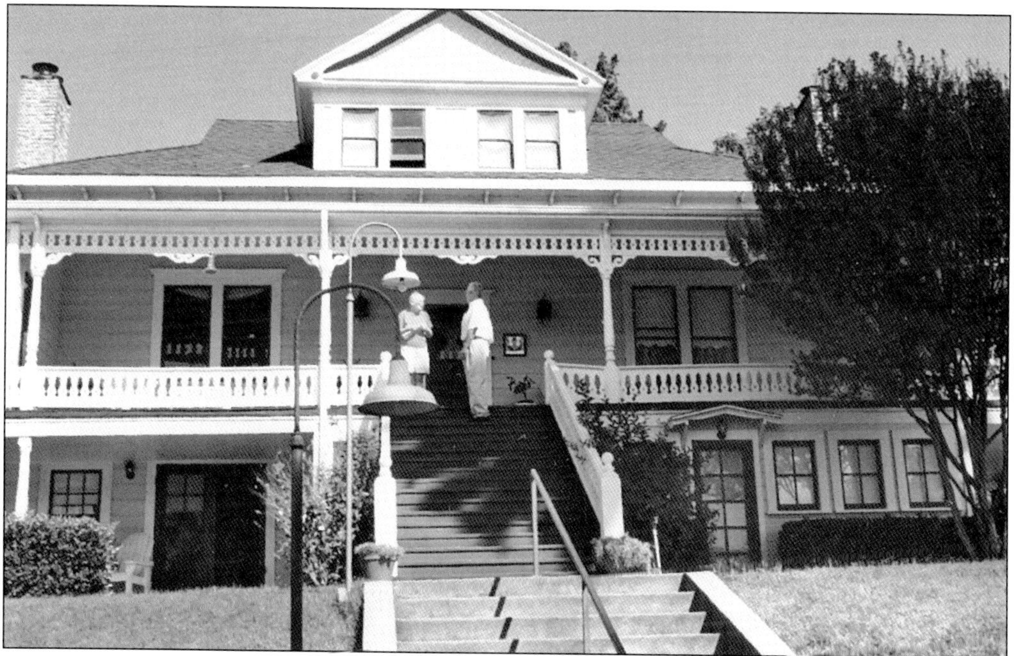

In the late 1900s, the Wohler Ranch was sold to Raford Peterson, and it continued to be a hop ranch until the late 1940s. The Raford House Inn, as it is known today, is used for a bed-and-breakfast, and the owners are Dane Pitcher and Rita Wells. The history of the house is amazing, being the biggest hop ranch in the county (some say in the California) and giving a new start in life to so many immigrants. (Courtesy of the Dave Henry collection.)

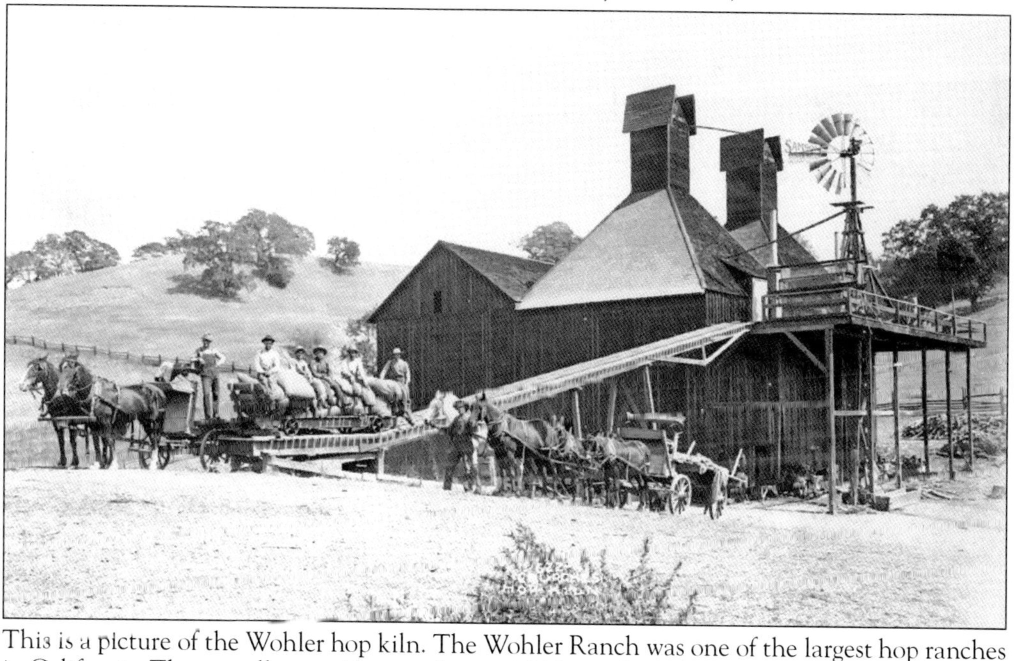

This is a picture of the Wohler hop kiln. The Wohler Ranch was one of the largest hop ranches in California. The payroll was said to total up to 1,000 people at the peak of harvest time. Raford Peterson held patents on a hop-picking machine, and he was the inventor of the first four-wheel drive, gasoline-powered tractor. (Courtesy of Frank Close.)

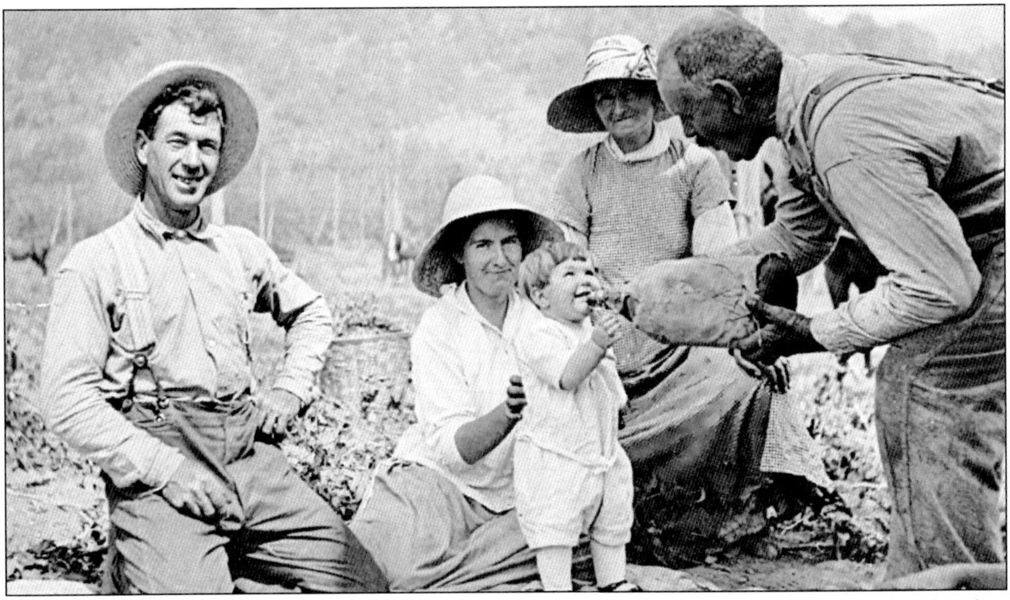

According to Virginia Van Keppel Hughes, "All through the 1900s, until the 1940s, many families spent the summer picking hops. They would camp nearby and work until the harvest was over. This picture was taken in the summer of 1916. Al Kimes is giving his granddaughter, Barbara Van Keppel (Wiebe), a drink of water from his burlap-covered jug while grandma Alice Kimes, mother Daisy, and father Cornelius Van Keppel looked on." (Courtesy of Virginia Van Keppel Hughes.)

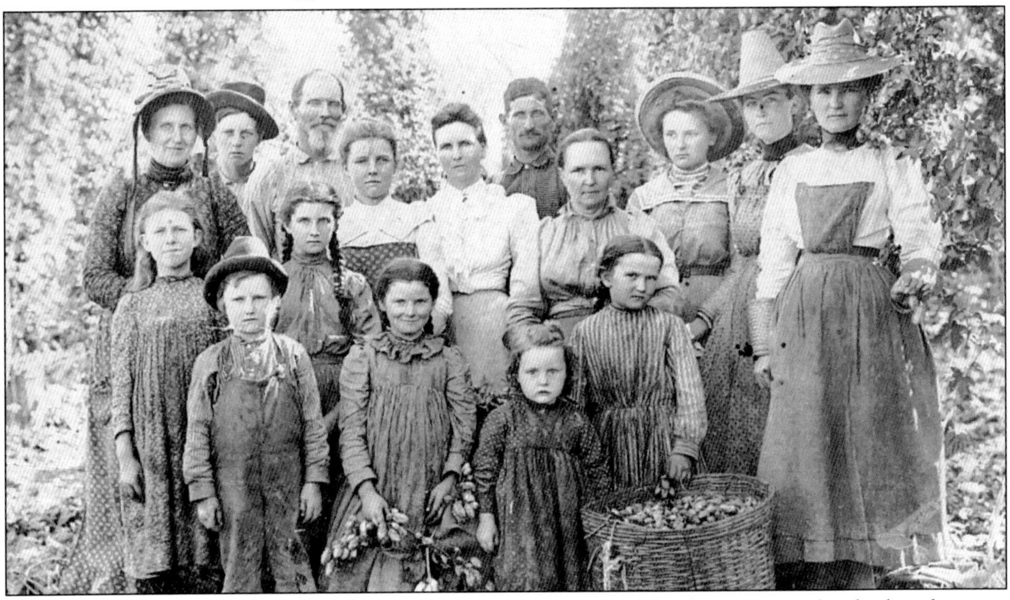

According to Ron Davis, "August 25th to September 15th was the short season for the hop harvest in West Sonoma County. The crew pictured here was mainly from two families, the Ross and the Coveys. The site of the harvest was the Weyhe Ranch located at the end of Ross Station Road and now the site of the Iron Horse Vineyards. Pictured are (from left to right, first row) unidentified, Mabel Ross (Abshire), unidentified, and Ada Ross (Yeager); (everybody behind the first row who can be identified) Sylva Ross (Douglas), Amanda Covey Ross, Ella Covey Ward, Tommy Ross, Alfred Ross, Hattie Ross Covey, and Lena Covey Estes." (Courtesy of the Ron Davis collection.)

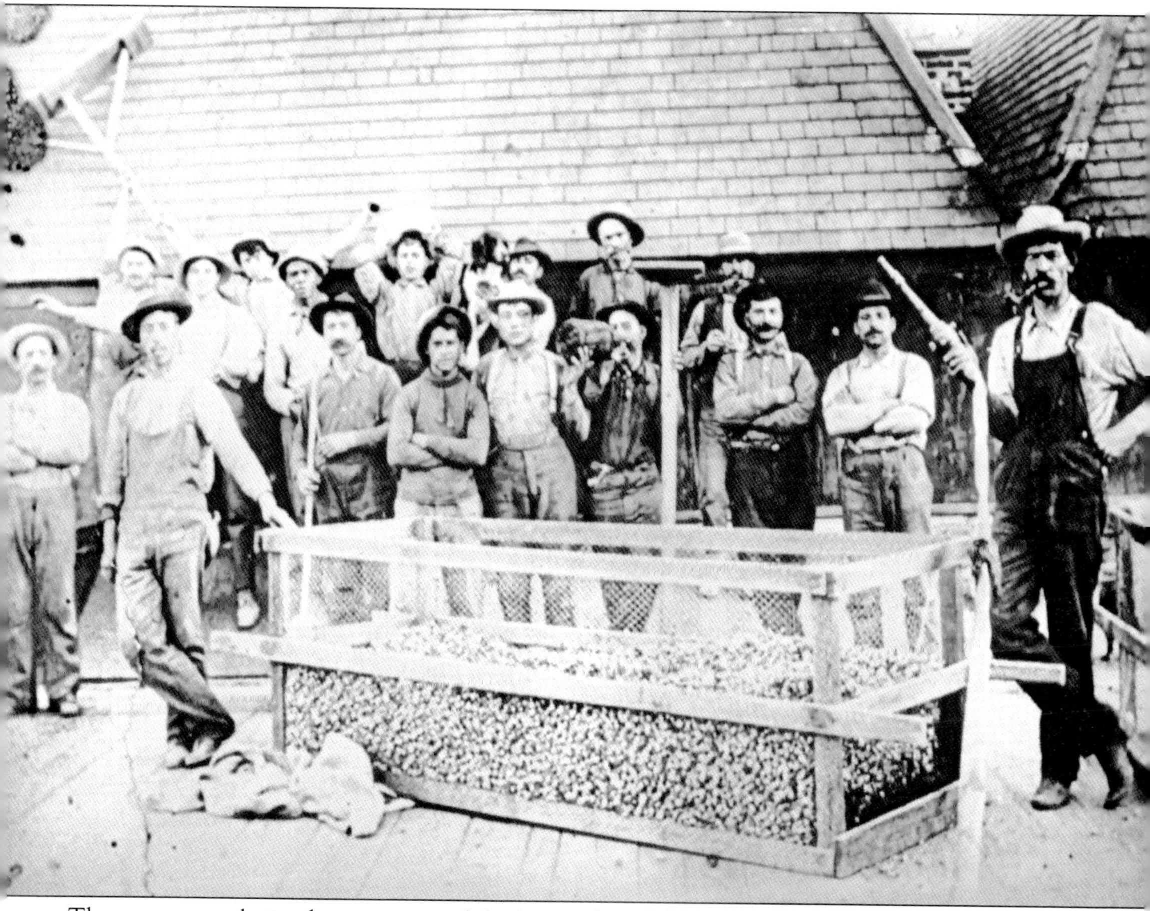

These men are drying hops on one of the largest hop fields in California, the Wohler Ranch. Pictured here from left to right are (first row) John Belotti, Cossimo Cinquini (hand on hop bin), Fernando Corsi, George Williams, Aristo Pelletti (lifting the jug), "Pupilo," unidentified, Dan Bertozzi, and Pio Cinquini in a jaunty pose; (second row) unidentified, Giuseppe Magri, Dick Cecchi (with broom), unidentified, Cesare Magri, Mariano Giannechini, Pietro Pelletti, and Dump Faudré. (Courtesy of Bob Aldridge.)

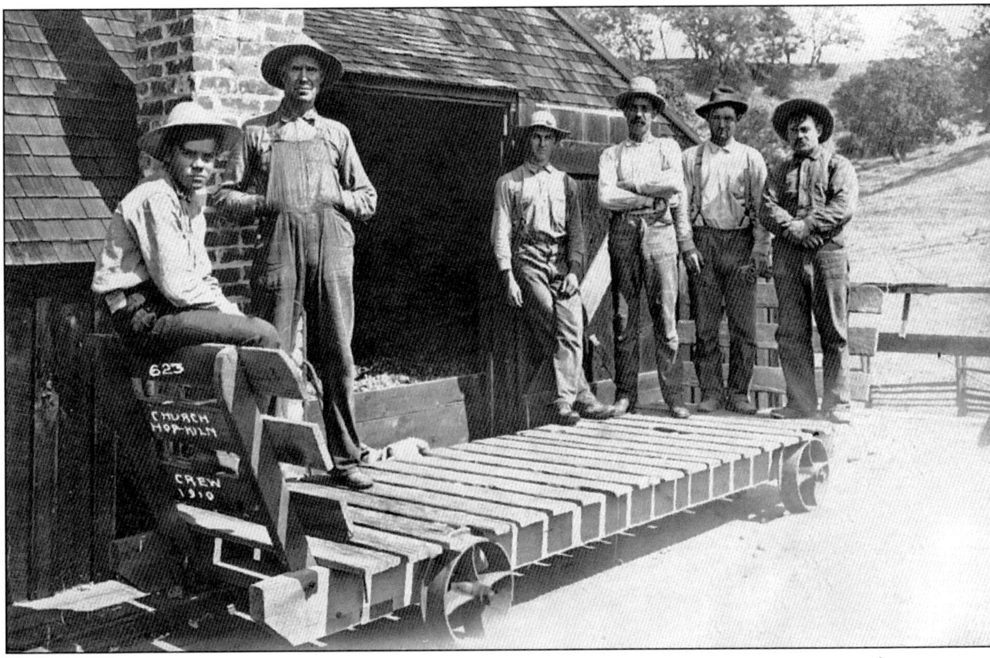

Over time, many farmers decided to grow hops because it was a profitable business. This is a picture of the Church hop kiln. This shows the crew of workers in 1910. (Courtesy of the Forestville Historical Society.)

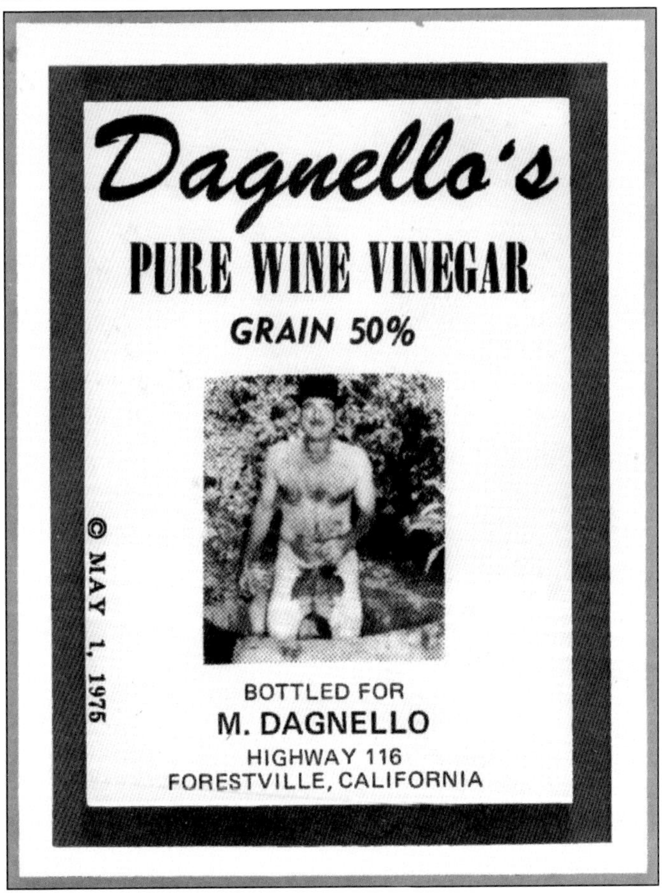

In 1975, Mondo Dagnello had his Dagnello's Pure Wine Vinegar Company on Highway 116. He had a wonderful sense of humor, as can be seen here with the old black derby hat he always wore and wearing nothing but a fig leaf. He surely sold lots of vinegar with this innovative label. (Forestville Historical Society.)

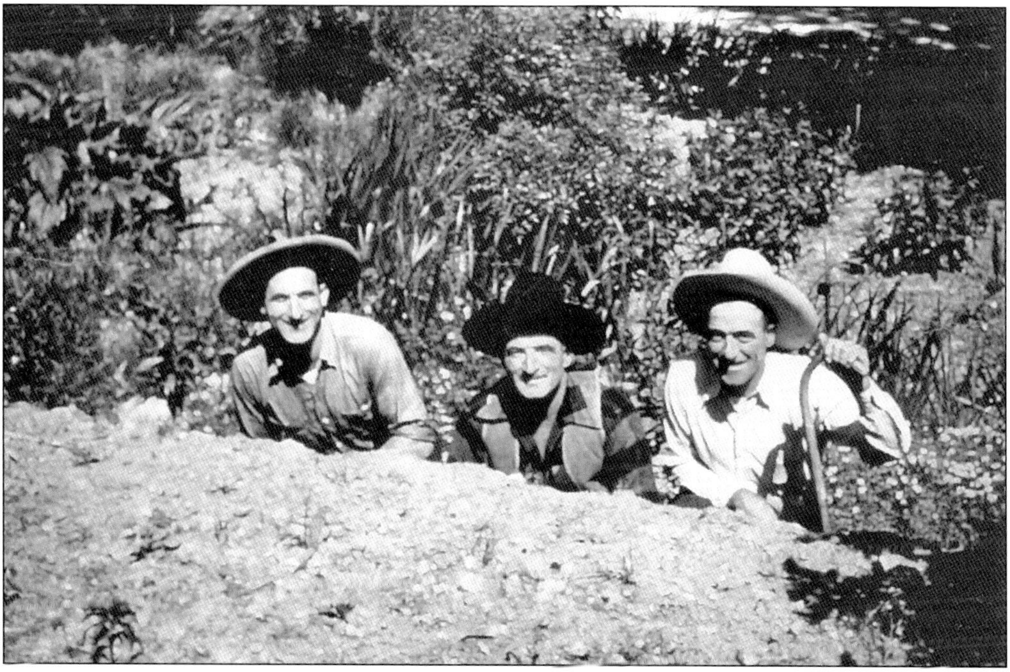

Mondo Dagnello and his brothers help build Santa Nella Winery. He later opened a store called Dagnello's Shady Rest Store in Pocket Canyon. (Courtesy of Gary Harris.)

Mondo Dagnello was born on May 17, 1916, at Cosmo Heights Station just above the Hacienda Bridge. He attended the Mountain View School and had many stories about growing up during Prohibition with his 12 brothers and sisters. This picture shows him at work, busy with his profession. He was quite a character. In later life he used to call the Forestville Club his office. (Courtesy of Gary Harris.)

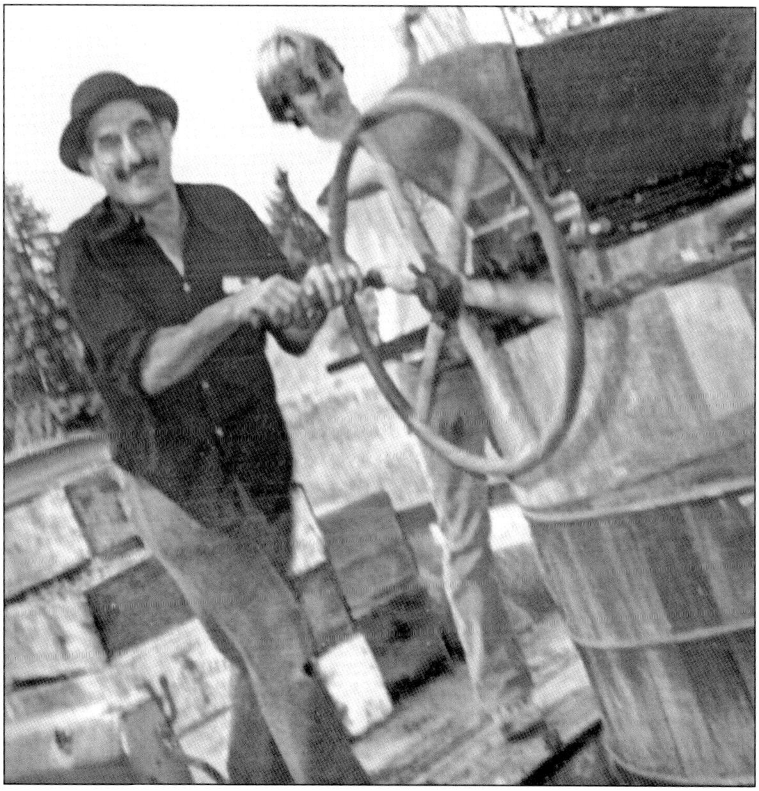

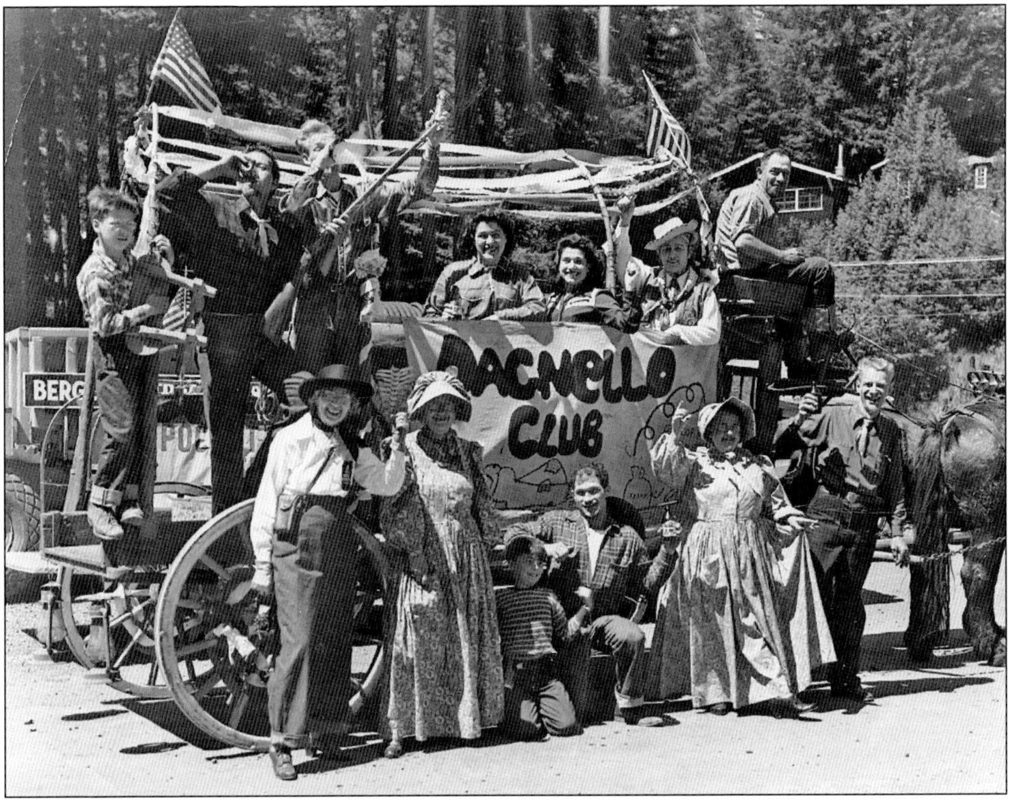

Mondo Dagnello always had lots of friends, and they are all together at the Stump Town Day's parade with a float for his tavern, the Dagnello Club, which was located across the street from the Santa Nella Winery. (Courtesy of Gary Harris.)

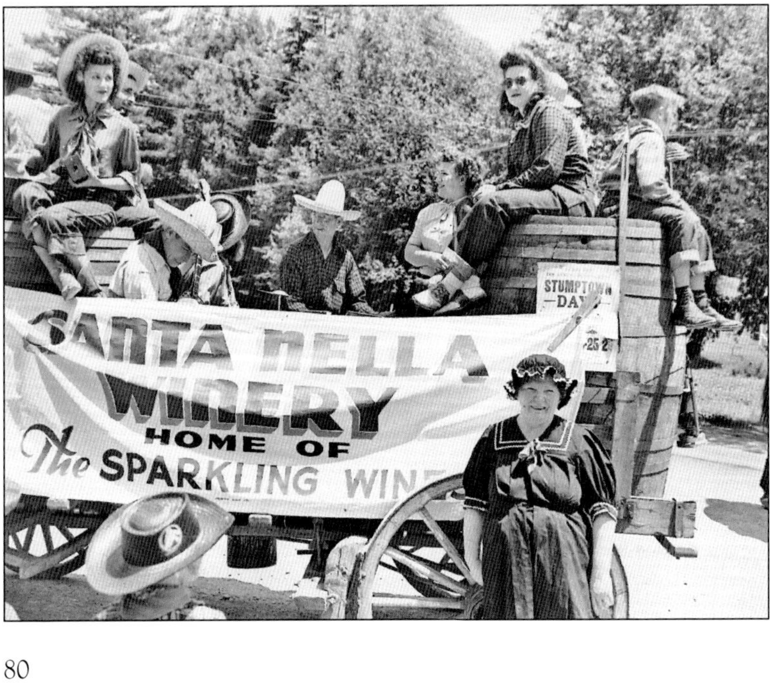

Santa Nella Winery was started in the late 1880s by Joseph Prosek. It had many owners, but in 1954 it was bought by the Korbel Winery. This picture was taken at the Stump Town Day's parade and from left to right above the banner are Iris Speer, Rose, Mary Dagnello, and Silvio Albergi (in the middle) playing his drums. (Courtesy of Lavon Speer Covington.)

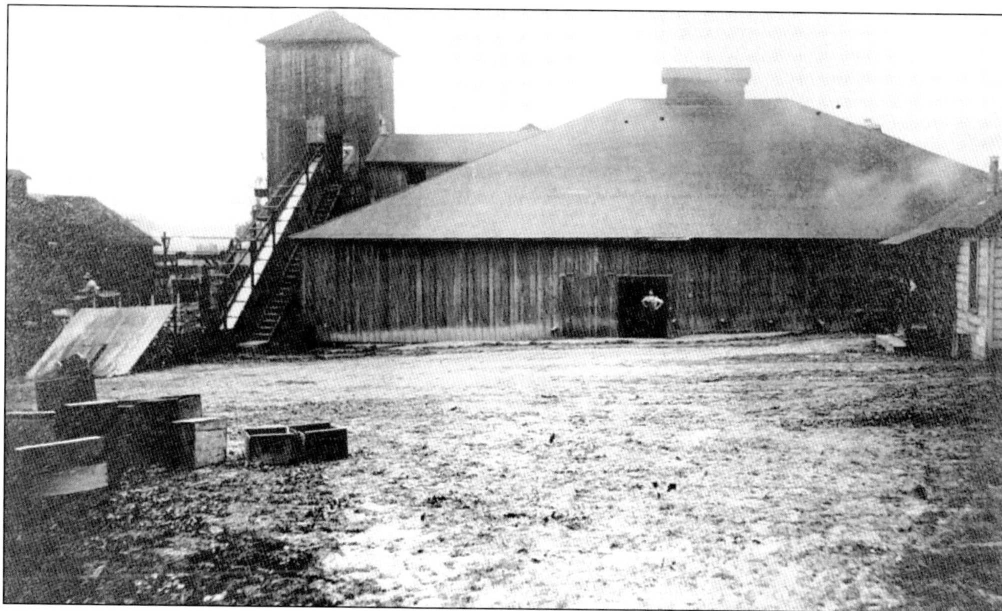

Charles Lehn arrived in Forestville in 1867 and went into partnership with Captain Cooper growing a vineyard and two acres of orchard. Captain Cooper selected mission vines, and Lehn operated the vineyard until a while after the death of Captain Cooper. In 1872, he built a winery with a capacity of 80,000 gallons of wine. His son William Lehn took over the winery in later years. During the 1906 earthquake, Billy Lehn said they lost 100,000 gallons of wine in their two wineries. H. Meranda wrote that part of the wine ran into the creek, and their bull was on a bender from drinking so much of it. This winery later became the Petri Winery and later the Electro Vector Company. (Courtesy of the Dave Henry collection.)

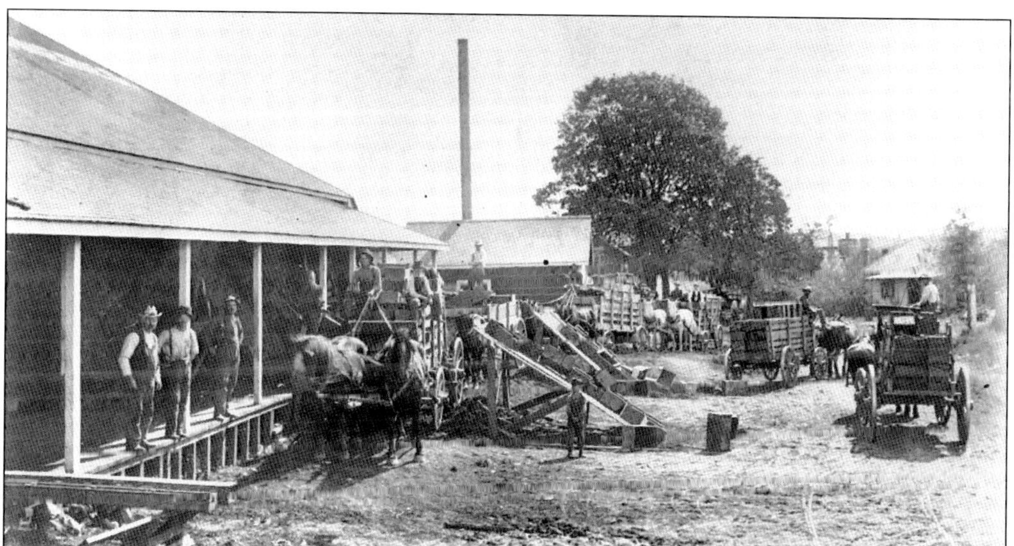

Many fine wines must have passed through the Trenton Winery. This area continues to be one of the best wine areas of Sonoma County. Unfortunately, the winery burned down after this picture was taken. (Courtesy of the Dave Henry collection.)

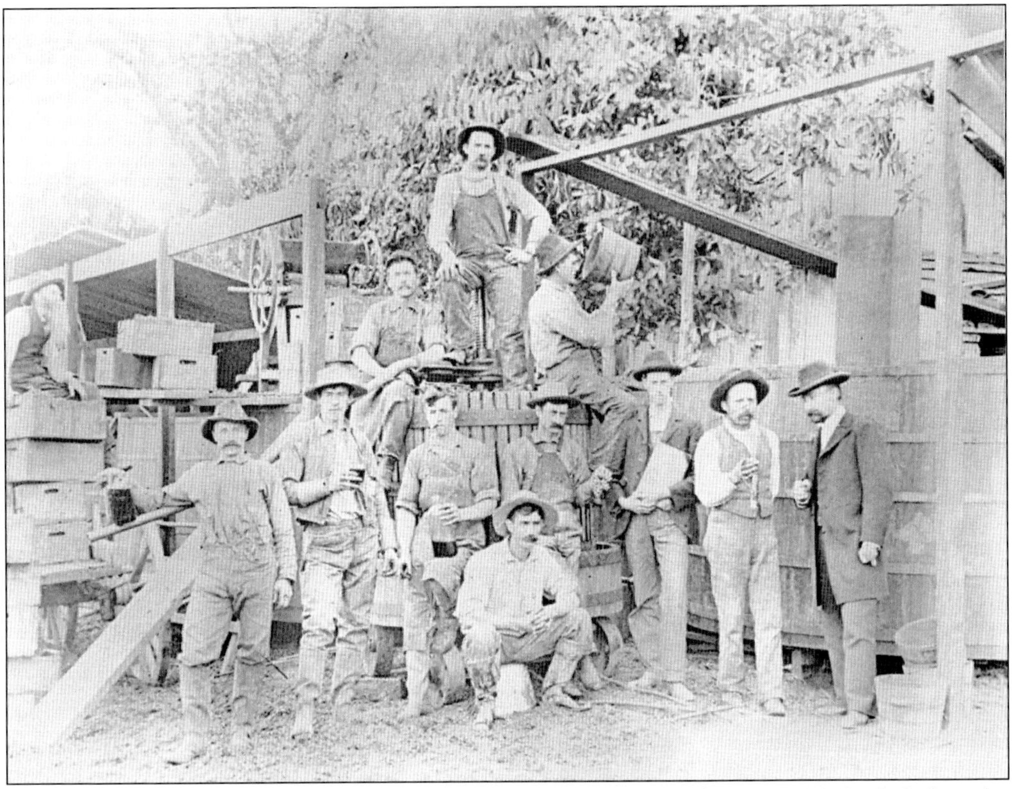

Dr. Mathey was busy with making wine when this picture was taken in 1890. Included in the shot are Bert Marley, Press Marley, Bill Anderson, Tom Norton, Jake Holms, Dr. Mathey, and Milliard Barnes (seated). (Courtesy of the Bob Aldridge collection.)

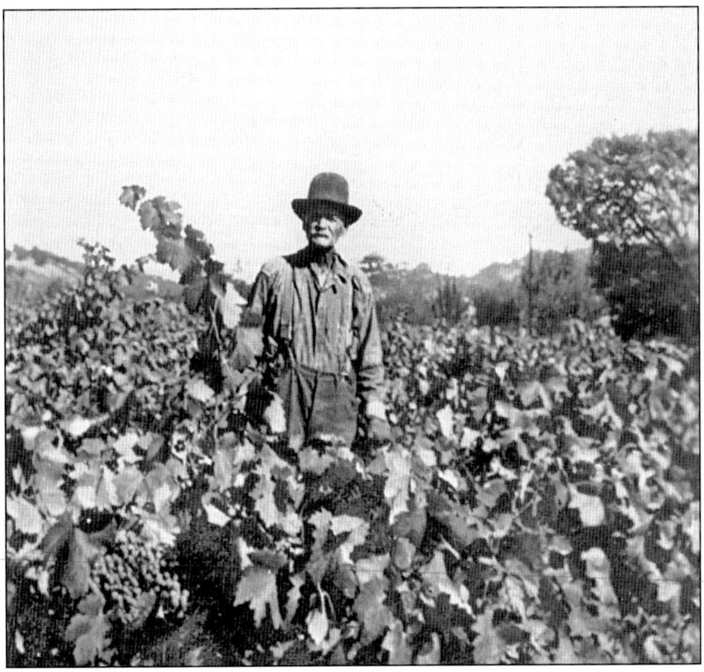

This is a picture of Martino Fava in his vineyard. After he and his brother left their home in Italy and settled in the Russian River Valley, they bought 40 acres with a view of Mount St. Helena. They started a mother barrel for vinegar in 1919 and another in 1925 that Marcucci Farms still uses today. (Courtesy of Phil Marcucci.)

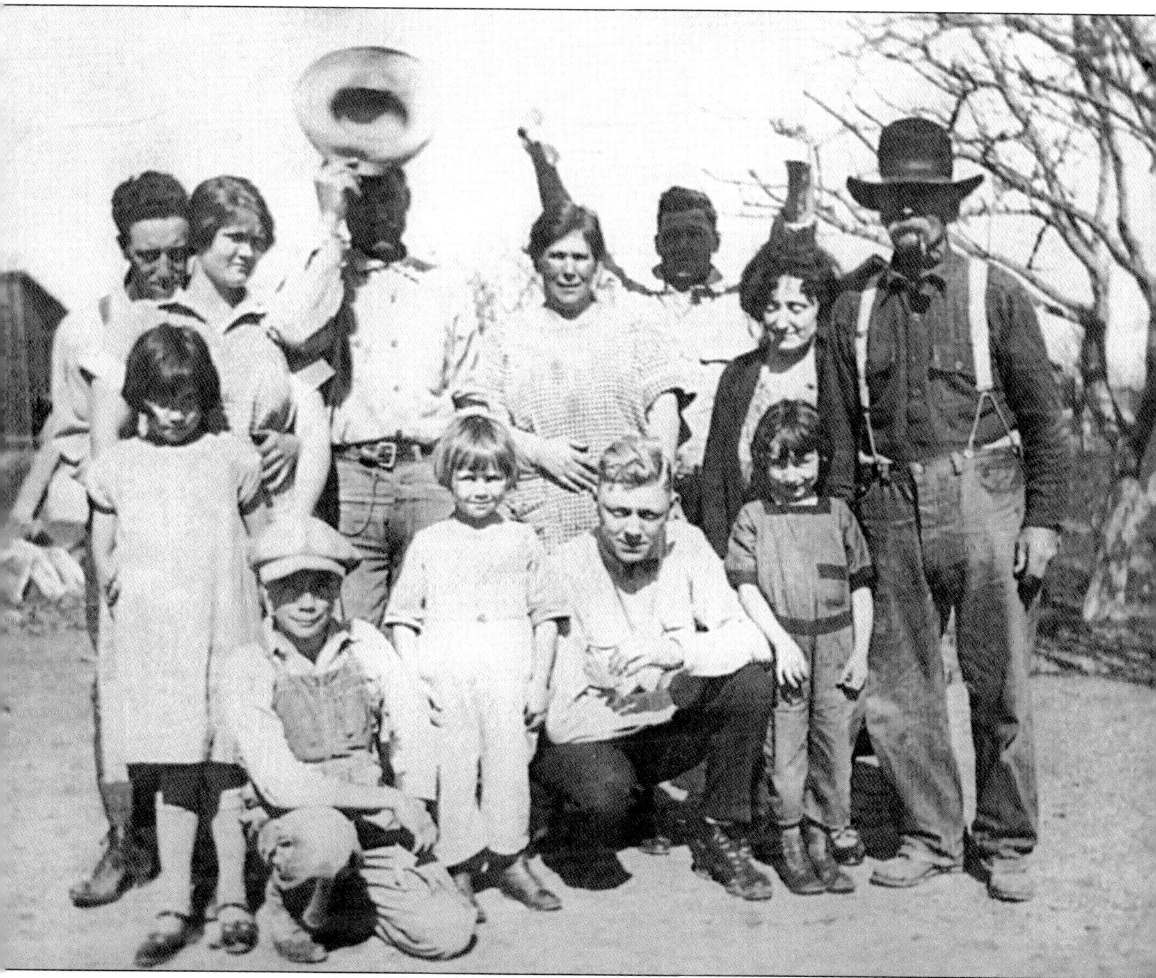

Martino and Larenzo Fava sailed around Cape Horn from Lucca, Italy, to San Francisco in the early 1880s and settled in the Trenton area of Forestville. In 1907, they had their first grape harvest. Today Phil Marcucci, great-grandson to Martino Fava and his family, continue the tradition of growing fine grapes for wine and vinegar. Pictured here are, from left to right, (first row) Verna Papera (daughter of Victor and Lala, granddaughter to Martino Fava), Angelo Fava (son of Angelina and Lorenzo Fava), Susie Fava (daughter of Angelina and Lorenzo Fava), unidentified man, and unidentified child; (second row) Victor Papera (son-in-law to Martino Fava), Lala Papera (daughter to Martino Fava, wife of Victor Papera), Lorenzo Fava (brother to Martino Fava), Angelina Fava (wife of Lorenzo Fava), unidentified man, unidentified woman, and Martino Fava (father to Lala Papera, brother of Lorenzo Fava). (Courtesy of Phil Marcucci.)

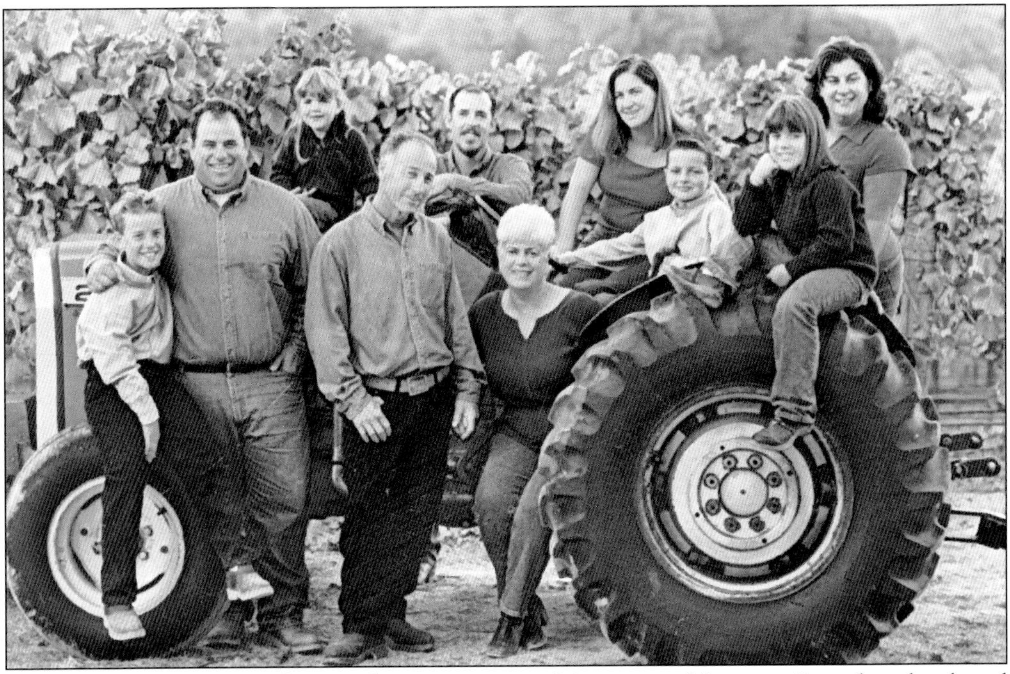

What began as a dream of two Italian immigrants, Martino and Lorenzo Fava, has developed into the Marcucci Farms and Fava Brothers Vineyard, run by Phil Marcucci and family. Seen here from left to right, the family is (first row) Nicholas Avilla, grandson; Matt Avilla, son-in-law; Phil Marcucci, husband; Cheri Marcucci, wife of Phil; Jake Petersen, grandson; and Haley Avilla, granddaughter; (second row) Amanda Petersen, granddaughter; Jeffery Petersen, son-in-law; Jackie Petersen, daughter; and Stephanie Avilla, daughter. (Courtesy of Cheri Marcucci.)

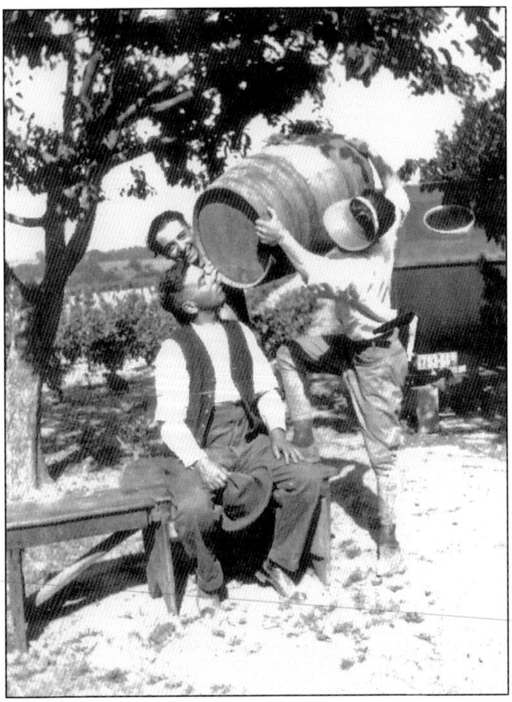

According to Phil Marcucci, "During the 1920s Prohibition years, all alcohol sales were stopped by the BATF [Federal Bureau of Alcohol, Tobacco, and Firearms] but most European families applied for a special permit from the BATF, which allowed them to make up to 200 gallons of wine. Most wineries during this time became very creative with their sales." (Courtesy of Phil Marcucci.)

Five

SAVING SOULS

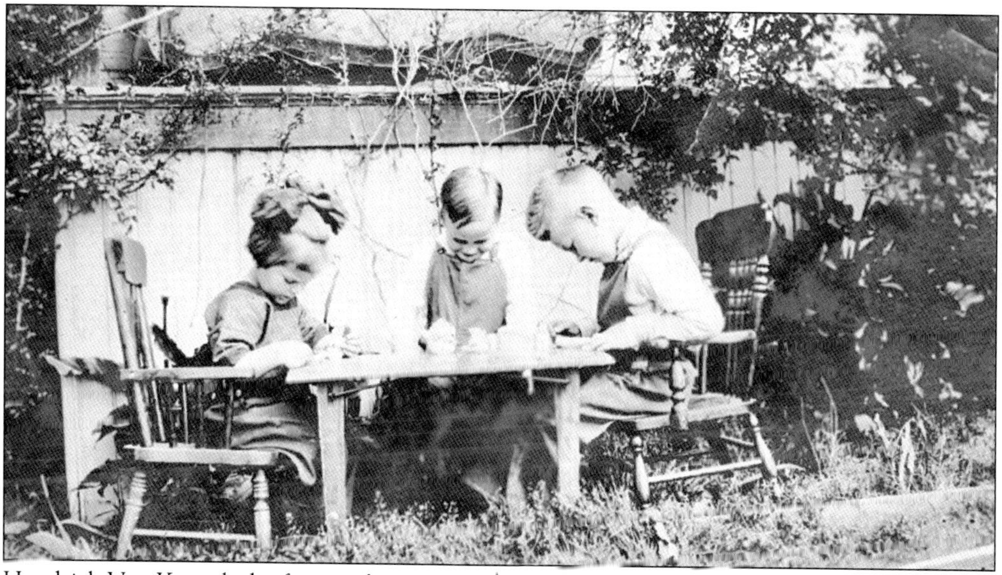

Hendrick Van Keppel, the famous furniture maker; his sister, Alice Van Keppel; and a neighbor boy are saying their prayers before lunch. The Van Keppel children were Seventh Day Adventists who attended church in Sebastopol. This was after the Adventist church closed in 1878. Hendrick and Alice were born in 1914 and 1916, respectively. The picture was taken in front of the John Van Keppel home on Van Keppel Road. (Courtesy of Virginia Van Keppel Hughes.)

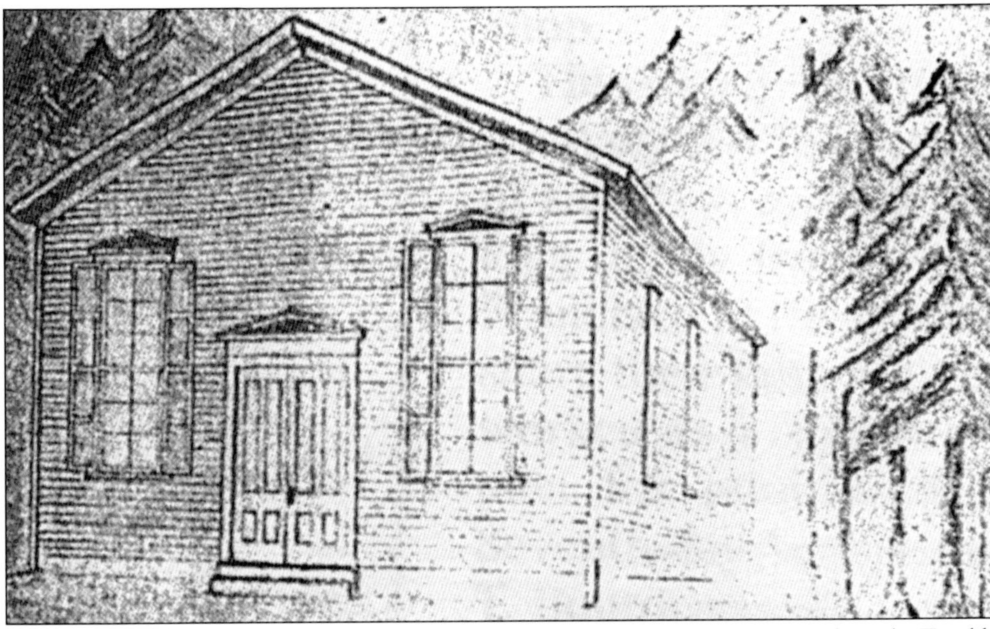

The Green Valley Seventh-Day Adventist Church was built on the property across from the Terrible T and next to Mom's Apple Pie. It was the second Adventist church built in California. William Tommy Ross and Sarepta Ross were regular attendees of the church. Tommy Ross writes of Ellen G. White (the founder of the Seventh-Day Adventist Church) speaking to the congregation twice. The church was only in existence for eight years when the congregation moved to Sebastopol. The property was later sold to J. W. Bramham. (Courtesy of Dave Bramham.)

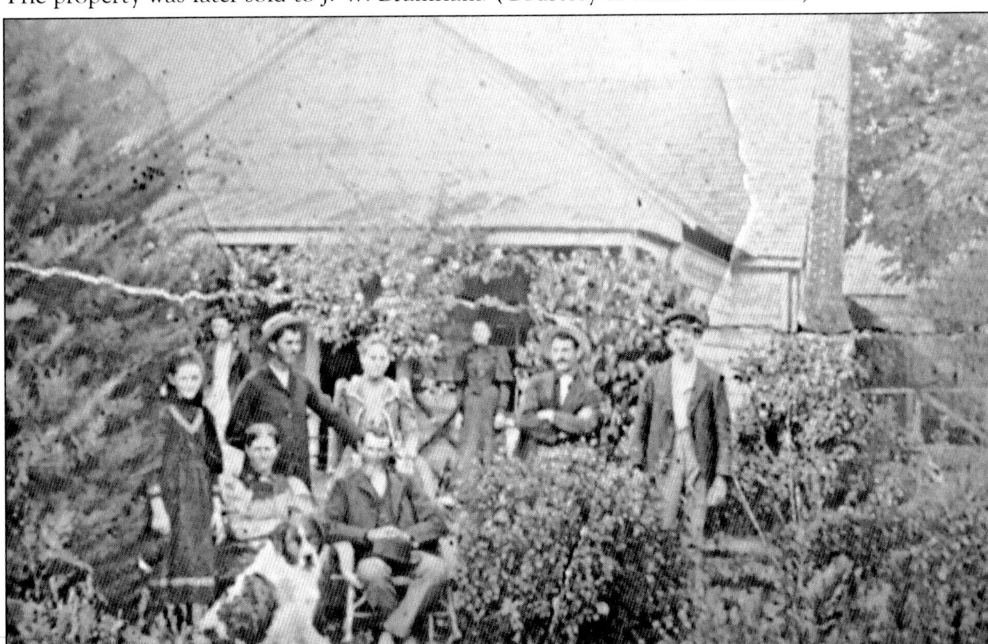

In his journal, William Tommy Ross wrote that he and Sarepta Ross went to the Green Valley Seventh-Day Adventist Church almost every day. Many speakers who came from far away stayed at their ranch house before ministering at the church. (Courtesy of the Dave Henry collection.)

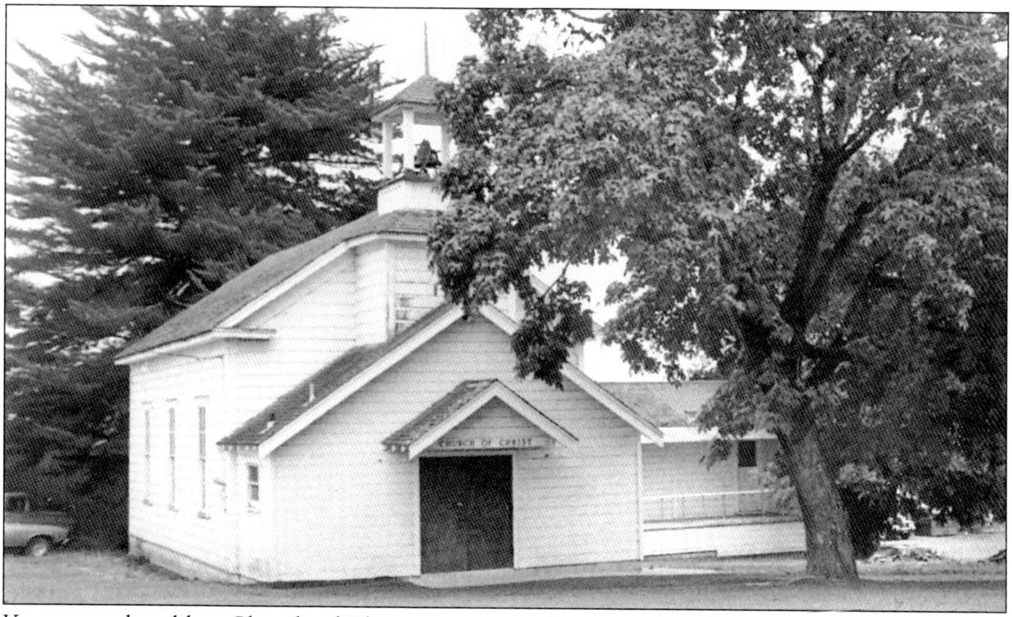

Known as the oldest Church of Christ in western America, this church was established out of the Restoration Movement in 1873, with James Logan preaching at the Redwood School until the church could be built. In 1879, George and Mary Schaumberg donated a lot on which to build. Uriah and Sarah Covey donated the lumber to build the first church. During the 121st anniversary of the congregation, the three living elders, Ross Yeager, Matthew Smith, and Noble Rogers, were in attendance. (Courtesy of the Dave Henry collection.)

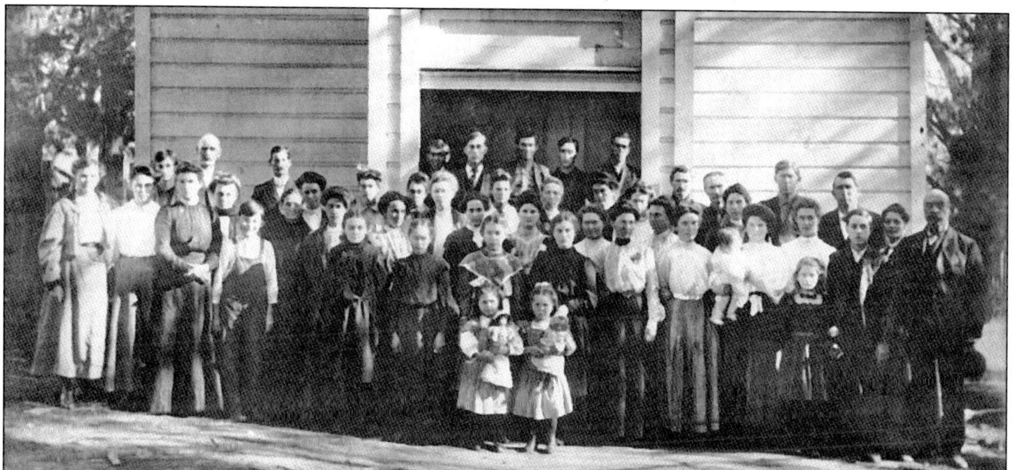

This picture of the Church of Christ was taken in 1908. Included in this image are (from left to ight, in front) Zola Covey and Helen Evans holding their dolls; (everyone behind them who can be identified) Myrtle Evans, Clara Smith, Amanda Covey Ross, Bill Green, Delecia Davis, Ralph Elder, Ruby Evans, Ada Ross, Lizzie Powell, Lee Covey, Mabel Ross holding Eunice Ross as an infant, Lu Donna Love, Clyde Burnett, John Given, Kenneth Ross, Bertine Mulkey, Dorah Davis, Ruth Parnell, Sylvia Davis, Elsie Peterson, Sylva Ross, Vern Evans, Lizzie Powell, Nellie Ross, Maggie Given, Mrs. Earnest Love, Benjamin Franklin Flesher, Alfred Ross, Jessie Parnell, Mandy Davis, Nola Davis, Ollie Fouts, Settie Fouts, Maude Bacon, Allie Fouts, Harmon Covey, Jake Fouts, minister Earnest C. Love, Dell Davis, and George Davis. (Courtesy of the Ron Davis Collection.)

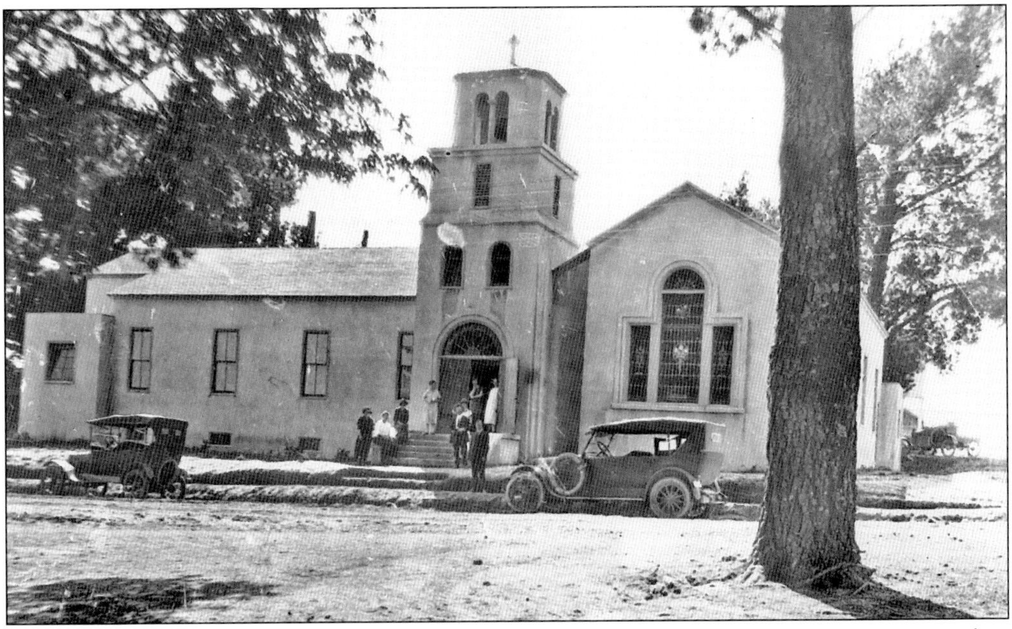

When the Forestville Methodist Church built a new home, it took from 1924 until 1929 to complete it. In 1929, before the Great Depression, many church members were worried about being able to pay back the money borrowed to build the new church because of crop damages to local farmers. James L. Case, the treasurer and retired minister of the Methodist church, sent letters to many wealthy philanthropists across the country, two of which were the Rockefeller foundation and JCPenney. Case's effort was not in vain, as several sent donations. The church building cost an estimated $12,250, but the architect, R. S. Tuttle, only charged $125 for his work. R. Livingston Wolfe was the church pastor during the dedication in 1924. Prior to the establishment of a fire department, the town used the church bell to warn of a fire. (Courtesy of Hal Wood and Verna Case Tischer.)

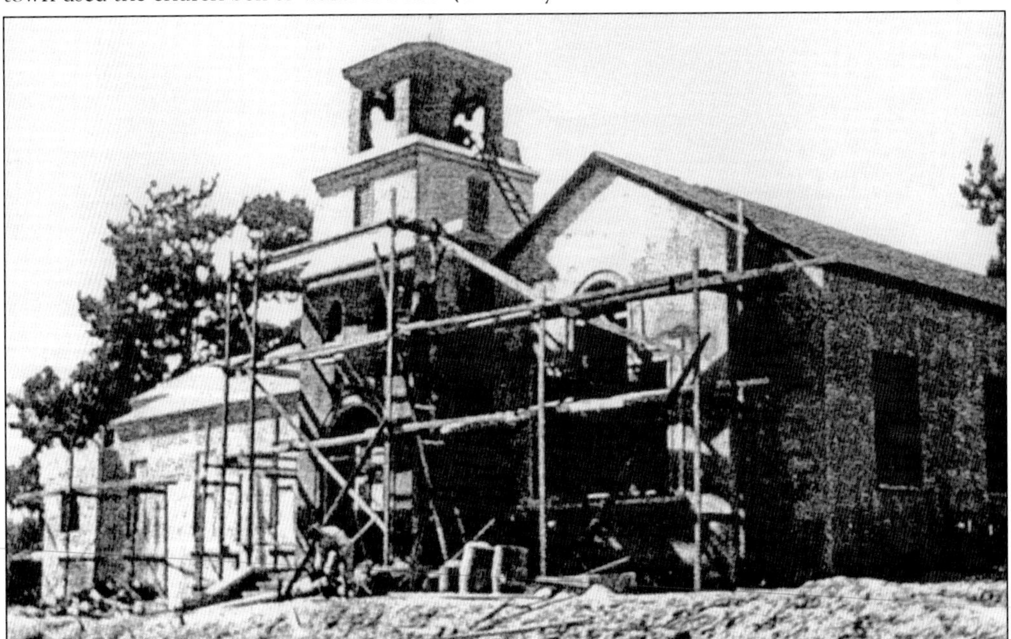

Six

Training Minds

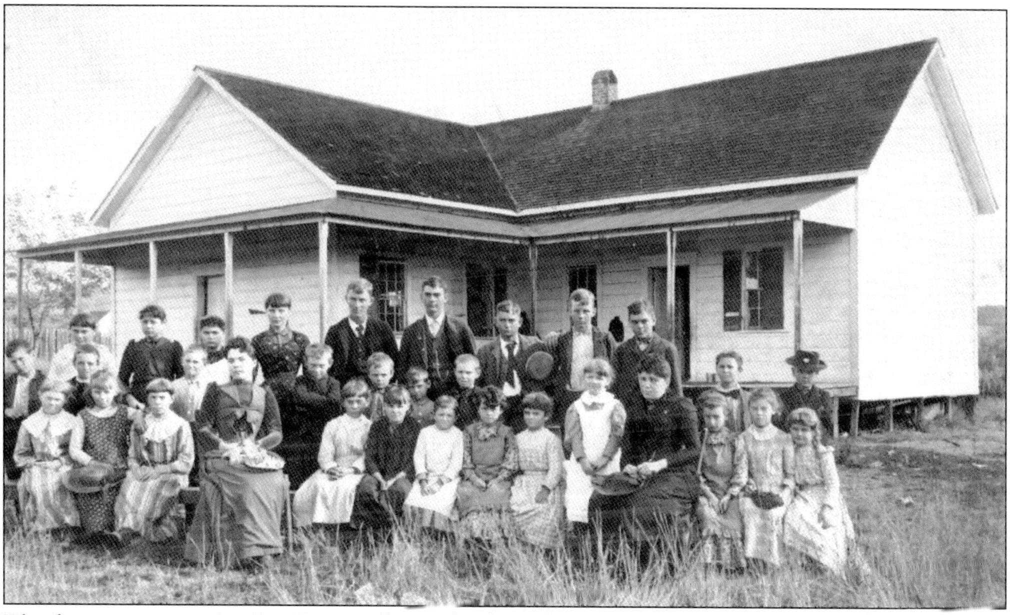

The first grammar school in Forestville was built in the 1890s and was called the Redwood School or Harbine School. The school stood behind the present-day Forestville Elementary School, close to Travis Road. The teacher was Eva Kennedy. The tallest student standing in the back row (fourth from right) is Francis (Frank) William Jewett. The teacher and student married on Christmas Day 1894. Kennedy was born September 10, 1870, and Jewett's birthday was on May 9, 1871; it made for a good town story during this era. (Courtesy of the Dave Henry collection.)

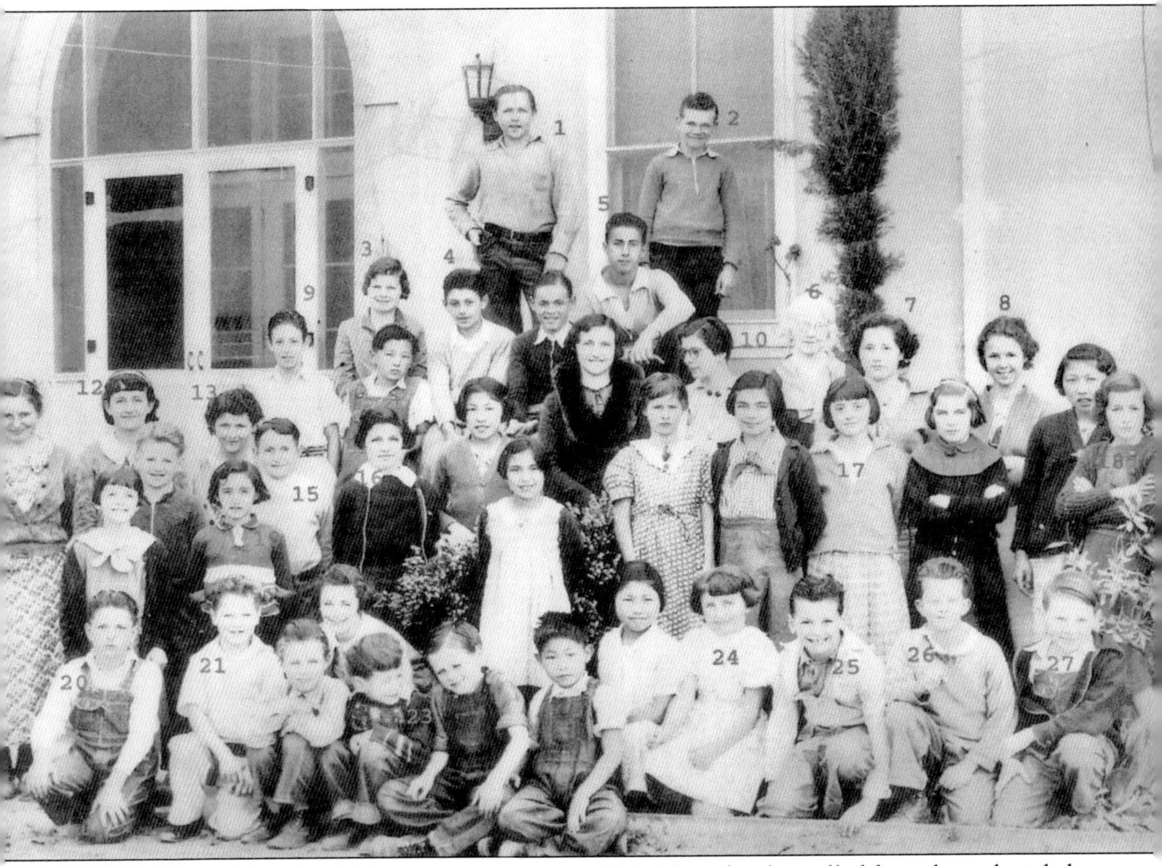

This picture of the Vine Hill School was taken in 1937. The school enrolled first- through eighth-grade students. Starting in numerological order are: (1) Roy Mefford, (2) Hugh Ingle, (3) Richard Vannucci, (4) Virginia Calvert, (5) Orval Bacci, (6) Miss Fondehn (the teacher), (7) Eva Albiani, (8) Sue Fava, (9) Lloyd Papera, (10) Miss Parsons (teacher), (11) Thelma Bertolucci, (12) Algia Bertolucci, (13) Adeline Frati, (14) Cliff Calvert, (15) Pat Bertolucci, (16) Evely Vellutini, (17) Anita Vannucci, (19) Evelyn Taveras, (20) Robert Papera, (22) Lorraine Pelletti, (23) Raymond Oliver, (24) Theadora Bertolucci, (25) Bob Entzminger, (26) Vernon Shaw, and (27) Calvert. The people without numbers are unknown. (Courtesy of Phil Marcucci.)

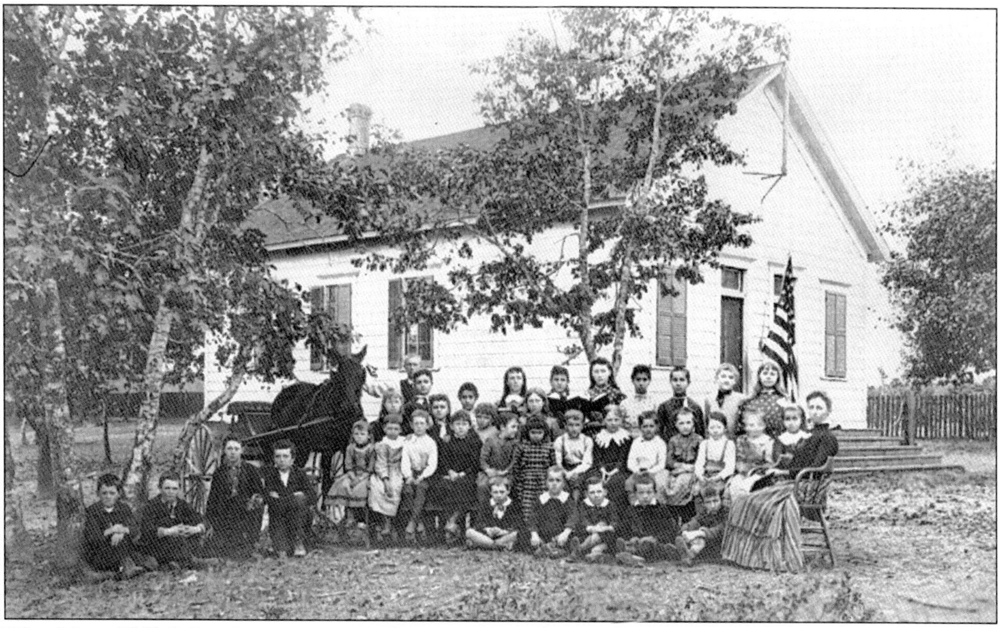

This Vine Hill School picture was taken c. 1891. The teacher was Mrs. Wells, and some of the students seen are Frank Vannucci, Albert Elmore, Bay Elmore, Harry Surryhne, Lizzy Surryhne, Josie Pilkington, Elva LeMay, Chet Pitkin, Alice Griffith, Guy Griffith, ? Ramos, ? Easter, and ? Matos. (Courtesy of Bernice Yeager.)

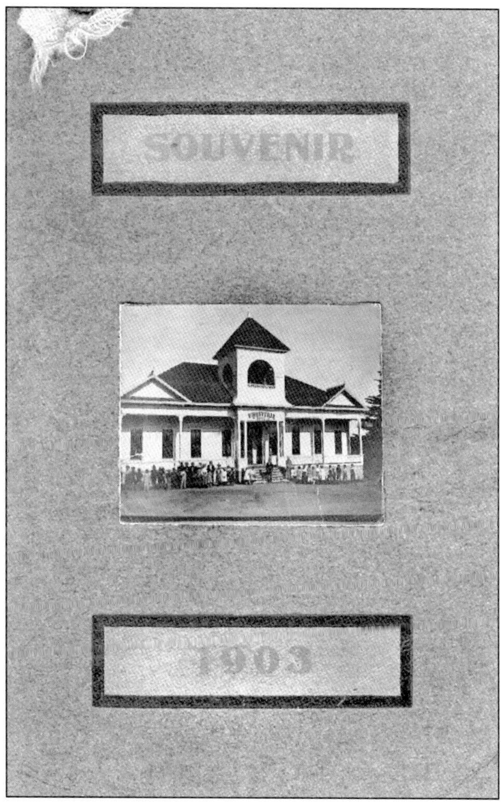

F. G. Kelly was the Forestville School principal during the 1902–1903 school year. Several people have saved these treasured memories of their years at Forestville School. (Courtesy of the Dave Henry collection.)

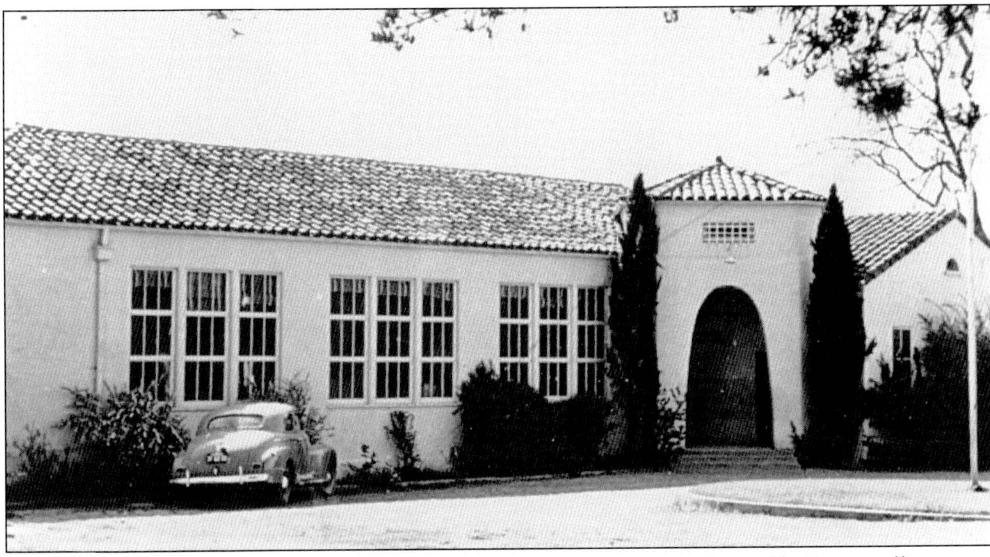

In December 1934, after the school had burned down, a cooperative formed by Forestville citizens rebuilt it. From starting the cooperative to finishing the school, the total time was about one year. (Courtesy of the Dave Henry collection.)

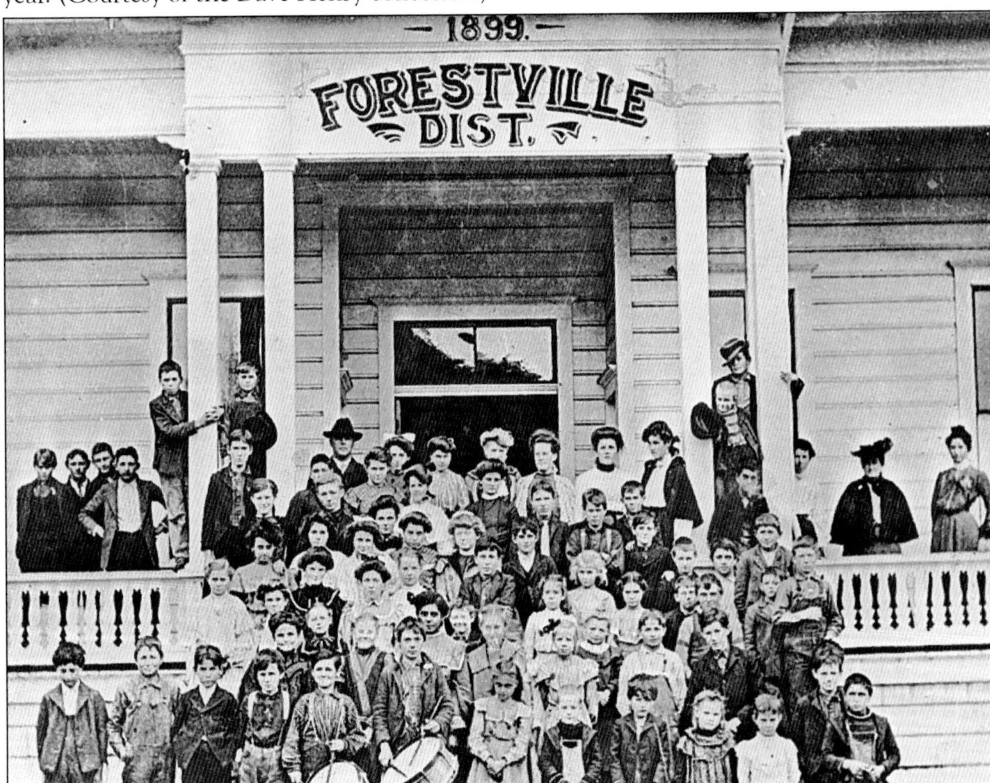

In this 1904 Forestville school picture, Burton Travis said his mother is on the extreme right with a cape and hat. Mrs. Worth, the lady to Travis's right with the black hat, is the teacher. Ed Kimes is in the back with a hat. (Courtesy of the Dave Henry collection.)

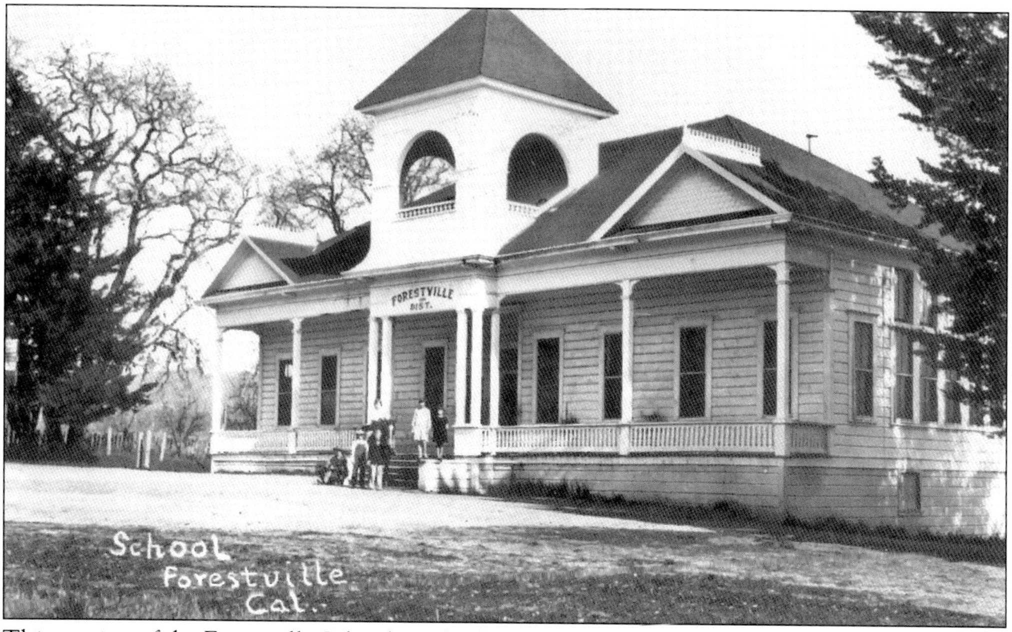

This version of the Forestville School was built in 1899 and burned in 1933. The old bell couldn't be found after the fire. Warren Templeman remembers his grandmother, Linda Bushnell, telling about how the Native American children always left school during lunch recess. One day they followed the children and found them eating acorns under a tree. The mystery was solved—they were just enjoying the food of their heritage. (Courtesy of the Dave Henry collection.)

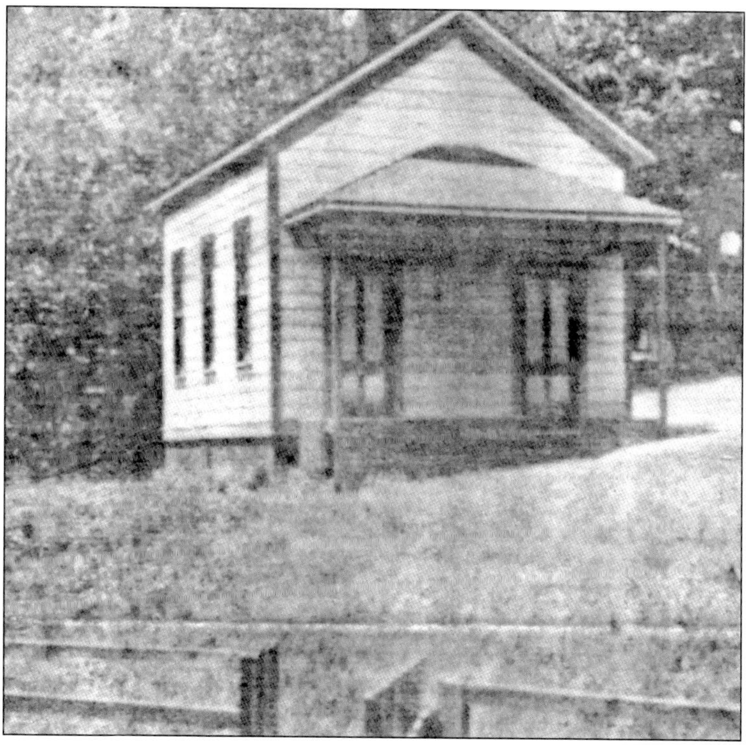

Merrit School was located in the hills above Mirabel Park, a one-room schoolhouse serving first grade though eighth. The teacher was Beulah Miller Lance. She lived in Fulton but took the train to Mirabel, where she lived during the weekday at the Hamilton Litton home. The date the school was built is unknown, but Eda Giusti attended in 1893, and it merged with Forestville school in 1924. (Courtesy of the Dave Henry collection.)

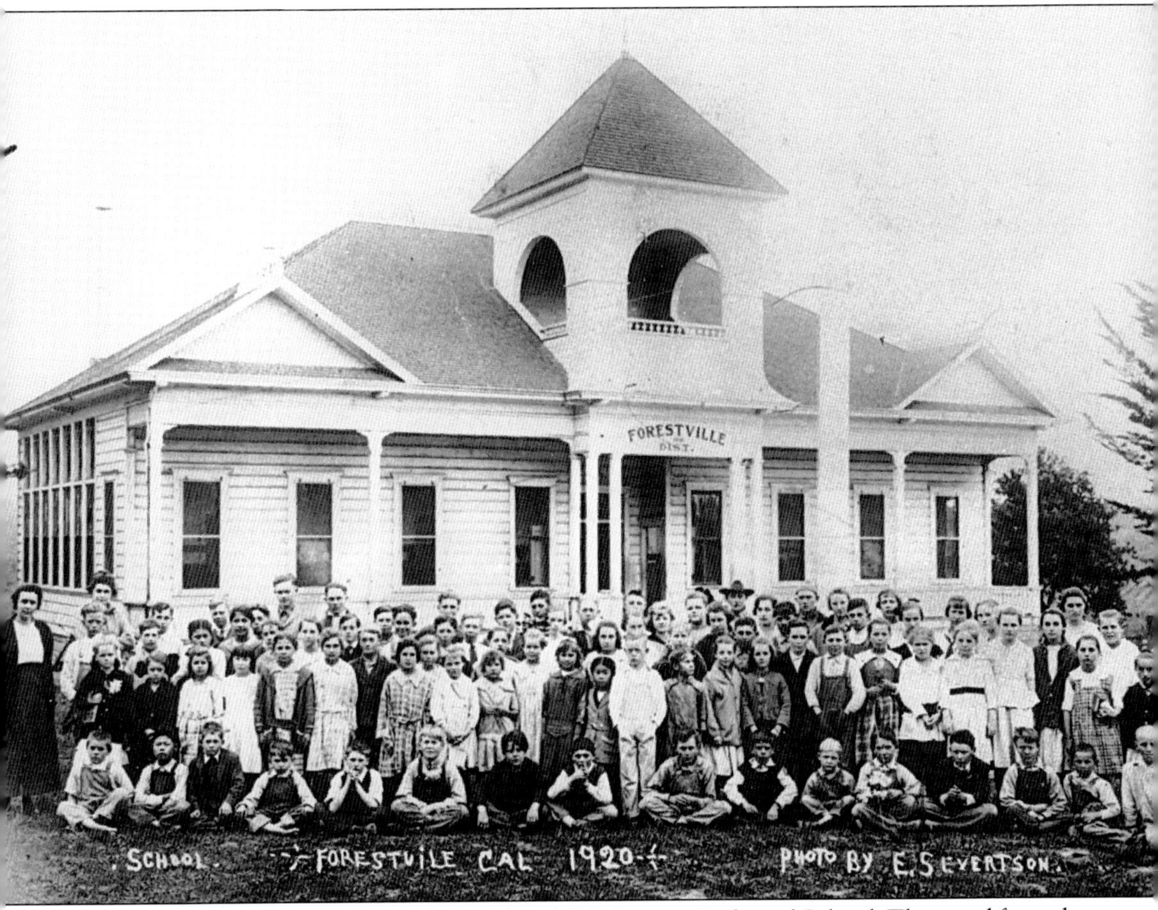

This school was built in 1899, replacing the old Harbine or Redwood School. The wood from the old schoolhouse was sold and used to build a barn on the Evans place, which was just across from Mirabel Road on the hill overlooking the town. This version of the Forestville School burned to the ground in 1934. People who attended the school in those years remembered going to the Methodist church for classes until a new school could be built. Most of the work in rebuilding the school during those Depression years was done by the Forestville Construction Association, which was created and made up of citizens of Forestville to save money and help unemployment. (Courtesy of Bob Aldridge collection.)

Seven

WHEELS AND RAILS

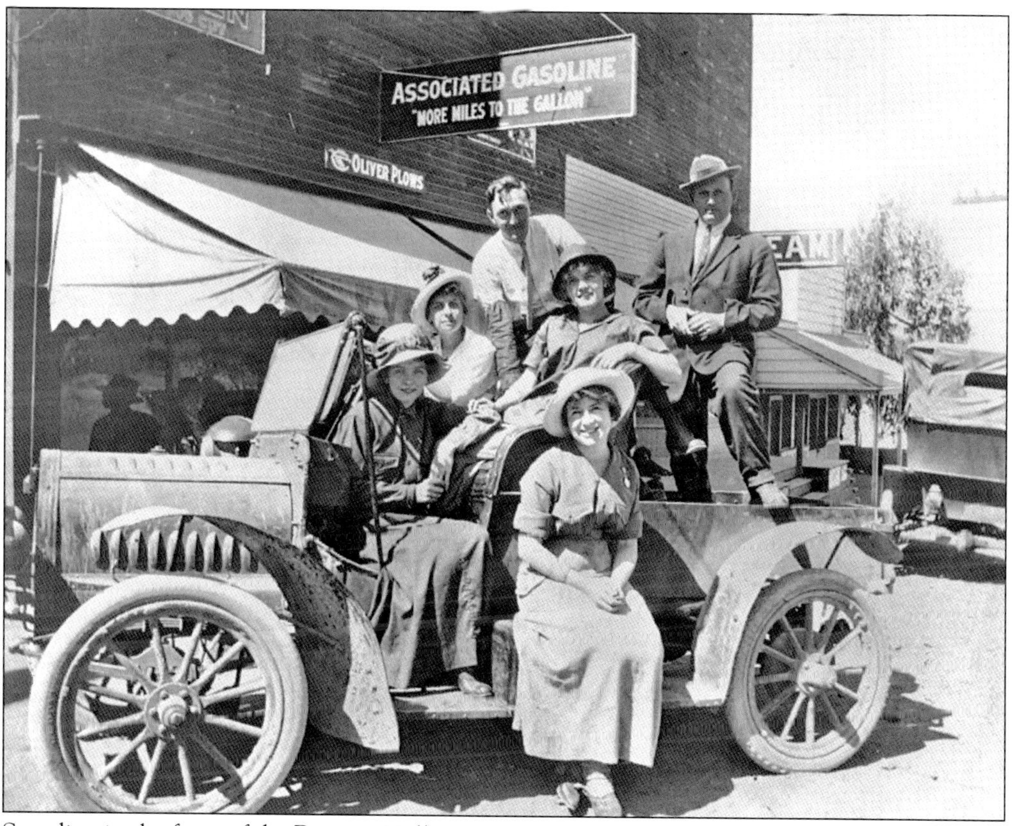

Standing in the front of the Dinucci Hall in a Rambler (probably about a 1909 model) are Archie Hull (left) and L. D. Yeager (right). (Courtesy of Ross Yeager.)

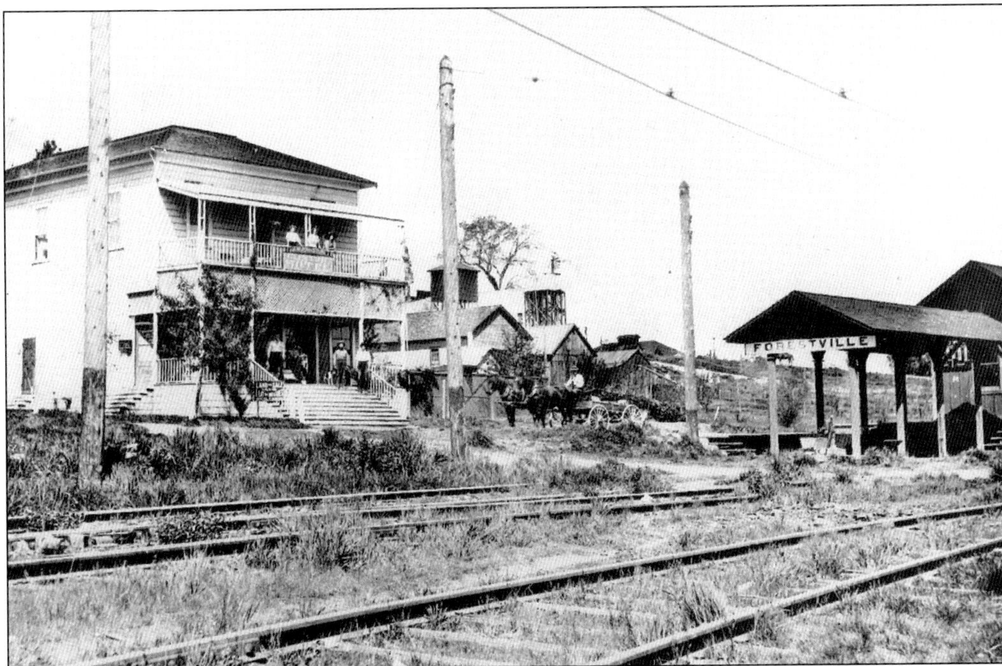

This hotel was originally the Johnson Hotel, located near where Carr's Drive In is located today. After the move, it was named the Electric Hotel, because it was across the street from the Petaluma and Santa Rosa Electric Railway Station. The P&SR Electric Railway was incorporated in 1903. (Courtesy of Lavon Speer Covington.)

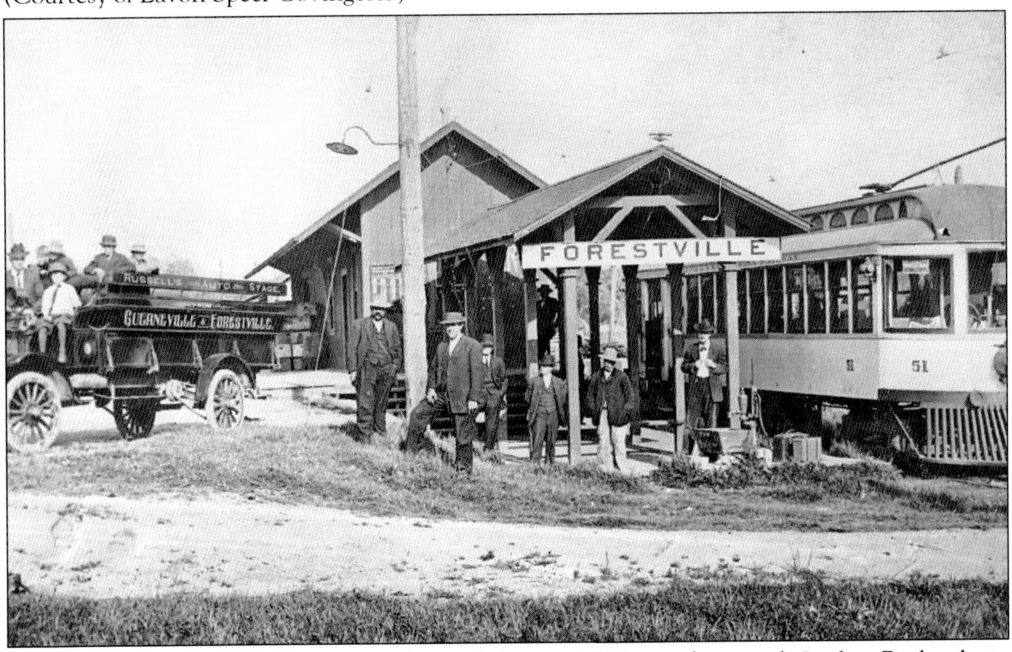

The P&SR Railway was started by John and George McNear, along with Luther Burbank, in order to ship fruit. A train carried the fruit from the farmland to the Petaluma River, where it was loaded on steamer ships to be taken as far away as the horn of South America. Forestville was the terminus of the P&SR Railway. (Courtesy of the Dave Henry collection.)

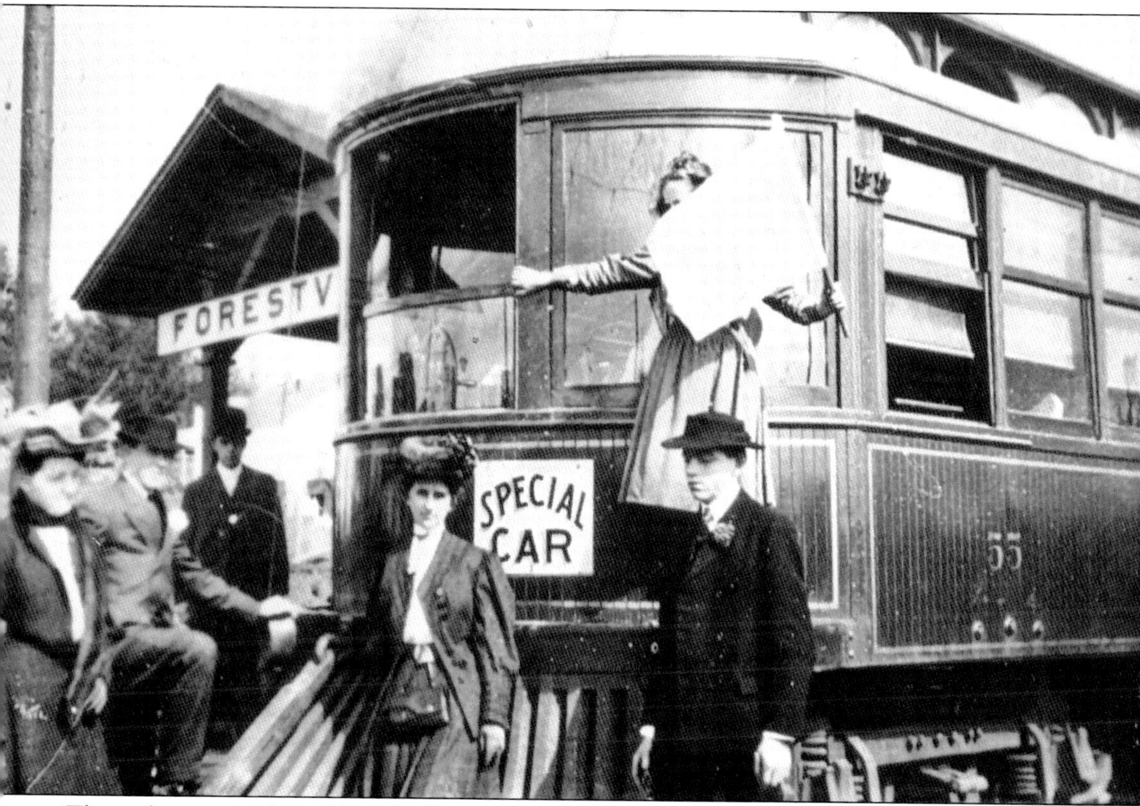

This is the inaugural run of the P&SR Electric Railway around 1905. The train carrying overnight freight service to San Francisco via the steamer ships from Petaluma was a much-needed service. Vacationers also rode the rail to their summer homes on the Russian River, and high school students rode it to Analy for their lessons. The train had a potbellied stove used to keep the cars warm during the winter. The old railway bed is now part of the West County walking trail. (Courtesy of the Dave Henry collection.)

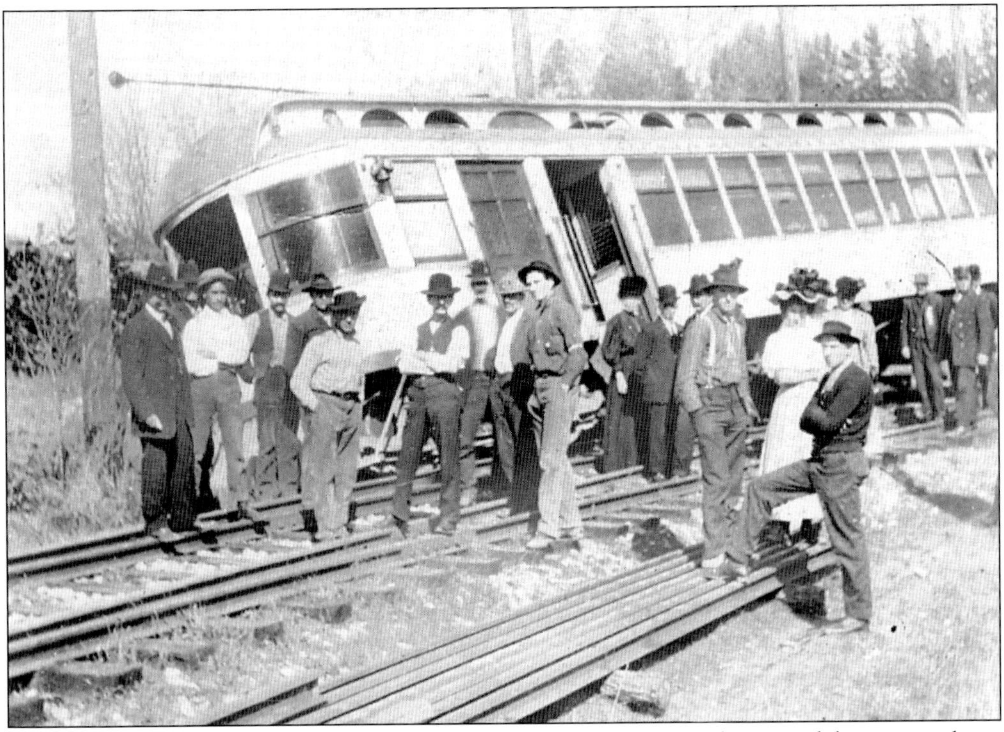

The P&SR Electric Railway derailed in 1920. It is not known how it happened, but it must have been interesting setting the train upright. (Courtesy of Ross Yeager.)

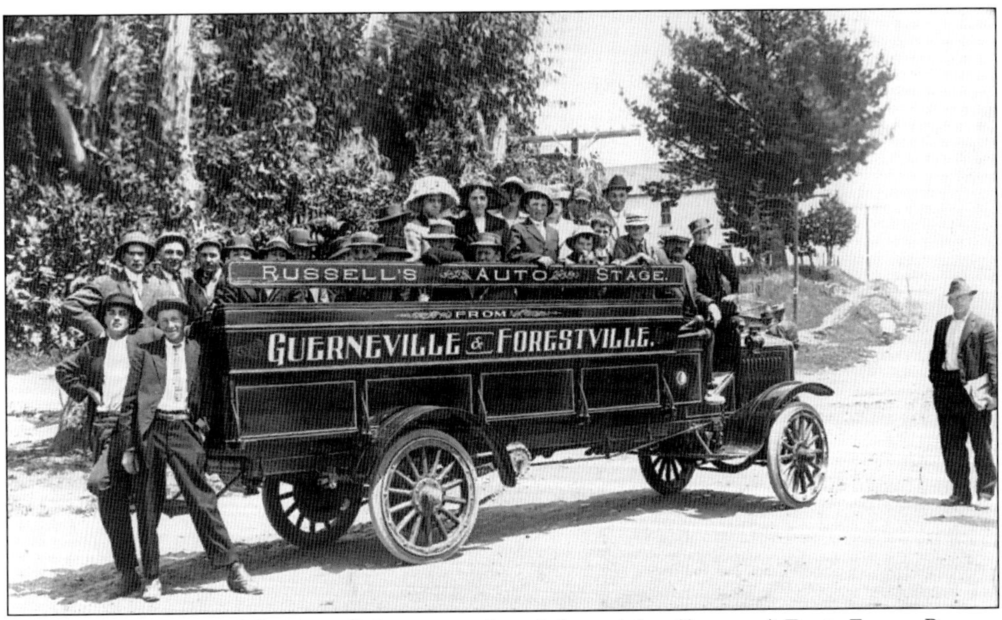

In this 1910 picture of the Russell Stage are, from left to right, (first row) Ernie Evans, Roscoe Fouts, and Jimmy Russell; (second row) Archie Hull, Mr. Evans, Pearl Russell, Allie Fouts, Ethel Close, Roy Wakeland, Frank Close, Clint Yeager, Everett Close, and George Ross. (Courtesy of the Dave Henry collection.)

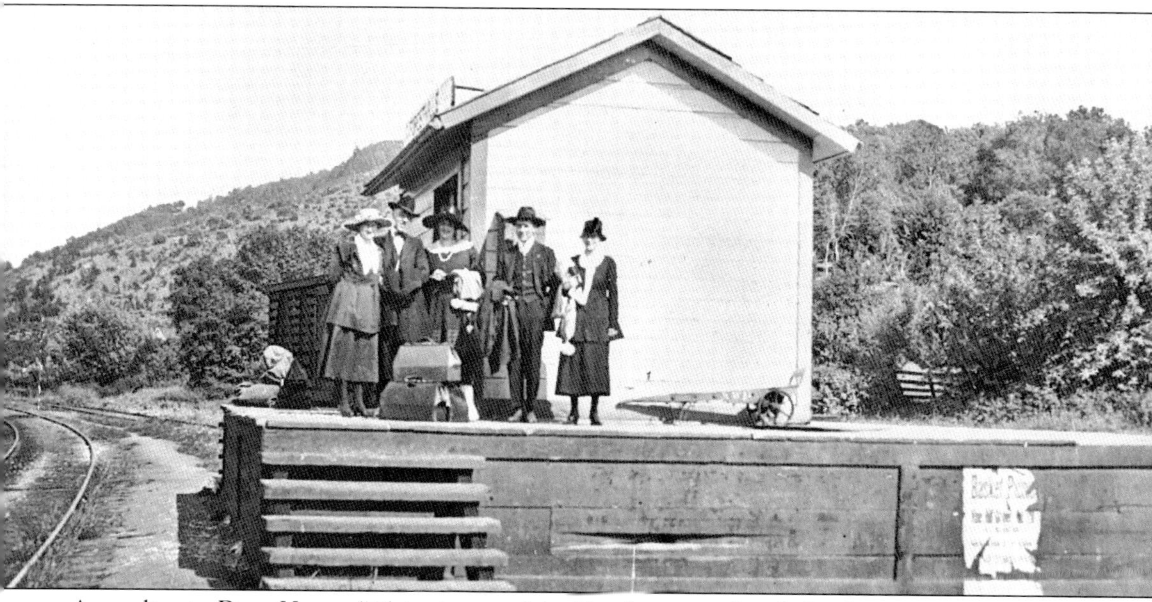

According to Dave Henry, "This picture of the Northwestern Pacific Railway station has, from left to right, Eve Clark, Fred Anderson, Pearl (Russell) Travis, Lawrence ?, and Gladys Clark waiting for the train to Santa Rosa. It was taken June 2, 1918. It faces east from the Farm House Inn where Trenton Road meets River Road. River Road was built on the old railroad right-of-way; the NWP being the standard gauge Iron Horse type with heavy, coal-smoke-belching cast iron engines. This station remained until after the trains ceased to run in 1935, then during a river flood it washed off its foundation to be rescued by Ted Rayner." (Courtesy of the Dave Henry collection.)

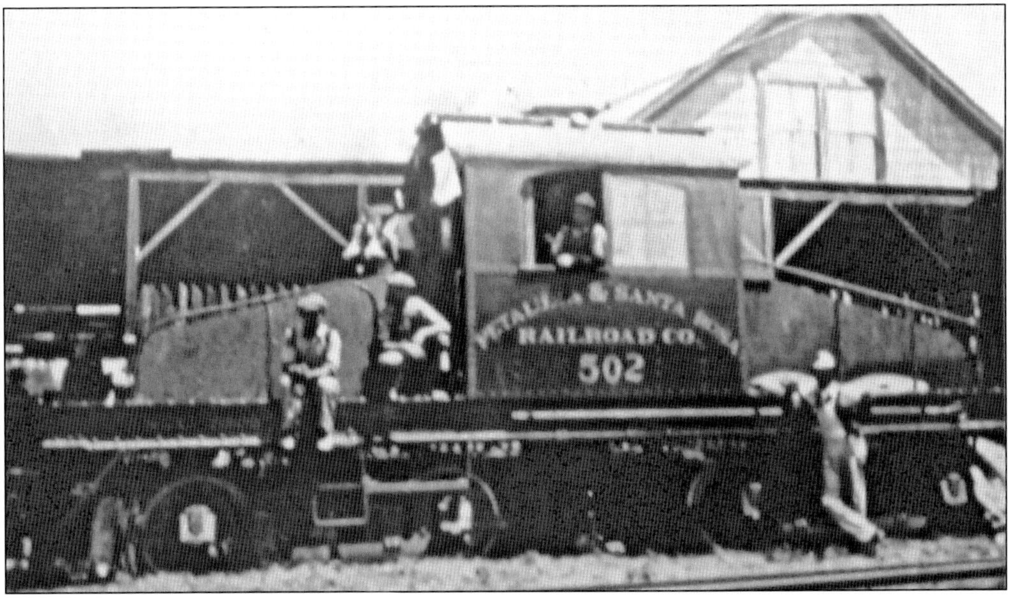

This steam-engine train was used on the NWP Railway. The picture shows the Forestville crew who worked on it. It was bought in 1921. (Courtesy of the Dave Henry collection.)

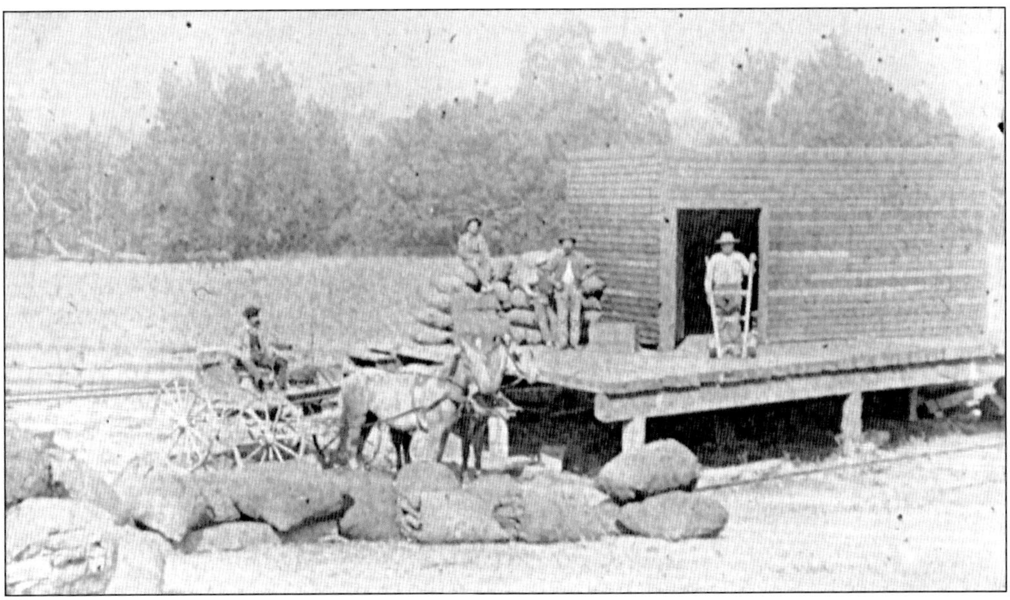

The NWP Railway depot was used to transport charcoal to larger cities. During a Russian River flood, the depot floated away in 1895 to Johnson's field, where the Farm House Inn is today. Shown in this picture is W. W. Travis driving a young, fast, prancing horse on the spring wagon. (Courtesy of the Dave Henry collection.)

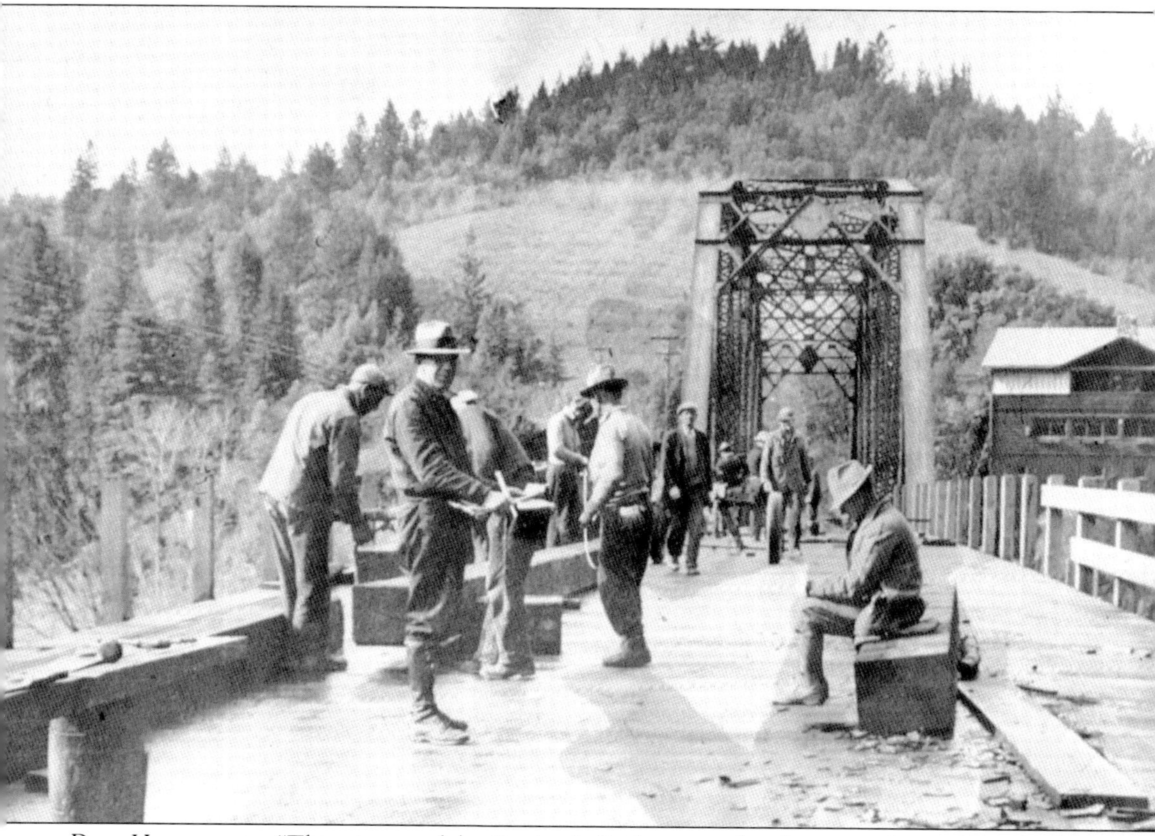

Dave Henry wrote, "This picture of the Hacienda Bridge was taken between 1944–46. With the cessation of rail service to the Russian River automobiles took the place of track and train. Here the men are resurfacing the Hacienda Bridge for rail-free traffic. The bridge is about three miles west of Forestville on River Road. A brass plaque on a girder on one end informs us the American Bridge Co. built the bridge in 1914. It replaced an earlier bridge that was in use by 1877. Timber harvesters at Korbel and Guerneville encouraged building the railroad. Teamsters driving goods the old way of transporting by ox-cart could take up to two days just to go to Petaluma." (Courtesy of the Dave Henry collection.)

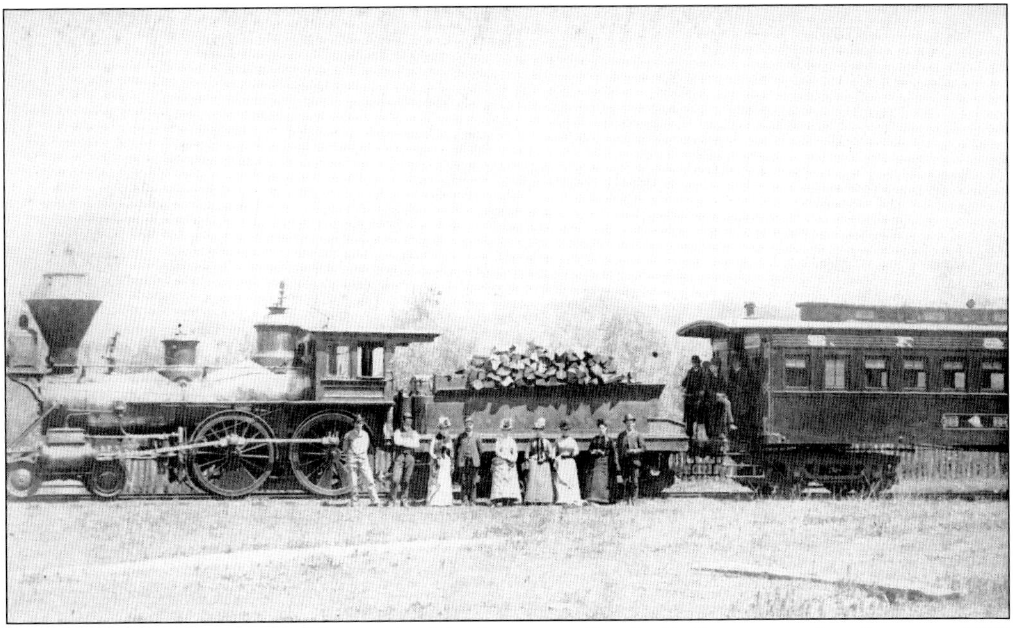

According to Dave Henry, "This is the Northwestern Pacific Railway sometime between 1876 and 1881. The NWP railroad built a branch line from Fulton to Duncans Mills and a Forestville depot near Mirabel Park. Mr. Guerne, the Korbels, Mr. Heald, Mr. Murthy, and M. Lundford were instrumental in bringing the train to Guerneville and Duncans Mills. They were all in the lumber business and needed a better way to move their lumber from the mills." (Courtesy of the Dave Henry collection.)

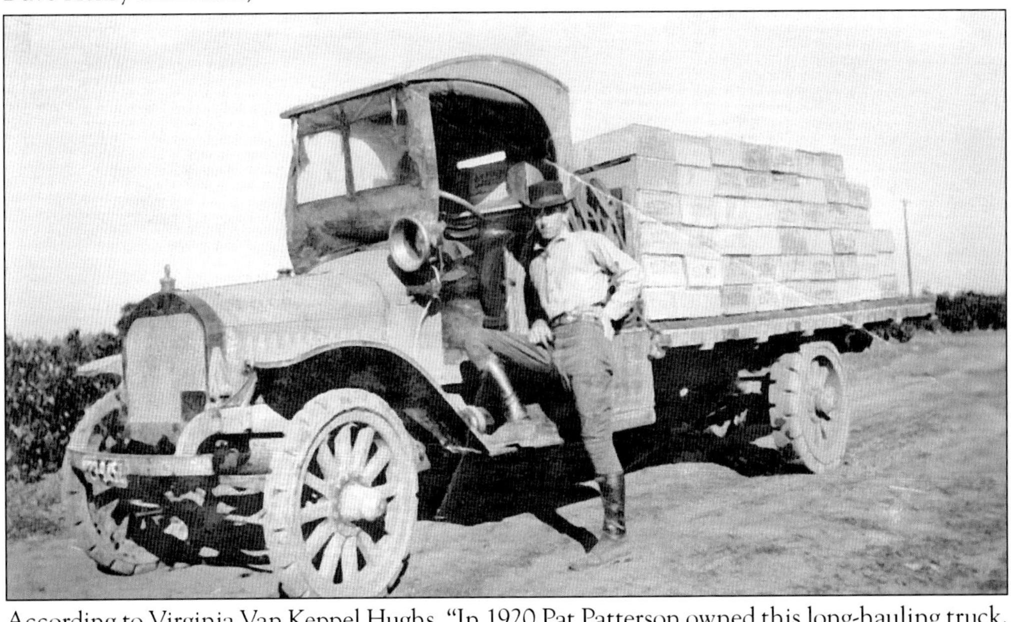

According to Virginia Van Keppel Hughs, "In 1920 Pat Patterson owned this long-hauling truck. It had solid rubber tires and a strong axle because many cars broke axles on the rutted dirt roads. Hauling trucks like this were used frequently to take groceries and household items out to the hop fields in nearby farms. Pat Patterson married Gertrude Kimes of Forestville." (Courtesy of Virginia Van Keppel Hughes.)

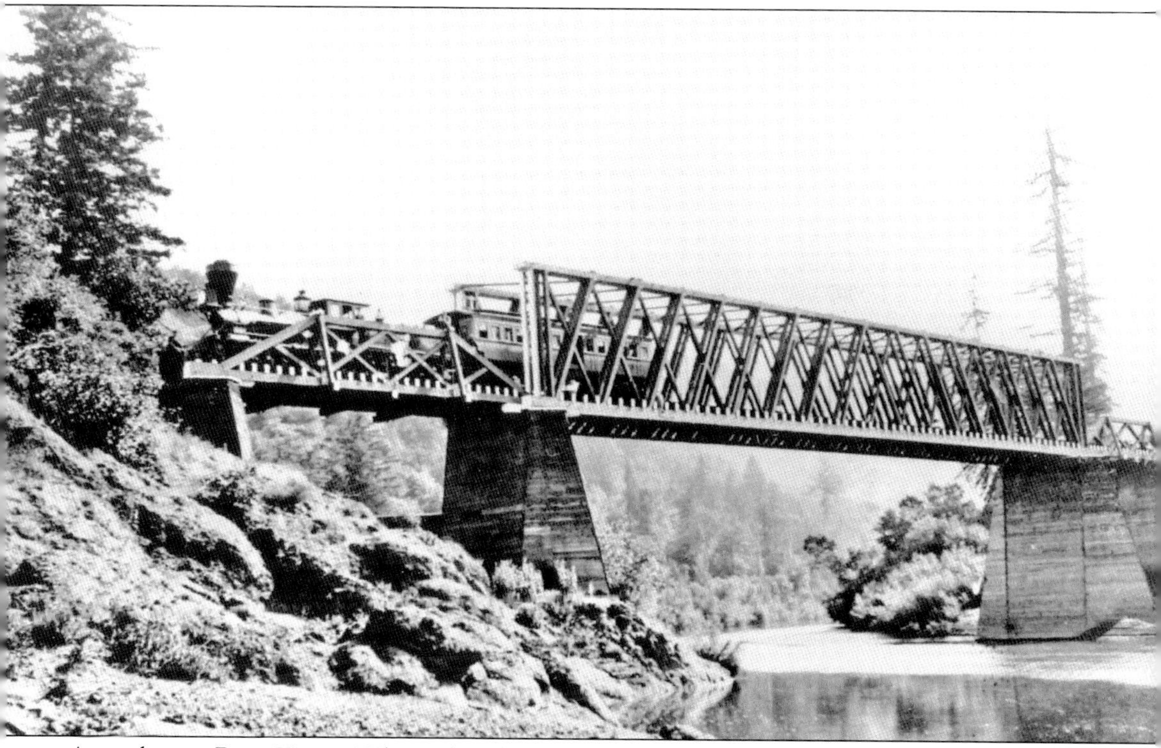

According to Dave Henry, "The earliest bridge over the Russian River at Cosmo, the Hacienda Bridge, was not built for heavy rail traffic. By 1914, the bridge couldn't bear the heavier weight of the trains—supports were getting weak. The photograph shows the four bridge supports to be made of wood as well as the floor of the bridge. It was strong enough for small trains but not the increasingly larger ones. A new steel bridge was built to replace it, and although now wider, it is the same bridge now used to travel in automobiles along River Road. Even in the high flood years, the 'new' bridge has always been high enough to be above the water, but sometimes, just barely." (Courtesy of the Dave Henry collection.)

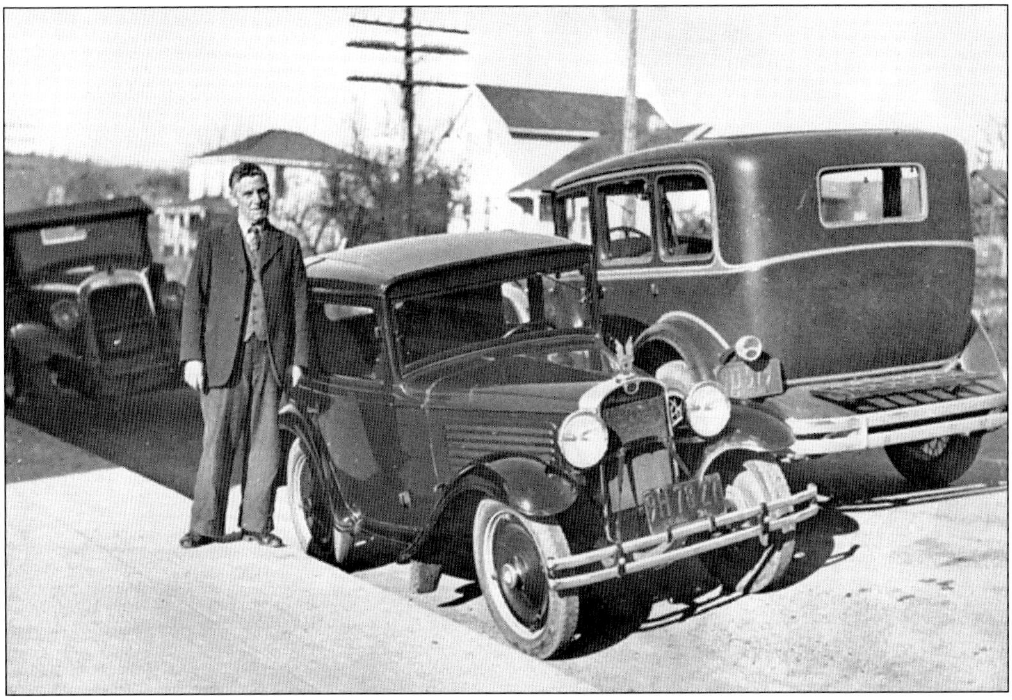

According to Dave Henry, "This is downtown Forestville in the early 1930s with Tom Silk, a local business man, standing in front of his store next to a new Austin Sedan. This car may have been considered the first of the compact cars manufactured by Austin Automobile Company of Grand Rapids, Michigan. In the background, the Templeman family lived in the house on the right and the home on the left belonged to the Armstrong family." (Courtesy of Lavon Speers Covington.)

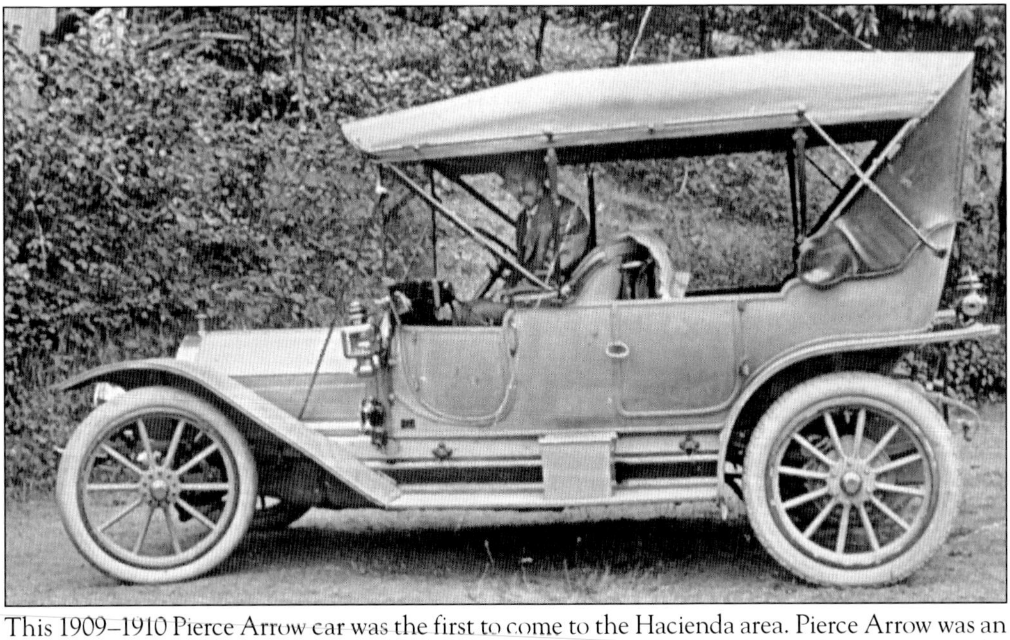

This 1909–1910 Pierce Arrow car was the first to come to the Hacienda area. Pierce Arrow was an American automobile manufacturer that built out of Buffalo, New York. Most of their automobiles were constructed for luxury between 1901 and 1938. (Courtesy of the Dave Henry collection.)

Eight

PLAYGROUND FOR SAN FRANCISCO

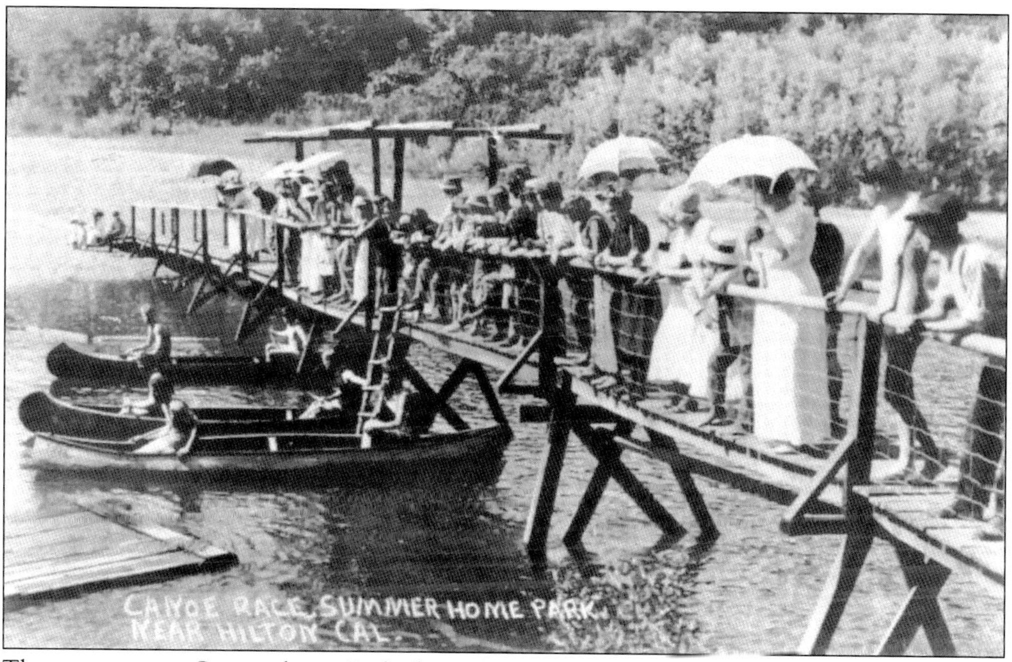

The canoe race at Summerhome Park, shown here in 1917, was just one of the activities included in the summer of fun. Summerhome Park is still near Hilton, which is just a little way past the Hacienda Bridge. It is on the other side of the river from Hilton and has been in existence since well before the 20th century. A number of the homes are still owned by members of the original families. The nearby town of Hilton is now gone, but the Hilton Park and campground are still doing well. (Courtesy of the Dave Henry collection.)

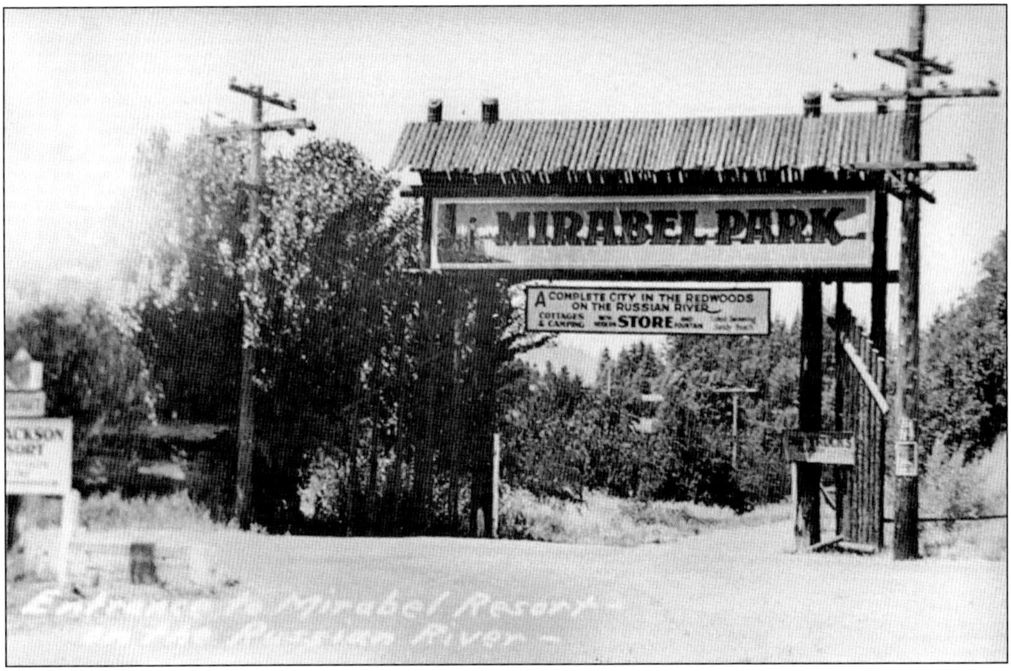

This is the old entrance to Mirabel Park. An artists' group from San Francisco who leased it from Fravir Bulton called it Camp Reverie. Jack London was one of them. They had it for three years before they had a disagreement with Bulton, and he suspended the lease. Another group from San Francisco rented it and named it Mirabel Park. (Courtesy of Bob and his sister Linda Burke.)

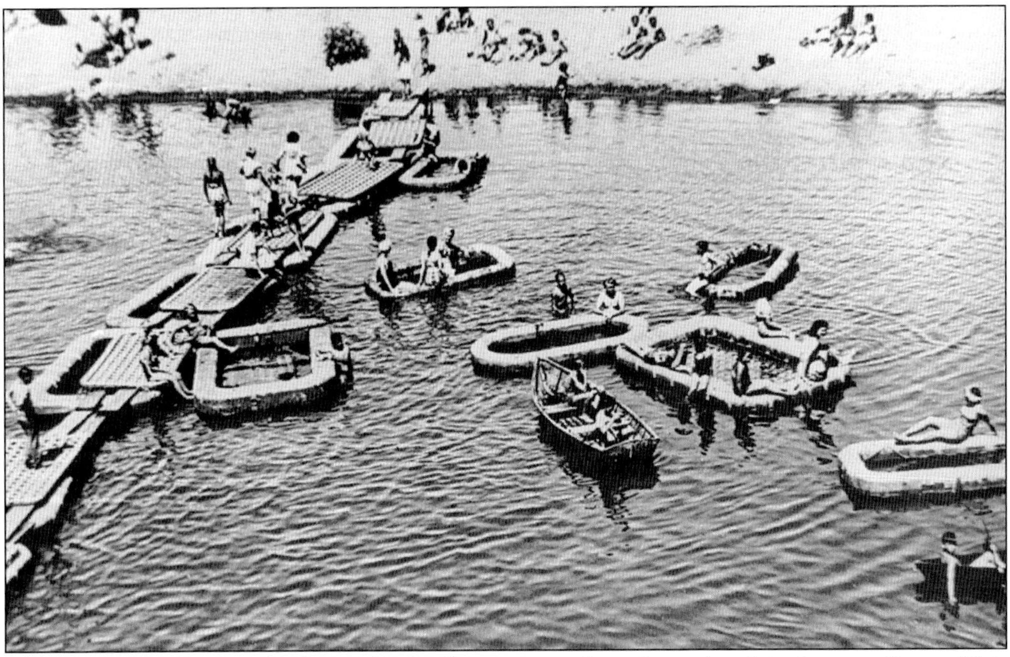

The pontoon bridge was built as a footbridge to get to the other side of the Russian River. This bridge was developed after World War II and was used for several years. (Courtesy of Bob and his sister Linda Burke.)

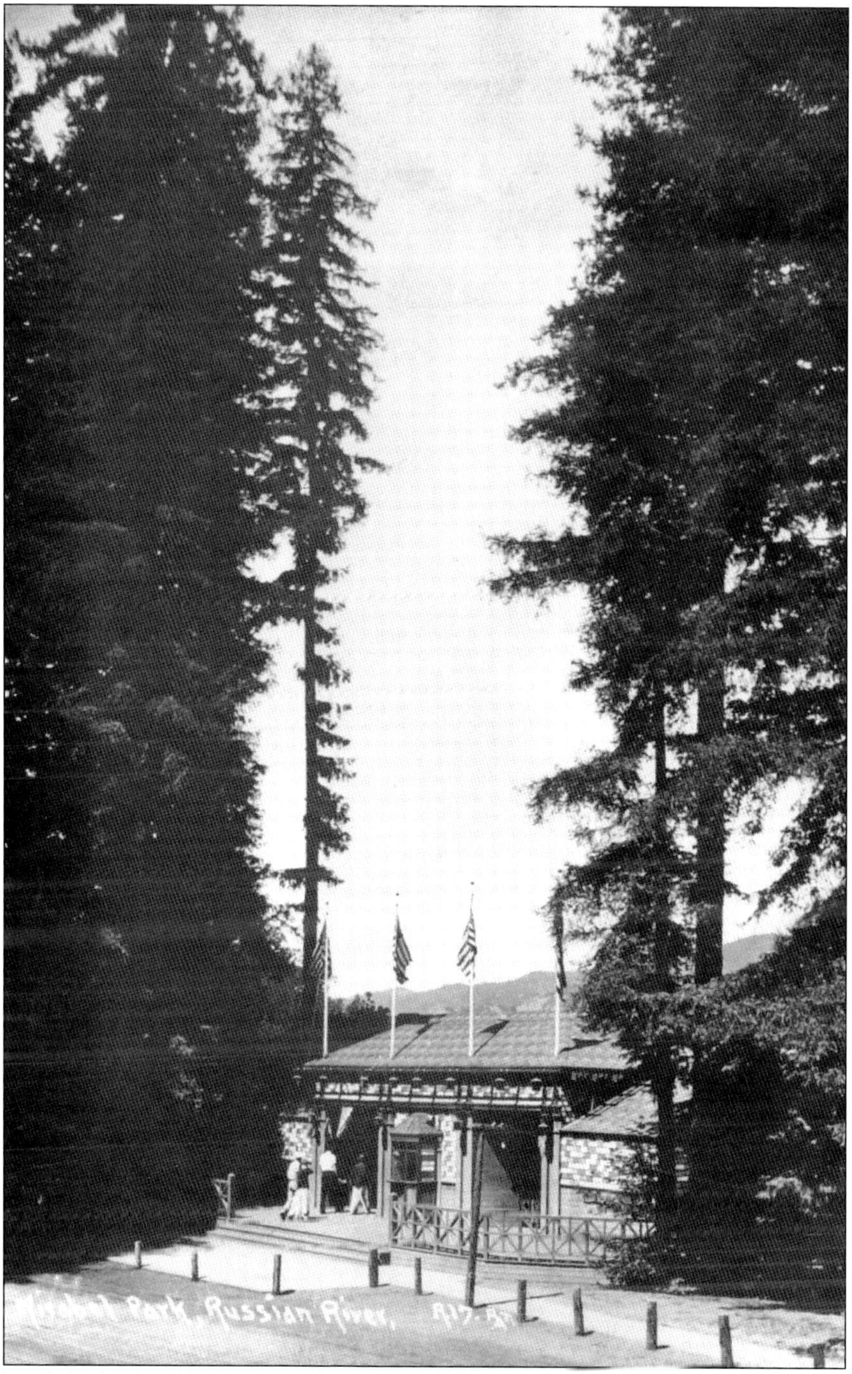

Mirabel Park had a dance hall where big names like Benny Goodman, Harry James, Glen Miller, Duke Ellington, Count Basie, the Dorsey brothers, the Dude Martin Western Band, and the local Russ Carwell came to play. On Sundays, there was dancing to the jukebox. The dance hall had bench seating around the perimeter, so there was always a place to sit after dancing. It also had a mirrored dance globe in the center that caught the light. (Courtesy of Bob and his sister Linda Burke.)

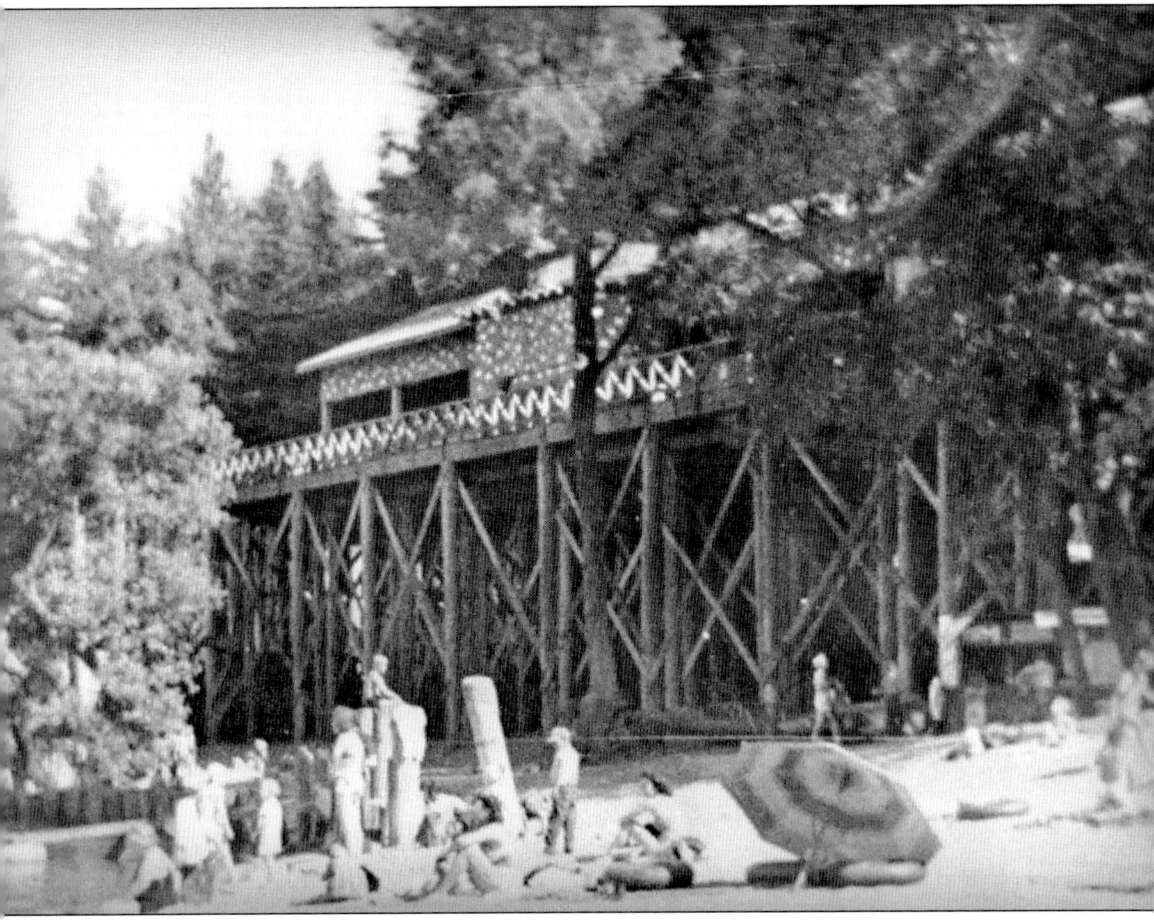

This picture is of Mirabel Dance Hall and the skating rink. It was lit up for nighttime entertainment on the river. When the Burke family ran Mirabel Park, the dance hall became a roller-skating rink. The dance hall had a stage that was elevated on several tiered levels. The fire department would always have its annual ball in the dance hall. (Courtesy of Bob and his sister Linda Burke.)

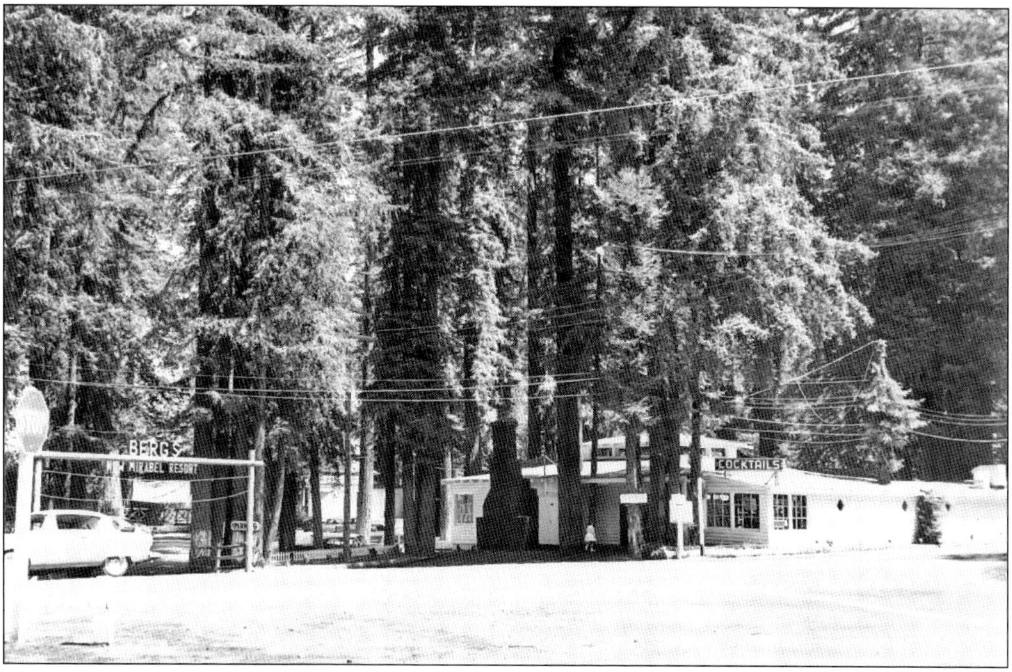

In the 1950s, Larry and Elvira Berg bought Mirabel Park and ran it for one season. The Burkes owned it before the Bergs and again after. Linda Burke said Don Hogue gave some of the Mirabel Park pictures to the Burkes. Charlie and Annie Kawa also owned Mirabel a few times. (Courtesy of Bob and his sister Linda Burke.)

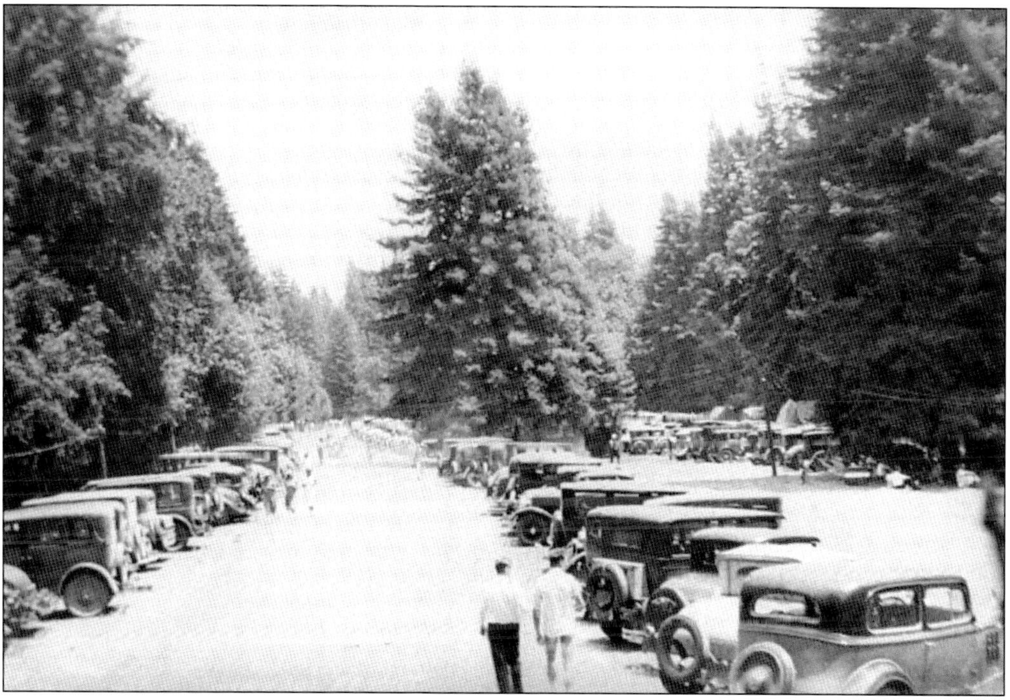

These early century cars were from the San Francisco vacationers who came to Mirabel Park to relax. The parking lot would hold up to 2,000 cars. (Courtesy of Bob and his sister Linda Burke.)

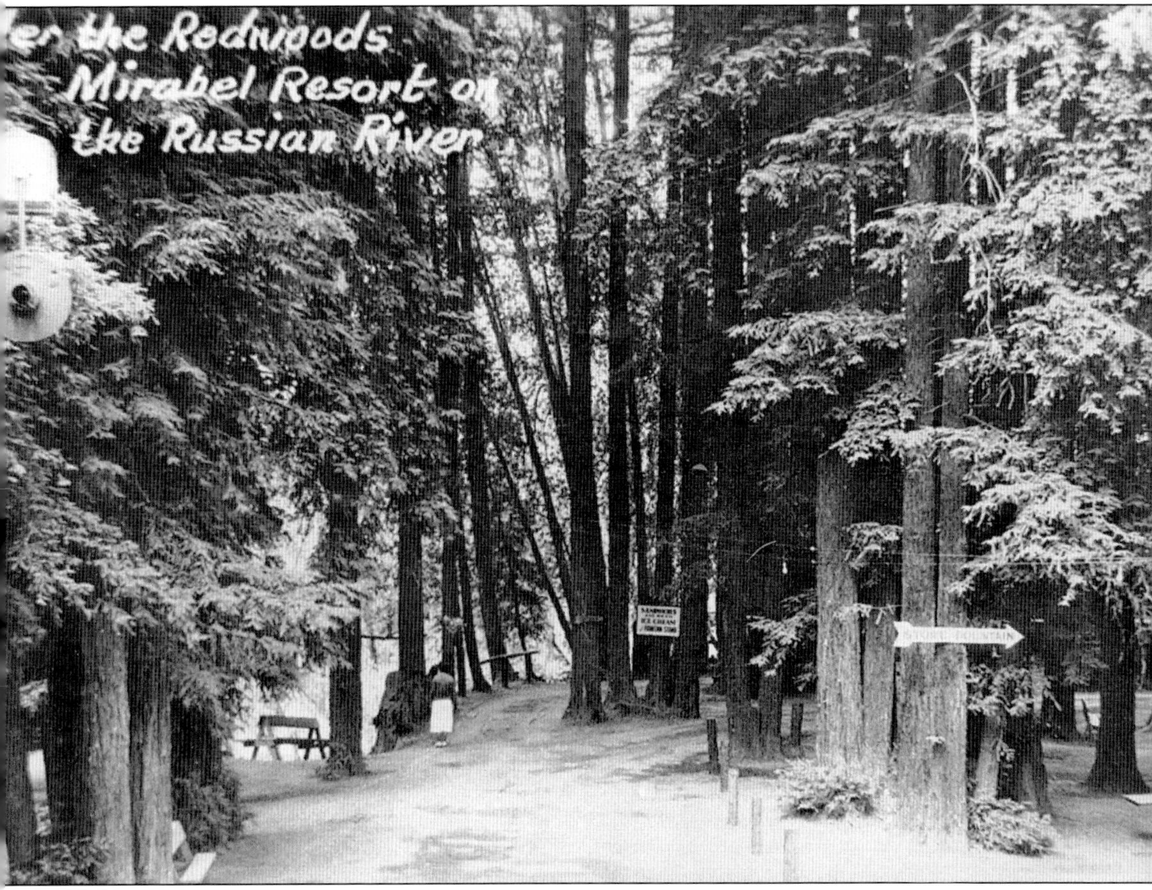

In this picture of Mirabel Park, one can see the old signal of the Fulton and Guerneville railroad. The railroad line ran in front of Mirabel Park where River Road is located today. The railroad continued until the late 1930s, and then the Hacienda Bridge became a car bridge. During World War II, the bridge was one lane; it became a two-lane bridge in 1946. (Courtesy of Bob and his sister Linda Burke.)

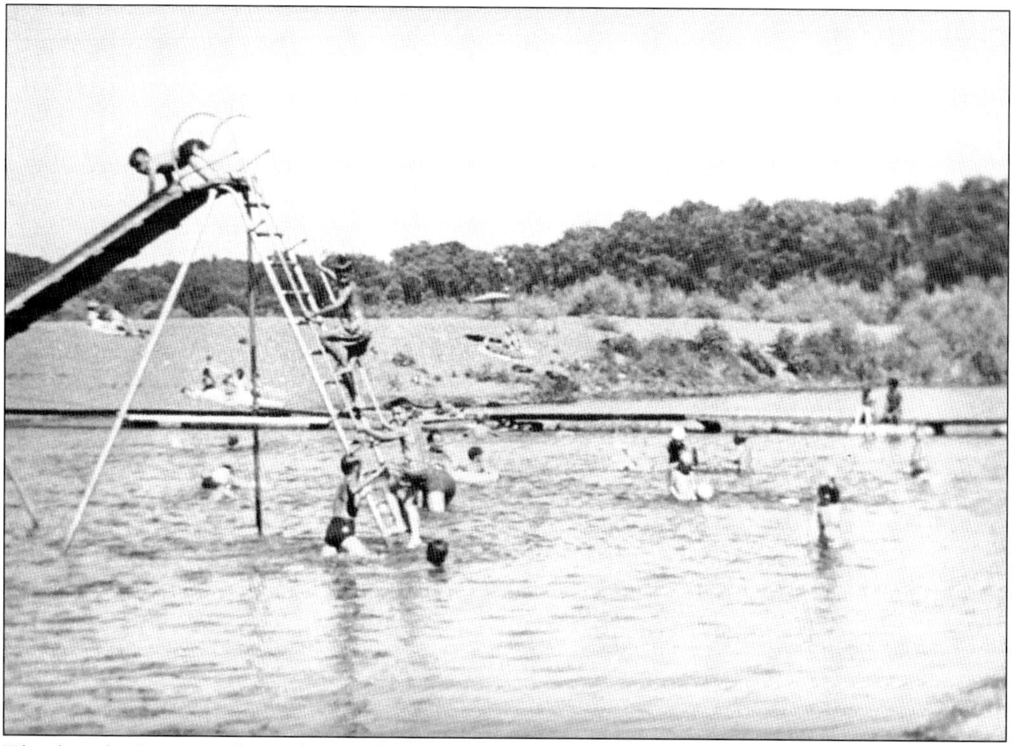

This beach playground was designed for enjoyment on the Russian River. Many people from San Francisco came to relax and enjoy the river. (Courtesy of Bob and his sister Linda Burke.)

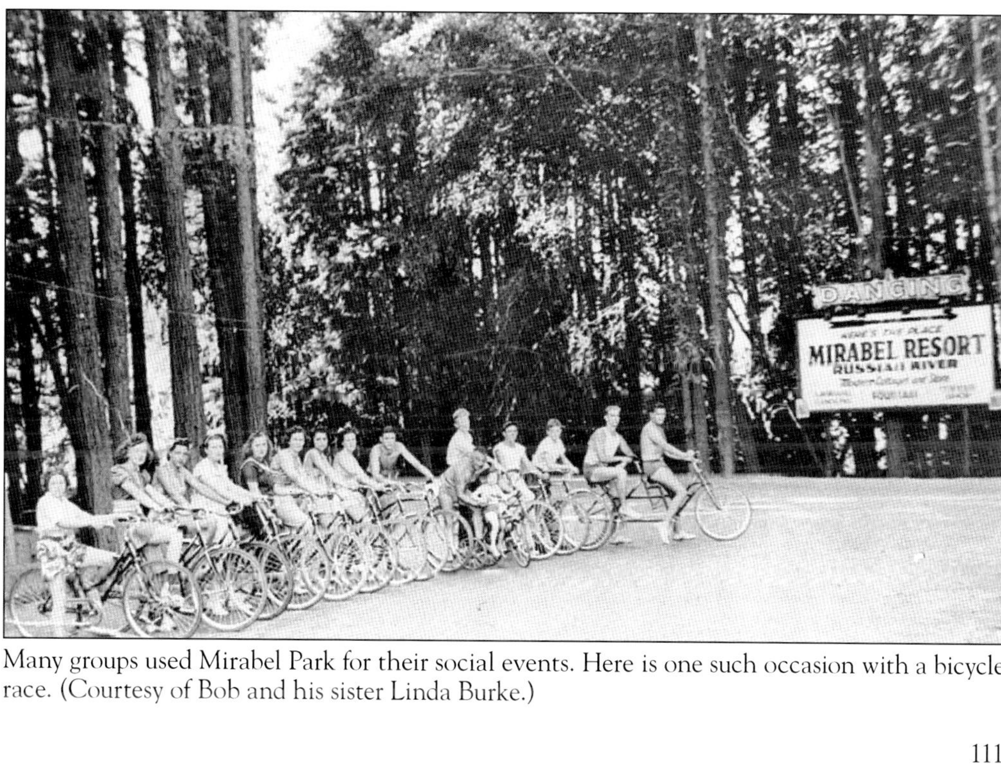

Many groups used Mirabel Park for their social events. Here is one such occasion with a bicycle race. (Courtesy of Bob and his sister Linda Burke.)

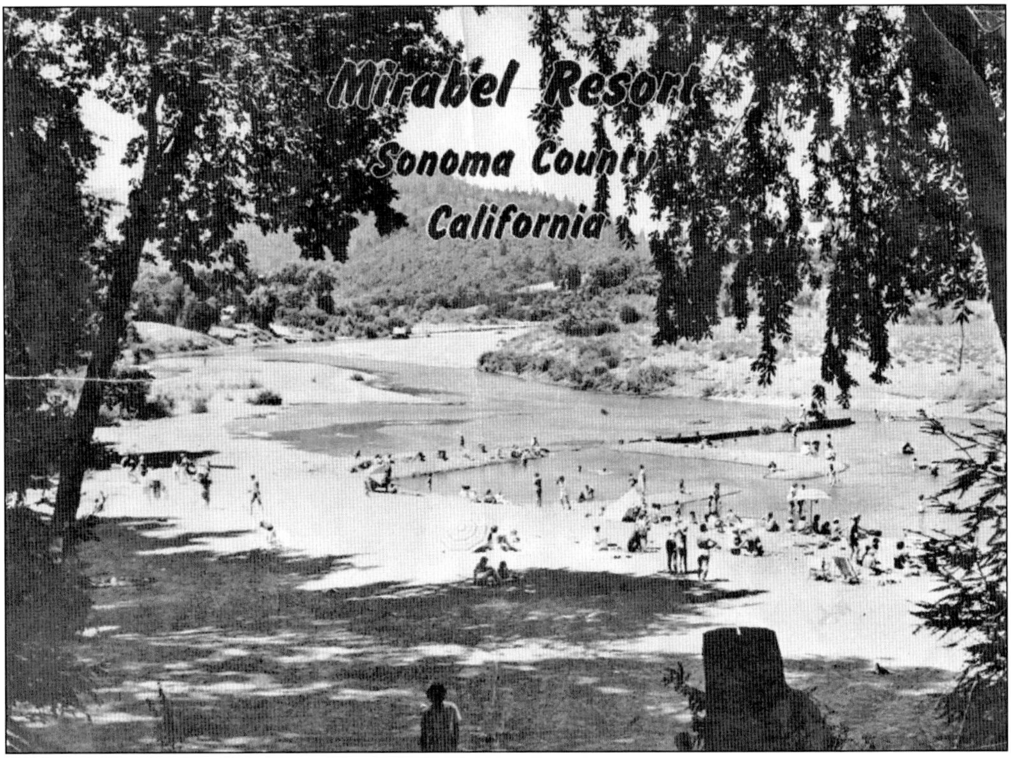

This view of Mirabel Park is the one used on the brochure. It shows the beauty of the beach and surrounding hillsides. It has one of the best beaches from which to swim the Russian River. (Courtesy of Bob and his sister Linda Burke.)

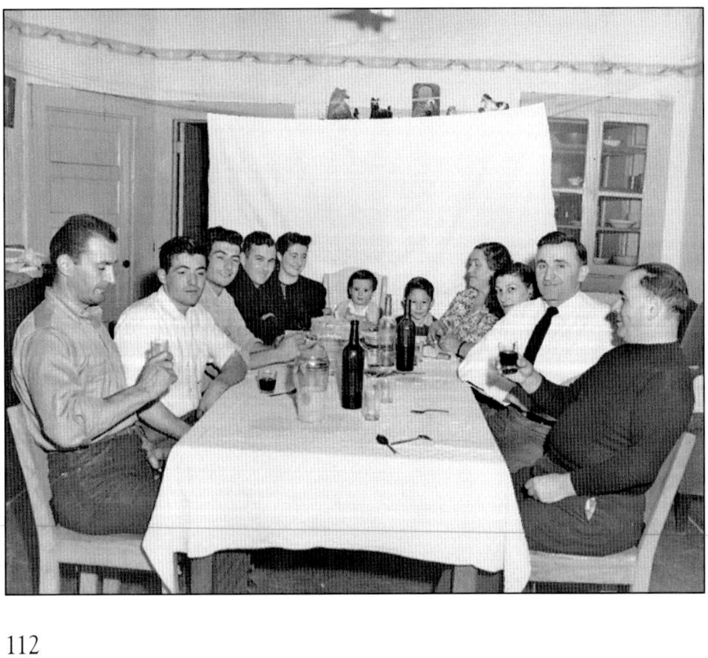

This is a family gathering of the Lacabannes, who owned the French resort on Mount Jackson. Pictured from left to right are unidentified, Emil Lacabanne, Louis Lacabanne, Robert Burke, MaryLu Burke, Bob Burke Jr. (at one year of age), an unidentified boy, Marie Lacabanne, and three unidentified dinner guests. Louis and Marie opened Mount Jackson in 1925 and served guests until the 1940s. (Courtesy of Linda Burke.)

MT. JACKSON RESORT

A secluded resort ½ mile from the Russian River

P. O. BOX HILTON, CALIFORNIA

Phone Forestville 2685

●

RATES

The following rates include breakfast, lunch, dinner, and lodging. The amusements and activities include swimming, dancing, tennis, etc., and are free.

Three Meals Daily

Daily per person 2 in Room	Daily per person 1 in Room		Weekly per person 2 in Room	Weekly per person 1 in Room
$5.50	$6.00	Cabins with hot and cold water, private toilet and shower	$32.50	$35.00
5.00	$5.50	Cabins with running water, public toilet and shower	$27.50	$30.00

CHILDREN'S RATES

Age	Weekly	Daily	Age	Weekly	Daily
1-2	$ 2.00	$ .50	7	12.00	2.50
2-3	7.00	1.50	8	13.00	2.75
4	9.00	1.75	9	14.00	3.00
5	10.00	2.00	10	15.00	3.25
6	11.00	2.25	11	17.00	3.50
			12	20.00	4.00

Wine included with meals.
Iron and sulphur springs on property.
We prepare lunches for beach parties.
Barbecue under the Redwoods every week.
Transportation furnished to beach, to and from bus stop.
Greyhound bus service daily from San Francisco to Hacienda.

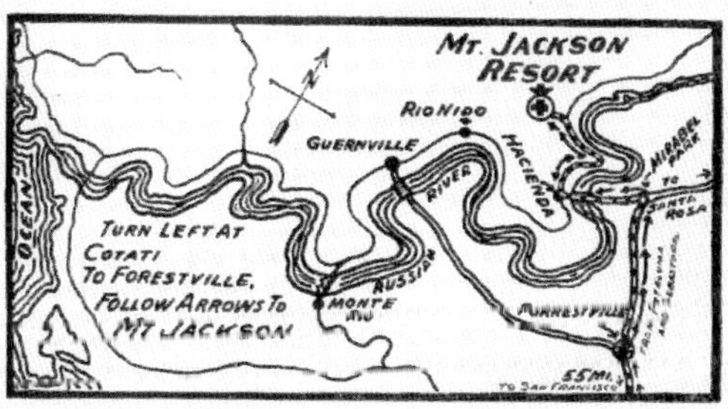

During Prohibition, many people gathered at the resort to partake of dinner and wine. When the federal agents came into the resort, the band would sing a French song that warned patrons to put their wine away until the agents had left. The resort had cabins to rent. Louis and Marie were excellent French chefs, but when the demand was too high, they had French chefs brought in to help. The food was always the best quality. The resort had a one-lane bowling alley, a creek-fed pool, and a dance floor. In 1943, the cast of Alfred Hitchcock's *Shadow of a Doubt* stayed at Mount Jackson. They were Teresa Wright, Joseph Cotton, Macdonald Carey, Patricia Collinge, Henry Travers, and Wallace Ford. (Courtesy of Bob and his sister Linda Burke.)

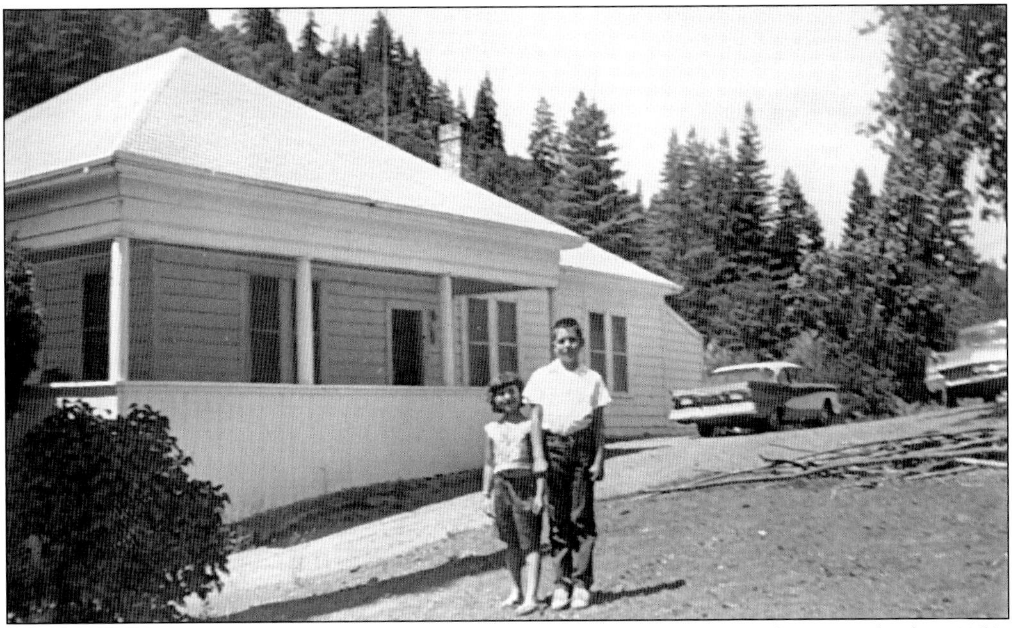

This is the home of the Lacabanne family, who ran Mount Jackson Resort. Shown in this late 1950s picture are Louis and Joan Lacabanne, the grandchildren of Louis and Marie Lacabanne. The resort no longer stands on Mount Jackson, but the old farmhouse still does. (Courtesy of Louis Lacabanne.)

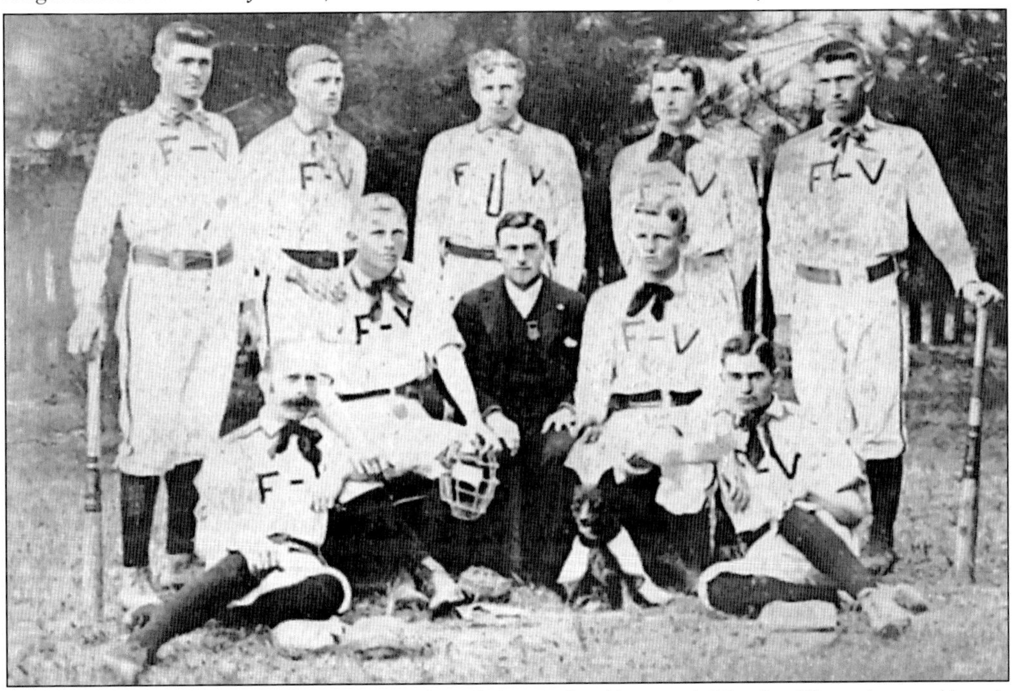

The Forestville Tigers baseball team are, from left to right, (first row) Charles Oliver (second base), Walt Rickert (catcher), Tom Silk (manager), Mark Rickett (pitcher), and J. E. Jewett (shortstop); (second row) A. V. Anderson (first base), Charles Rickett (center field), Ira Fallon (left field), Harmon Covey (right field), and Henry Thomas (third base). The team proudly includes their mascot, Pronto. (Courtesy of the Dave Henry collection.)

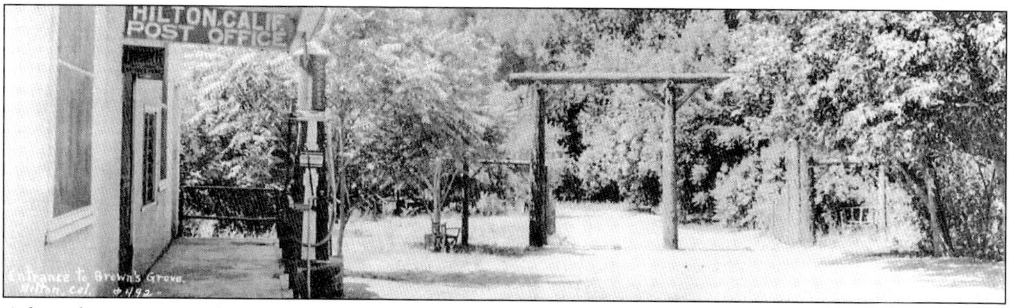

After the 1906 earthquake, Hilton Park became a thriving brick-kiln business to supply San Francisco with brick to help rebuild the city. In the 1930s, the area became the Hilton family campground. It was a mail and passenger stop on the Northwestern Pacific railroad line, which served the Russian River before 1935. Railroad workers used Hilton as their camp. It had its own post office, general store, gas station, dance hall, hotel, and bar. Hilton continues to be a popular boating, fishing, and camping recreation area. The current owner, Don Fulkerson, has improved it and made it a great place for family fun. (Courtesy of Don Fulkerson.)

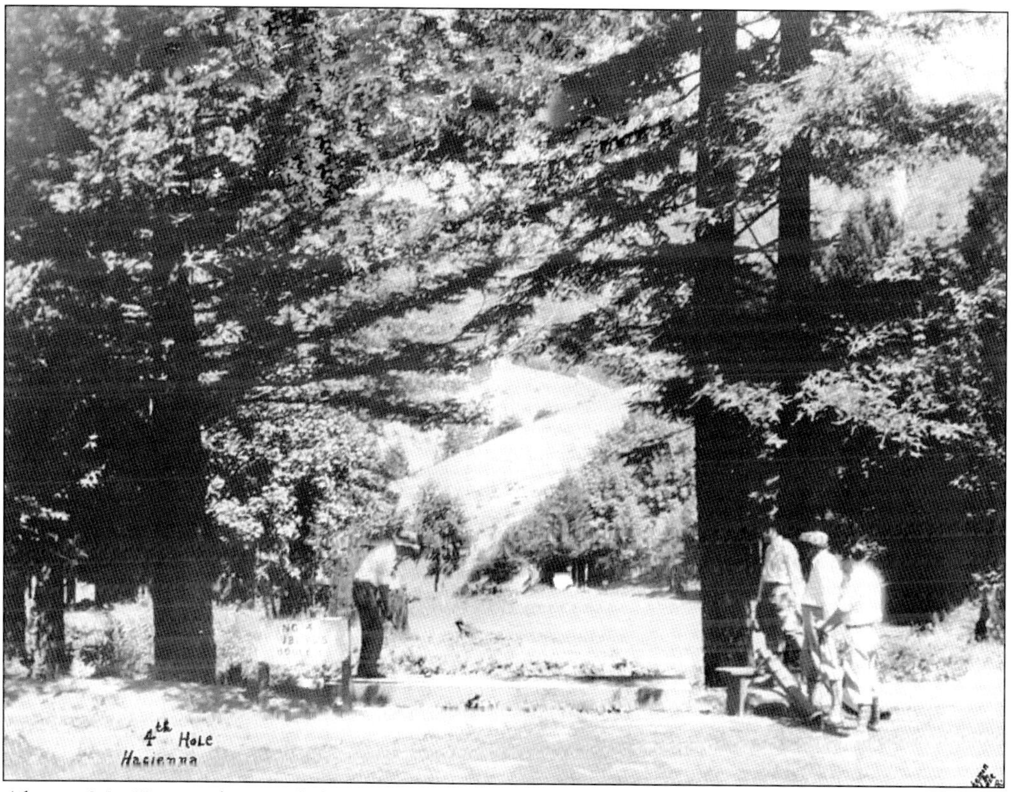

Alistair MacKenzie designed the Hacienda Golf Course. He also designed the Northwood Golf Course, as well as the famous Augusta National and Cypress Point in Monterey. (Courtesy of the Dave Henry collection.)

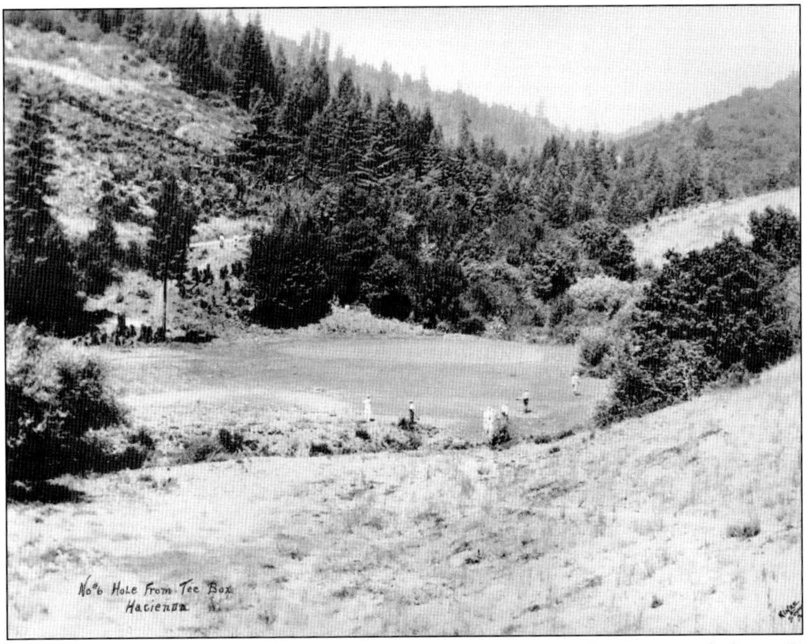

Alistair MacKenzie, who designed the Cosmo Golf Course, was born in Yorkshire, England, in 1870. After studying to become a doctor, he decided to design golf courses. He wasn't a good golfer but enjoyed the design work so much he wrote the book *Golf Architecture* in 1920. His designs were noted for their sensitivity to the natural surroundings. He was also good at designing a course that accommodated players with different levels of ability. *Sports Illustrated* called him "golf's greatest architect." His Cypress Point was rated the fourth greatest golf course in America. He designed Northwood Golf Course for the Bohemian Club to use during their encampment. (Courtesy of the Dave Henry collection.)

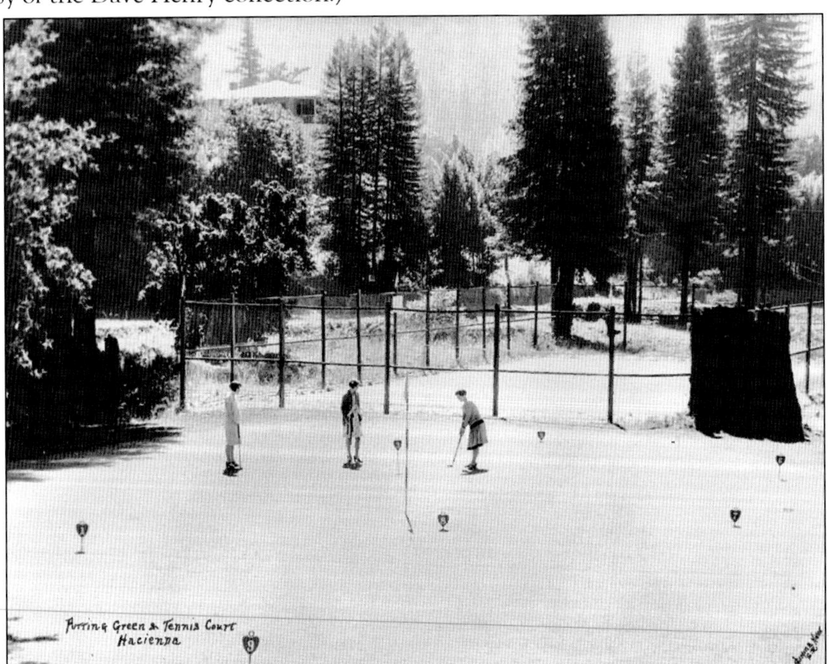

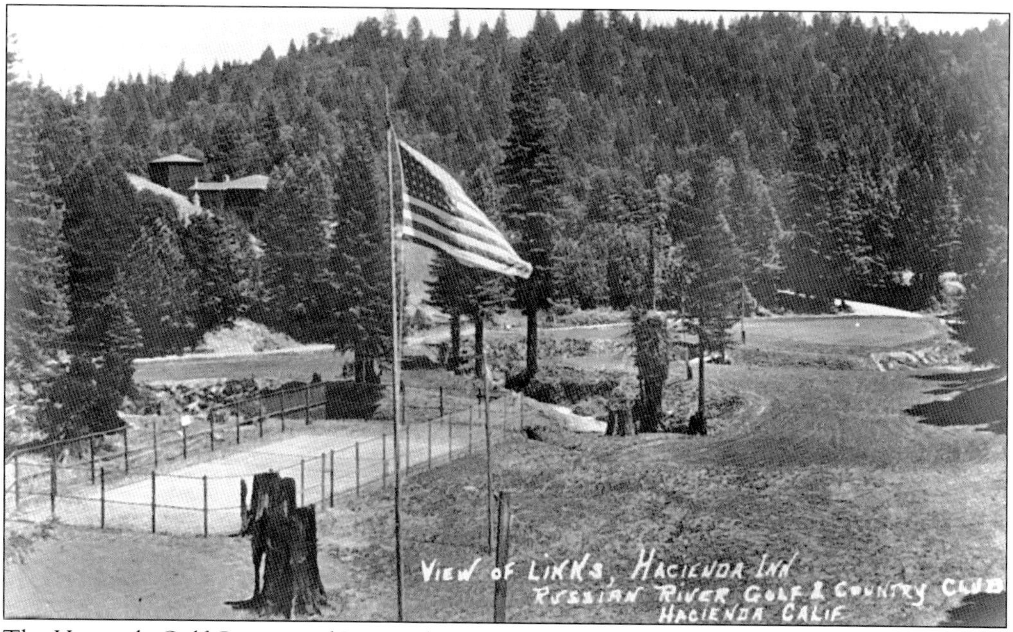

The Hacienda Golf Course and Hacienda Inn (later known as Skippy's restaurant) were located just below the camping area. Camping platforms were on the hillside for summer campers to pitch their tents and enjoy the outdoors. They offered stables for horseback rides by the river. (Courtesy of the Dave Henry collection.)

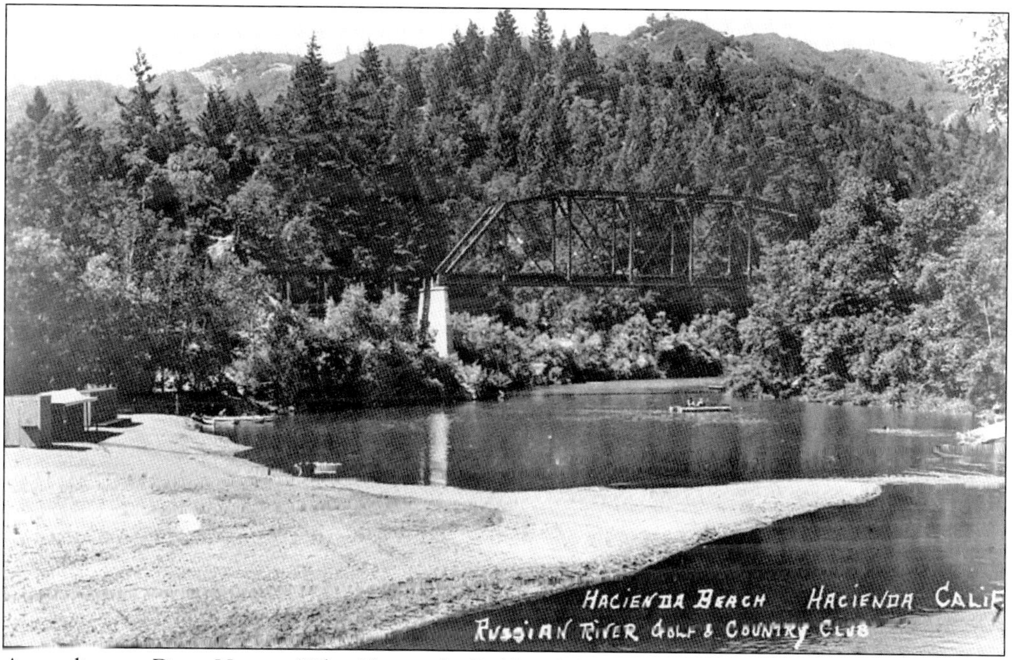

According to Dave Henry, "The Hacienda Golf and Country Club was originally a farm that was lived on by the McPeak family. Mrs. McPeak was born in the house that was on the inn property. It was a working farm with livestock and vineyards. According to a story told to me by Mrs. McPeak some years ago, the pig once got into the late season fermenting grape grapevines and became quite inebriated." (Courtesy of the Dave Henry collection.)

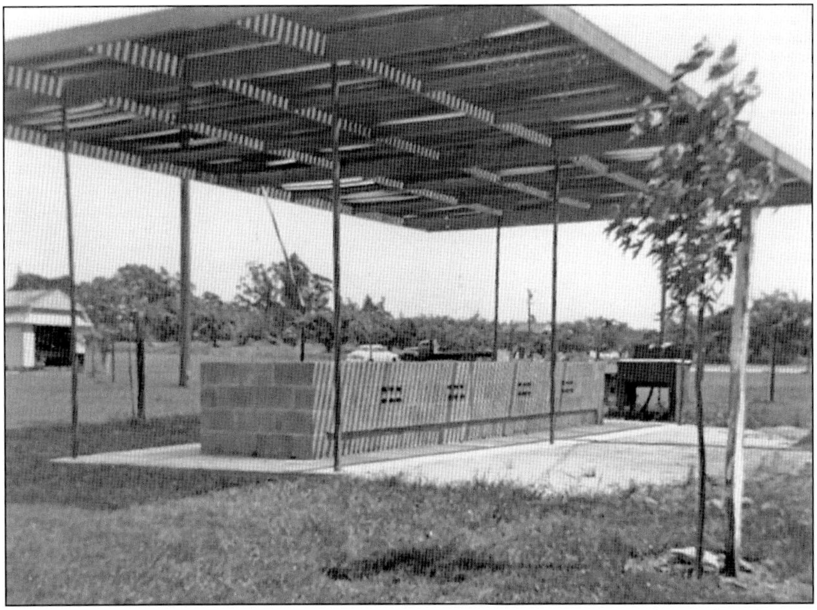

In 1959, Bob Aldridge and Frank Anderson had the idea to start something for the youth of the town, so they formed the Forestville Youth Betterment Association to buy property and build a park. The first official meeting was March 11, 1960, at Ilo Tolley's house, which was originally the Losson Ross home. George Ross, Andy Anderson's father-in-law, loaned them money to purchase most of the property from Paul Speer. Five years later, Darleen and Paul Speer Jr. sold another four acres to the park. Sometime after that, Lavon Speer Covington and Wayne Speer donated 1 acre of land. Fund-raisers for the park were started. Conrad Bowman built the pump house. Angelo Mancini built booths for the park to use as carnival booths. The founding members of the Youth Park were George Ross, Bob and Marda Aldridge, Frank (Andy) Anderson Sr., Catherine Baldacci Carson, Marvin Davis (fire chief), Dick Ehlert, Martha Garfield, Elva Jarvis, Ken Johnson, Claudia McDermott, Francis Rose, Steve Stephens, John and Molly Thelan, Ilo Tolley, and Irvin Wise. (Courtesy of the Dave Henry collection.)

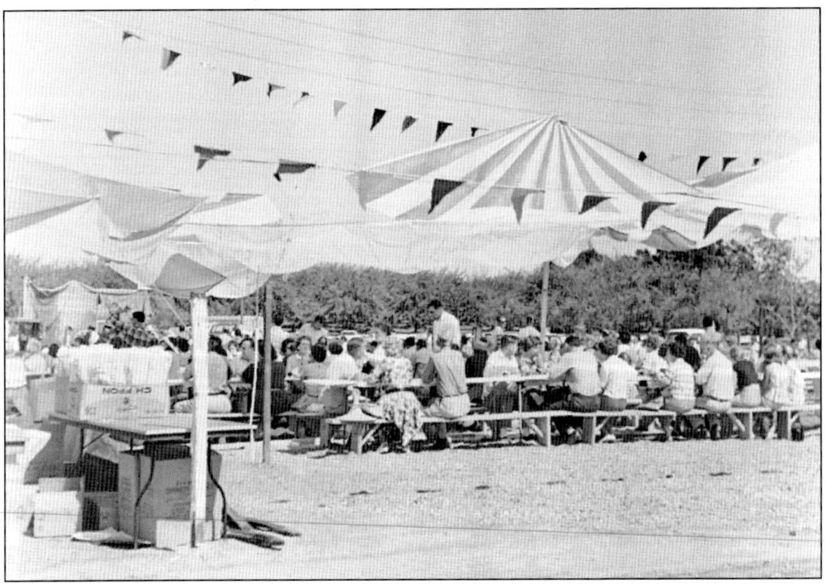

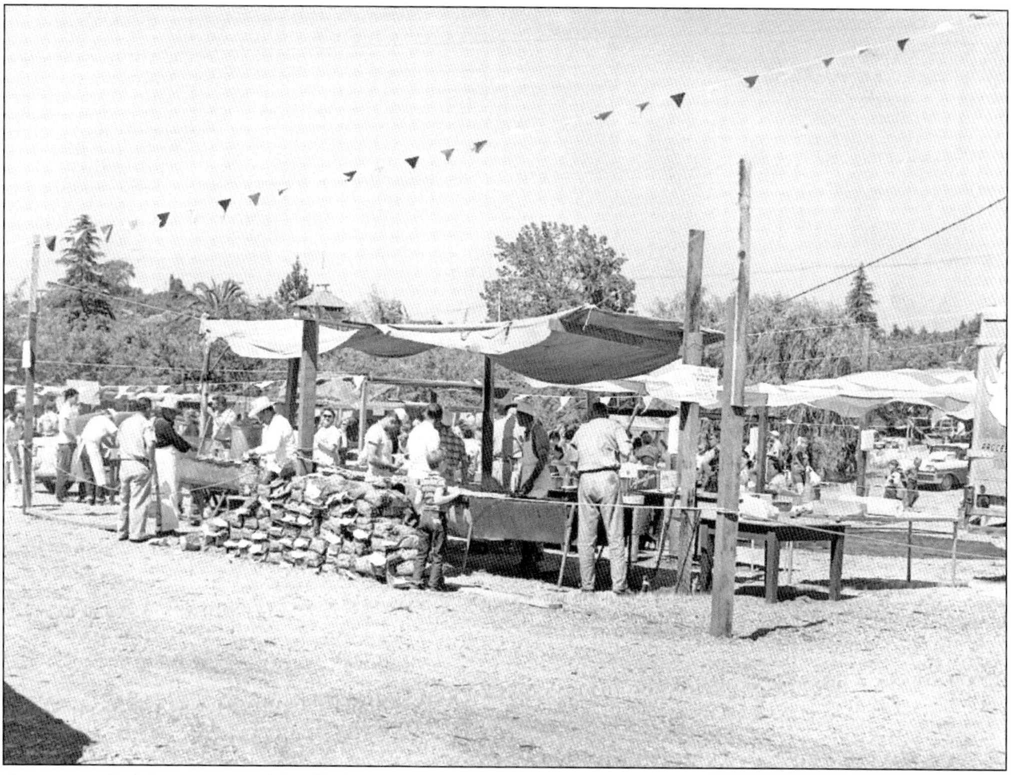

A group of citizens went skin diving for abalone to use for the barbeque. Eva Martinelli is one of the skin divers pictured here. At the first barbeque in 1960, the town put up large parachutes for shade. "One of the most attended and fun attractions was a dunk tank where people would pay to dunk well-known citizens," remembers Barry Aldridge. Many volunteers prepared the vacant area for the first barbecue. Temporary booths were constructed, and river stones from Mirabel Park were used for the barbecue pit. It became a yearly event and is still held to this day. The barbeque has gotten so large that people from all over Sonoma County come to have a steak or chicken dinner. It is a time for the community to get together and see friends. Forestville Youth Park is totally maintained by donations and the annual barbeque. Records from October 13, 1963, show profits of $2,018.37. This has continued to be a wonderful town-maintained park. (Courtesy of Sherry Martinelli.)

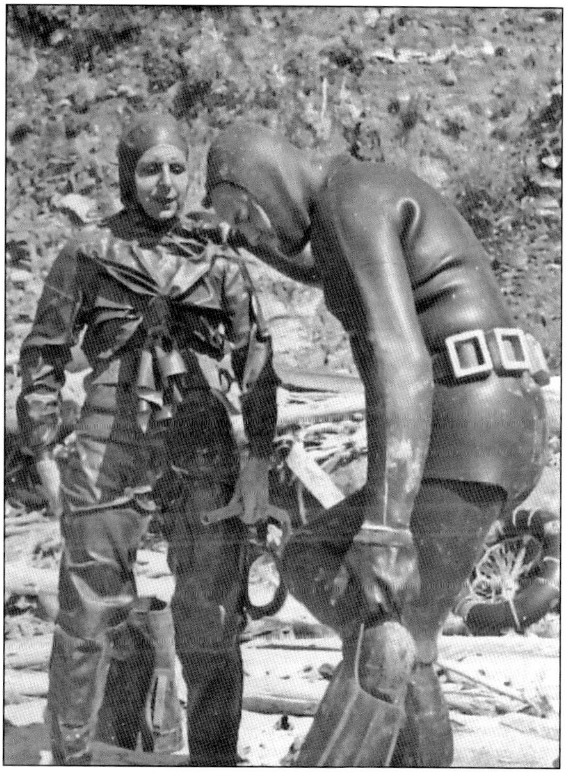

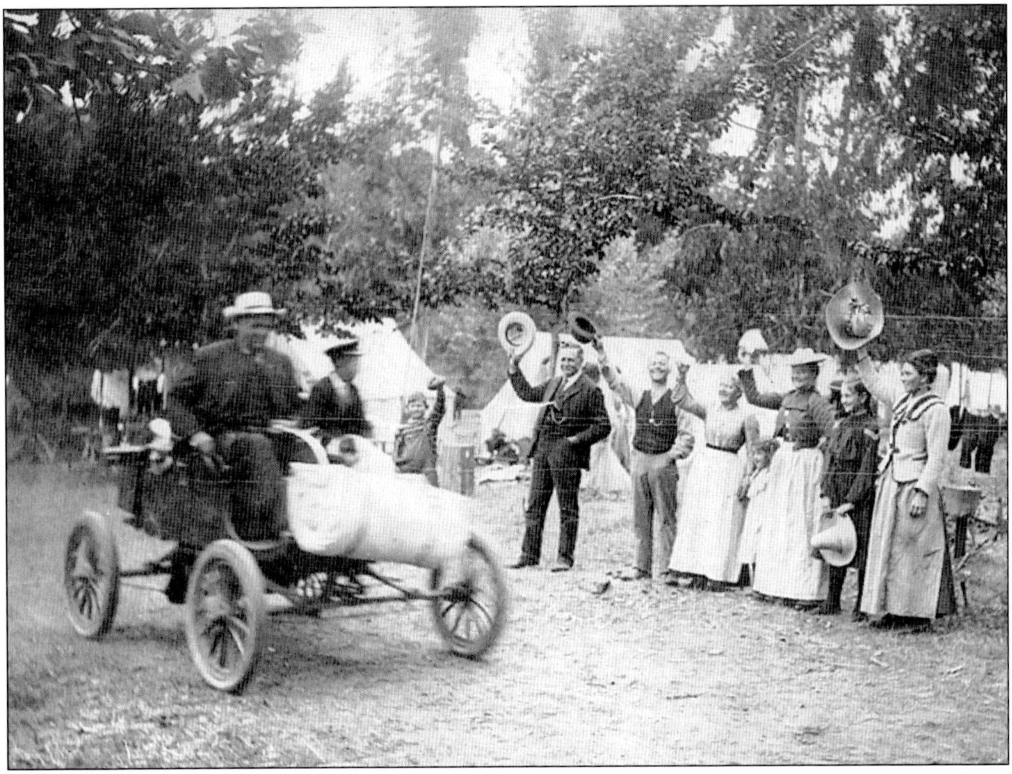

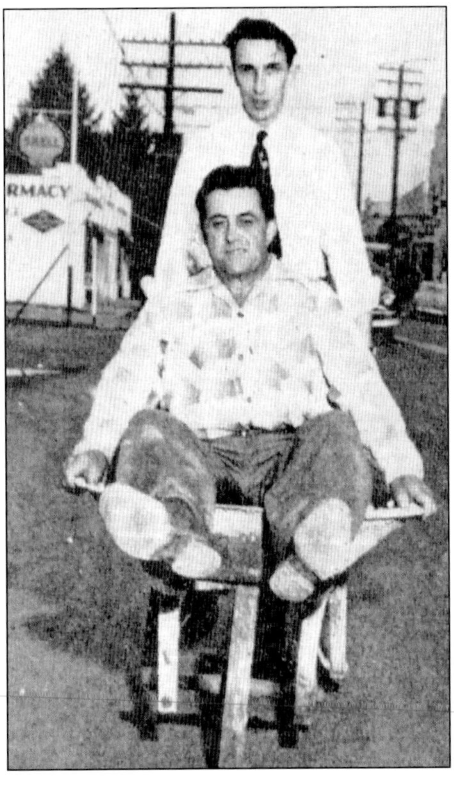

In 1908, the Luzamn Company manufactured a one-seat electric car with lever steering. In this picture, the proud owner adapted a carrier for his dog on the front. He is showing it off to some campers who are giving him a hats-off salute. (Courtesy of Florence Templeman.)

Bob Aldridge and Oscar Ludolff had a bet going. It was decided that whoever won the bet would be pushed down Main Street in Forestville in a wheelbarrow. During the 1952 presidential race, Bob Aldridge was a Democrat betting on Adlai Stevenson, and Oscar Ludolff was a Republican voting for Dwight D. Eisenhower. (Courtesy of the Dave Henry collection.)

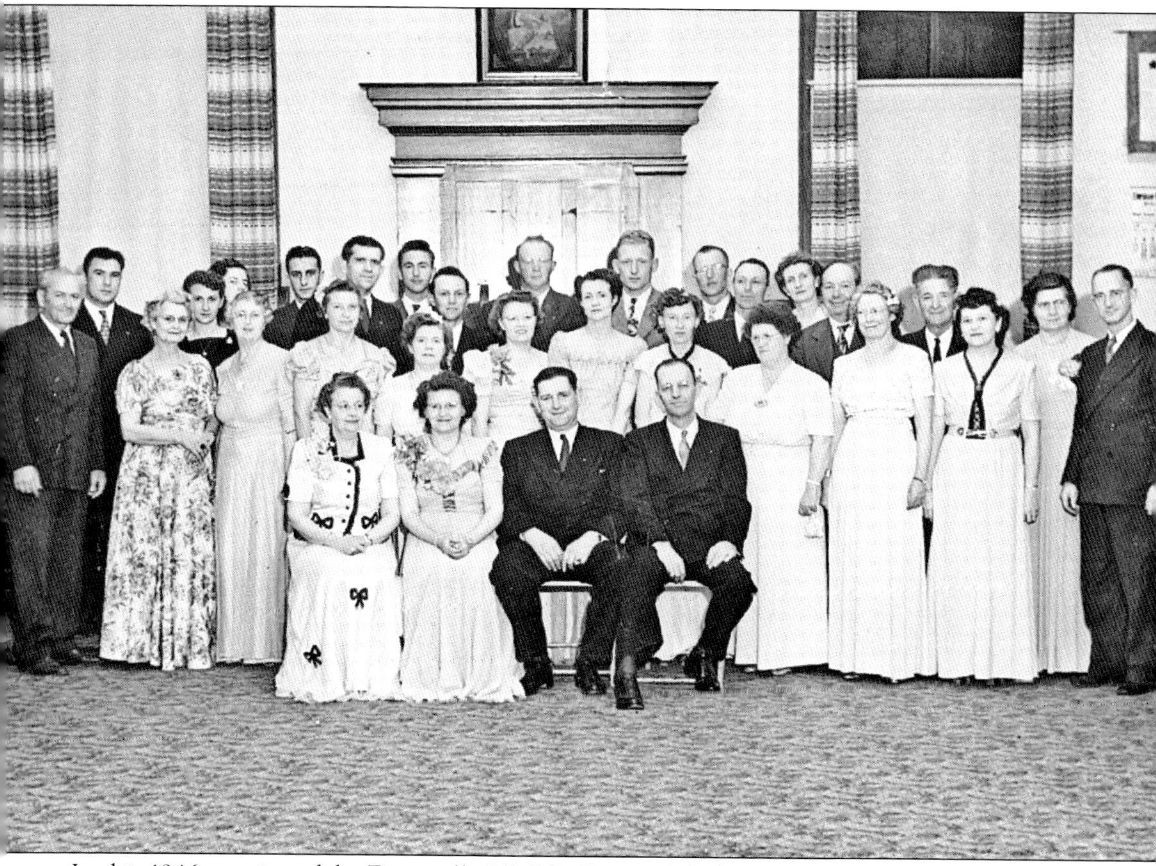

In this 1946 meeting of the Forestville I.O.O.F. (Internal Order of Odd Fellows), members pose with their wives. Pictured here are Burton Travis, Cliff Shultz, Frank Bledsoe, Milton Flesher, Norman Miller, Art Sorensen, Kenny Templeman, Jess Winkler, Cal Kimes (department grand master), Harry Barr, Walt Kimes, Bob Rutherford, Jerry Rowe, and Cecil Musser. (Courtesy of the Dave Henry collection.)

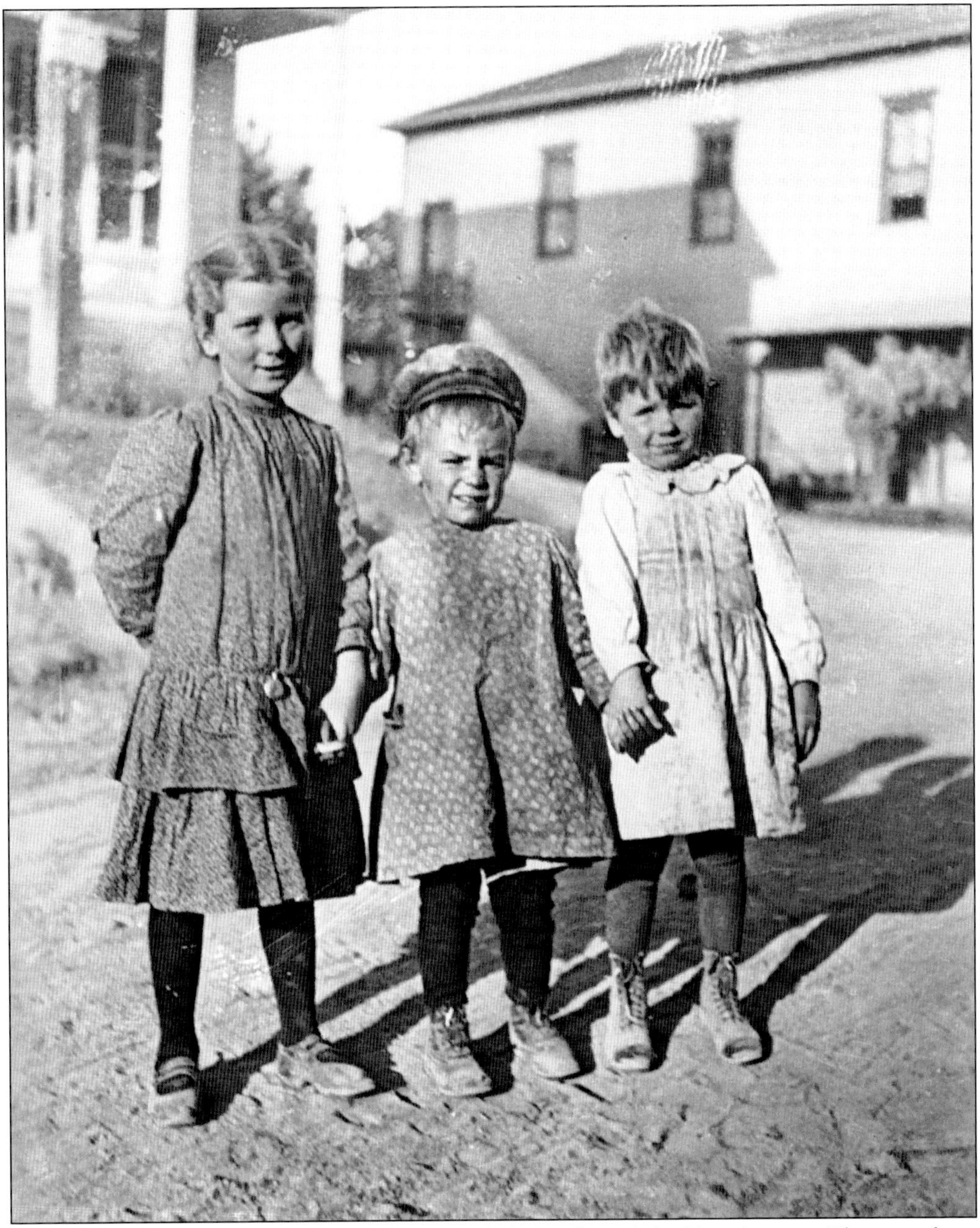

These three children are the offspring of the Clark family and the Templemans. They are, from left to right, Gladys Clark, Kenneth Templeman, and Wilma Clark. The Clark home is in back of them to the left and to the right is the Johnson Hotel, which later became the Electric Hotel when it moved by the train depot. (Courtesy of the Dave Henry collection.)

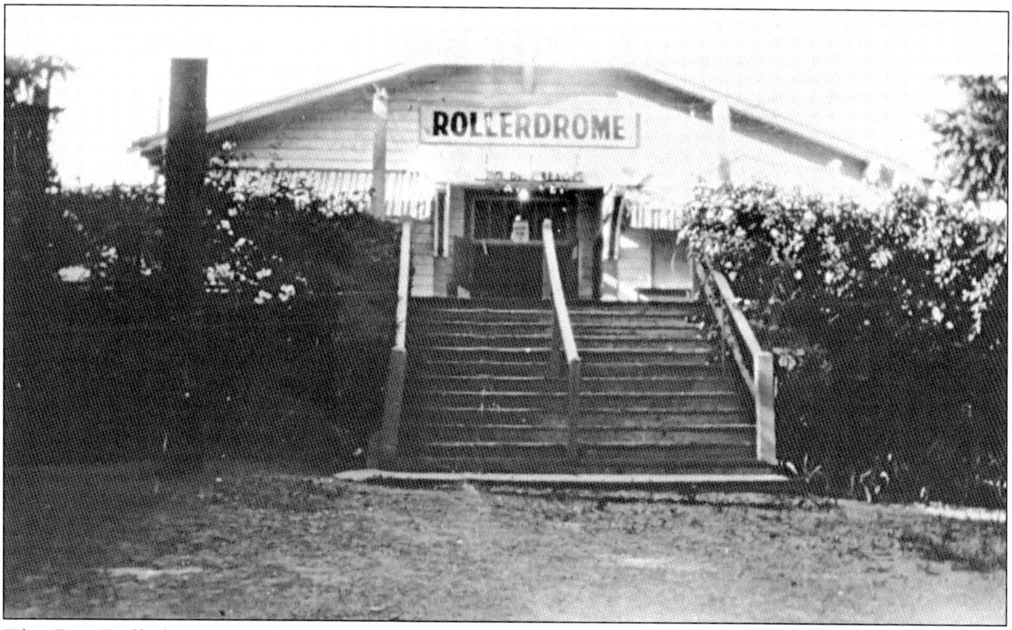

The Rio Dell skating rink was a dance hall until the mid-1930s. The Rollordome was located between Rio Dell Court and Rio Vista Road. People would come from as far as Santa Rosa to skate. Ross Yeager worked at the Rollordome during his youth. He remembers it being very busy at times. (Courtesy of the Dave Henry collection.)

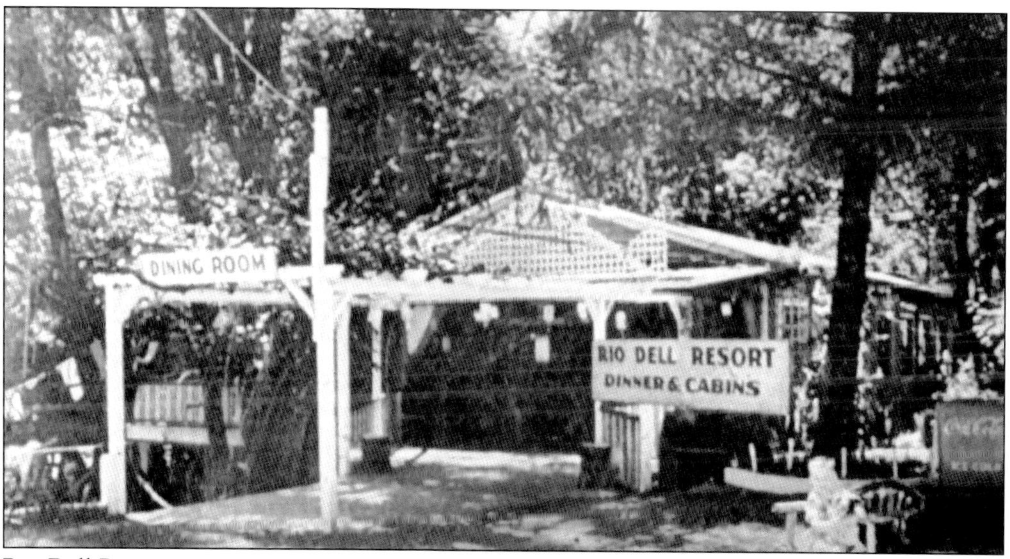

Rio Dell Resort was a summer vacation spot. It had cabins to rent out with a big ranch house, and it was located close to the Russian River. Rio Dell Resort was at the corner of River Road and Rio Vista Road. (Courtesy of the Dave Henry collection.)

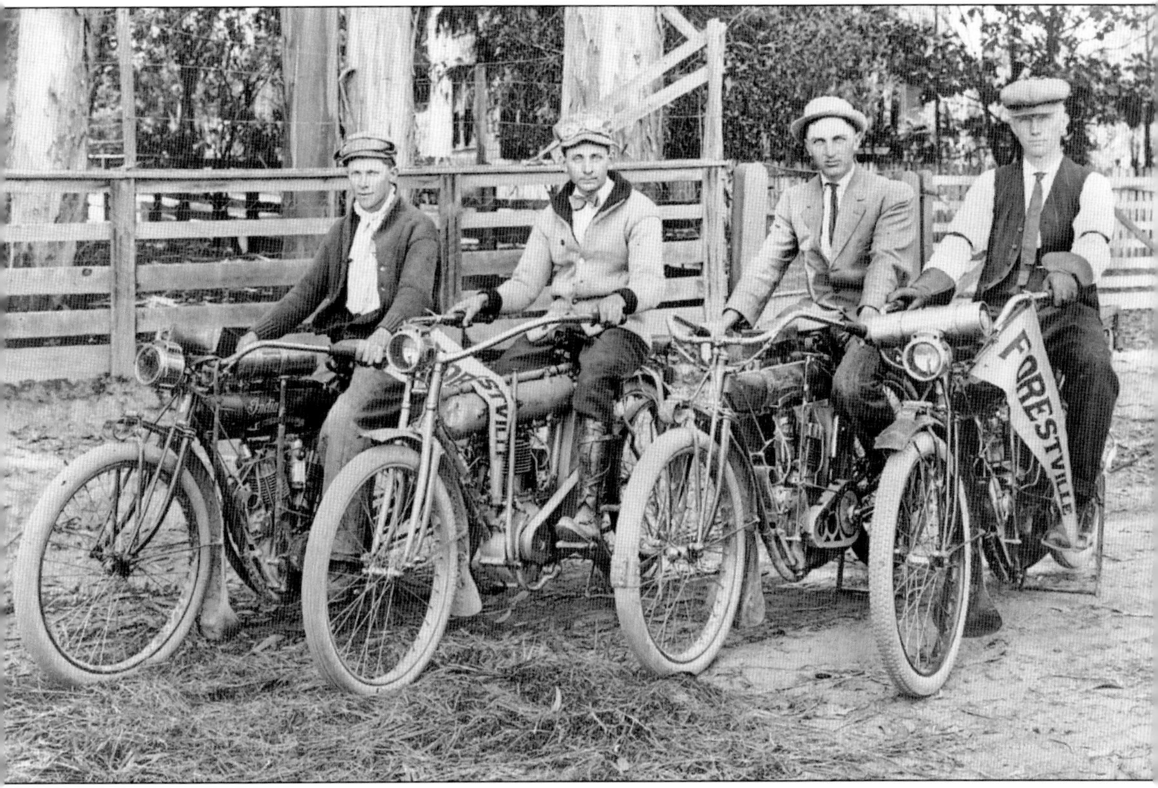

This photograph was taken in front of the Oliver home on Covey Road, just across from Van Keppel Road. The four young men found their motorcycles to be an improvement over the bicycle. They all had Indian brand motorcycles except Clint Yeager, who rode a Yale, which was very modern for 1912. They are, from left to right, Milton Hicks, Clint Yeager, Earnest Everett Close, and Clyde Fouts. (Courtesy of Ross Yeager.)

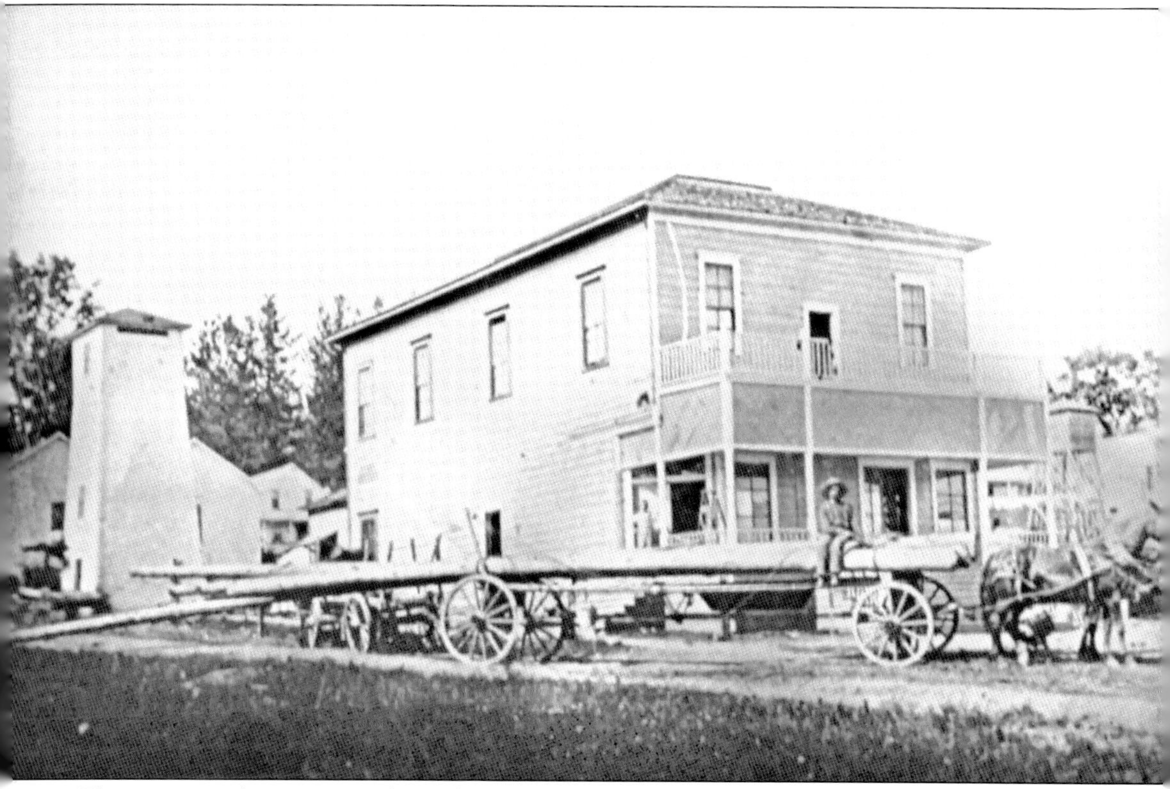

This picture, taken in 1904, shows the Forestville Electric Hotel. The building was formerly Jim Johnson's saloon and was moved down Main Street to the depot when the electric train came to town in 1904. Walt Morris is hauling poles for J. P. McConnell. This building later burned down. (Courtesy of the Dave Henry collection.)

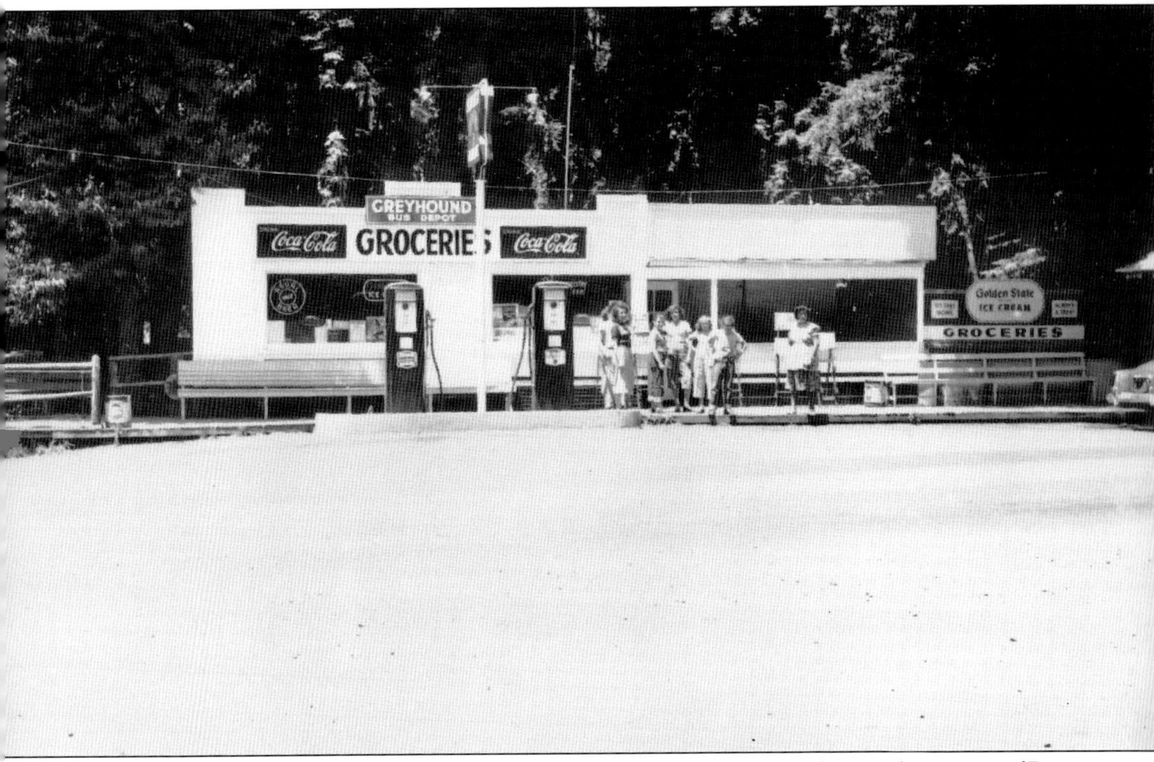

This 1950s picture of the Mirabel Grocery Store and Gas Station was taken at the corner of River and Mirabel Roads. This business served the needs of the people at Mirabel Park. Note that it was also the Greyhound bus depot. After the rails were taken up, Greyhound established a route to include the Russian River. For those who didn't drive, this was very convenient. During those years of big bands playing on the river, it was also possible to take advantage of a fine dance hall. (Courtesy of the Dave Henry collection.)

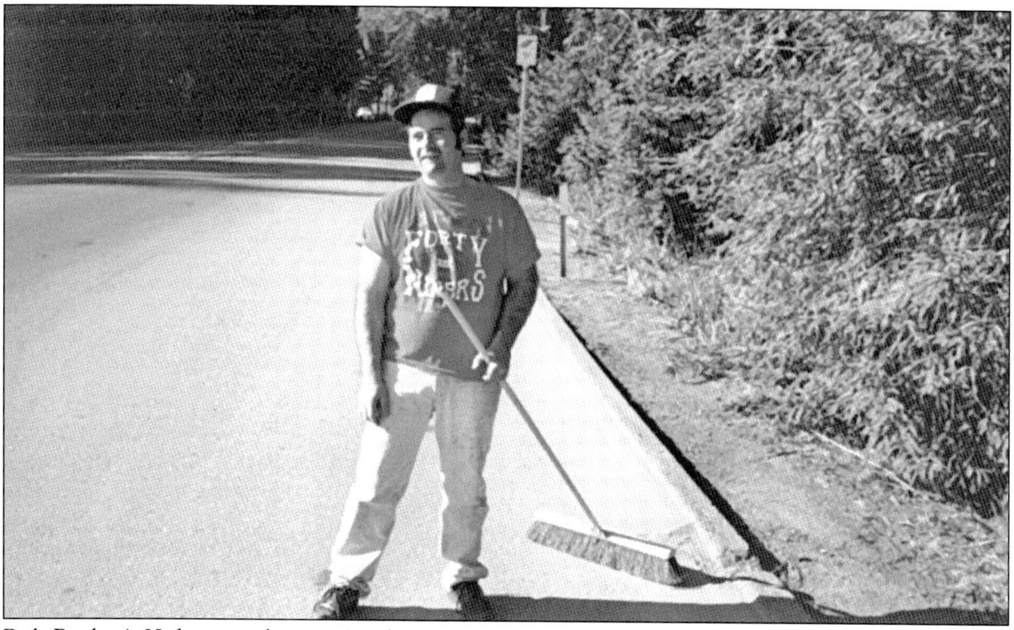

Bob Burkes's Kids started in 1967, when he was visiting some children in the hospital who had cancer and he thought it would be a great idea to bring some joy into their lives. He helps kids who are terminally and chronically ill. He also helps children who are blind, disabled, abused, diabetic, and autistic. His non-profit organization runs on donations. He has a barbeque every Wednesday evening between June and September for the kids and their families. From October through May, he has skating, bowling, trout fishing, field trips, pizza parties, and more. During the holidays, he has several fund-raisers at the Union Hotel in Occidental. Bob was honored by the Forestville Chamber of Commerce as the Citizen of the Year for selflessly helping those in need. He was also grand marshal in the Forestville Parade and has been given several humanitarian awards. This bus (below) was purchased from Forestville School and now is used for both Bob's Kids and Mirabel Park. (Courtesy of Louis Lacabanne.)

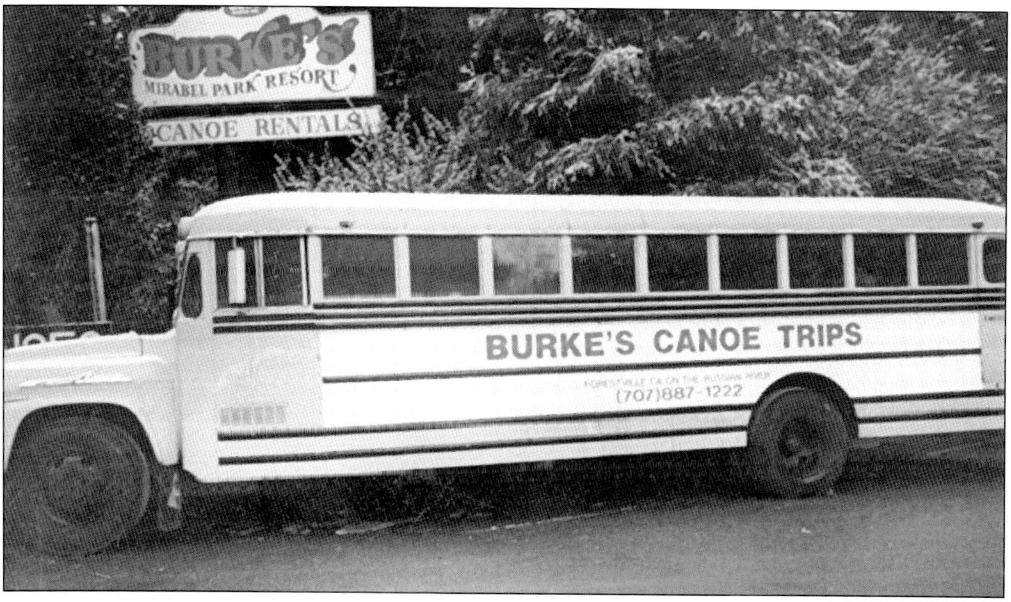